# Contents

For a catalog or book orders
call or write: Milestone Ministries
34207 Enos Dr., Halsey, OR 97348
Voice or Fax call 1-800-761-0234
or visit us at milestoneministries.com

# ROD and STAFF
# ENGLISH
# HANDBOOK

Rod and Staff Publishers, Inc.
Crockett, Kentucky 41413

Telephone (606) 522 4348

# Preface

When actual-life writing or speaking responsibilities come, a familiar, easy-to-use reference book is a welcome tool. It is our intent that you will learn to use this independent handbook efficiently during your school years. We hope you will have one with you as a tool when you leave school.

This handbook is unique because of its Christian character throughout. It is relevant to the life style of a people who are separate from sin.

We appreciate the help of many in bringing this vision to reality. Esther Neuenschwander wrote the basic text. Others have reviewed and edited the manuscripts. Our God is worthy of all glory and praise.

*—The Publishers*

# Introduction

Never does a day go by in which we do not use language. For most of us in North America, the language is English. We recognize language and the ability to communicate as a gift from God.

Our happiness depends upon our ability to communicate with God and with man; unhappiness results from the lack of this vital communication. Even our communications within ourselves—our thoughts—are made up of words. Let us study to keep all our communications acceptable to God.

There are many areas in which we can make use of language after we have mastered it. In speaking to one another, we as Christians use words that edify and encourage. Good grammar helps us to put the right feeling into what we say. Letter writing is another area where we can be useful in cheering or encouraging others. Letters can travel to other areas when we ourselves need to stay home. Not everyone writes a book or contributes to a periodical, but where is the man who never reads one? So both he who writes and he who reads with understanding appreciate the gift of language. This leaves no room for slovenly grammar in God's plan for communication.

The English language has many variations in punctuation and spelling. A word can also be used as a number of parts of speech. With all these irregularities, we can still detect a complete sentence, a subject, or a predicate. God has made our minds to grasp complete thoughts. We receive satisfaction when we have made our thoughts plain to others; conversely, we suffer when we cause misunderstanding.

Sometimes we are tempted to think that our grammar need not be precise. But remember that Bible truths are revealed with exactness. For instance. the two small commas in Luke 23:32 ("two other, malefactors, led with him") tell us that our Saviour was free from wrong. The commas make the word *malefactors* an appositive to *two other*, whereas the absence of commas would denote that Christ was also a malefactor. Never underestimate the rules of grammar!

The usefulness of this handbook reaches beyond formal education. It is also written to supplement the study of English grammar for those who are out of school, and to provide a reference for things we forget. Many hours have gone into its making so that it might be as complete as possible. Its arrangement is such that answers can be found easily.

The sections on Christian writing are detailed because the Lord constantly needs laborers in that field. May we look to God, who provided a plan for our salvation, and may we follow His bidding. May our sweet relationship with Him move us to write for His cause.

# GRAMMAR

# I. Parts of Speech

## A. NOUNS
1. Definition
2. Noun Classes
    a. Common Nouns
    b. Proper Nouns
    c. Abstract Nouns
    d. Concrete Nouns
    e. Collective Nouns
3. Noun Gender
    a. Masculine Gender
    b. Feminine Gender
    c. Common Gender
    d. Neuter Gender
4. Noun Person
5. Noun Number
    a. Singular Nouns
    b. Plural Nouns
6. Noun Case
    a. Nominative Case
    b. Objective Case
    c. Possessive Case
7. Noun Inflections
8. Noun Usage
9. Substantives

## B. PRONOUNS
10. Definition
11. Personal Pronouns
    a. Pronoun Case
    b. Pronoun Usage
    c. Antecedents
    d. Pronoun Declension
    e. Compound Personal Pronouns
12. Demonstrative Pronouns
13. Relative Pronouns
14. Interrogative Pronouns
15. Indefinite Pronouns

## C. VERBS
16. Definition
17. Verb Classes
    a. Regular Verbs
    b. Irregular Verbs
18. Verb Kinds
    a. Action Verbs
    b. Being Verbs
19. Verb Use
    a. Transitive Verbs
    b. Intransitive Verbs
        1. Linking Verbs
        2. Complete Verbs
    c. Auxiliary Verbs
20. Verb Inflections
    a. Verb Voice
        1. Active Voice
        2. Passive Voice
    b. Verb Mood
        1. Indicative Mood
        2. Imperative Mood
        3. Subjunctive Mood
    c. Verb Tense
    d. Verb Number
    e. Verb Person
21. Verb Conjugation
    a. Conjugation of the Verb *to Be*
    b. Conjugation of the Verb *to Grow*
    c. Conjugation of the Verb *to Be Grown*
22. Verbals
    a. Infinitives
    b. Gerunds
    c. Participles
23. Troublesome Verbs

## D. ADJECTIVES
24. Definition
25. Single-Word Adjectives
26. Adjective Phrases
27. Adjective Clauses

# H. INTERJECTIONS
### 51. Definition
### 52. Usage Guidelines for Interjections

# I. Parts of Speech

Our English words can be divided into eight groups called *parts of speech*. They are *noun, pronoun, verb, adjective, adverb, preposition, conjunction,* and *interjection.*

A *noun* is a word that names a person, place, thing, quality, or action.

A *pronoun* is a word that is used in place of a noun.

A *verb* is a word that expresses action or a state of being.

An *adjective* is a word used to describe nouns and pronouns.

An *adverb* is a word which modifies verbs, adjectives, and other adverbs.

A *preposition* is a word which shows the relationship between the object of the preposition and another word in the sentence.

A *conjunction* is a word which connects other words or groups of words or sentences.

An *interjection* is a word which expresses feeling.

The way a word is used in a sentence determines what part of speech it is. The same word may be used as several different parts of speech.

> *Cooking* is an art. *(cooking* used as a *noun)*
> The beef was *cooking* three hours. *(cooking* used as a *verb)*
> *Cooking* utensils are needed daily. *(cooking* used as an *adjective)*

## A. NOUNS

### 1.

### Definition

A noun is a part of speech that names a person, place, thing, quality, or action.

### 2.

### Classes

All nouns have been divided into two main categories: *common* or *proper.*

*2a.*

*Common nouns:* A common noun names *any* person, place, or thing.

| PERSONS | PLACES | THINGS |
|---------|--------|--------|
| man | desert | animal |
| cousin | home | water |
| attendant | inside | idea |
| doctor | school | flowers |
| baby | upstairs | time |

Doubtless you can think of sentences in which these common nouns could also be used as other parts of speech.

A.2a.

*2b.*

*Proper nouns:* A proper noun names a *specific* person, place, or thing. Proper nouns are always capitalized.

| PERSONS | PLACES | THINGS |
|---------|--------|--------|
| Mr. Clark | California | Civil War |
| Miranda | Sherman Hotel | Easter |
| American | Promised Land | Pilgrim's Progress |

Nouns can also be classified as *abstract, concrete,* and *collective.*

*2c.*

*Abstract nouns* name qualities, ideas, conditions, and all other things which cannot be perceived by the five senses.

**honesty, loyalty, perfection, misery, danger, bliss**

*2d.*

*Concrete nouns* name things which can be perceived by the five senses (sight, touch, smell, hearing, or taste).

**clouds, heat, fragrance, music, salt**

*2e.*

*Collective nouns* name a group of persons or a collection of things.

**audience, committee, family, flock, swarm**

# 3.

# Gender

All nouns have either *masculine, feminine, common,* or *neuter* gender.

*3a.*

*Masculine gender* denotes a male.

> **king, widower, rooster, ram**

*3b.*

*Feminine gender* denotes a female.

> **queen, widow, hen, ewe**

*3c.*

**A.3a.**

*Common gender* denotes either feminine or masculine or both without specifying which.

> **children, sheep, people, customers, relatives, assembly**

*3d.*

*Neuter gender* denotes all things not of *masculine, feminine* or *common* gender.

> **tree, chair, submission, fog, machinery, war, lesson**

## 4.

## Person

Nouns are always in the third person except for the rare times when they are used in apposition with first- or second-person pronouns. In such cases the person of the pronoun determines the person of the noun.

> "And I *John* saw these things, and heard them." (The noun *John* is in the first person because *I,* to which it refers, is in the first person.)
>
> You, *John,* must prophesy to many people. (*John* is in the second person because the pronoun, *you,* to which John refers, is in the second person.)
>
> *John* wrote the Book of Revelation. (*John* is in the third person. There is no pronoun to which John refers.)

## 5.

## Number

Number indicates whether the noun refers to one or to more than one. Nouns are either *singular* or *plural.*

*5a.*
*Singular nouns* name one person, place, or thing. They may name one group or one collection of things.

match, city, congregation

(1) Since a proper noun names a *specific* thing, it nearly always is singular.

King David, Red Sea, Israel

(2) Some nouns are singular in meaning although their form is plural.

A.5a.

civics—ONE SUBJECT
gallows—ONE STRUCTURE
measles—ONE DISEASE
Daily News—ONE PUBLICATION
Niagara Falls—ONE NATURAL WONDER

*5b.*
*Plural nouns* name more than one person, place, or thing.

eyes, matches, yards, secrets, cities

(1) Some nouns have no singular form.

scissors, suds, trousers

(2) Most nouns are changed from singular to plural by adding *-s* or *-es.*

bird—birds    girl—girls

(3) Nouns ending with *ch, sh, s, ss, x,* and *zz* are made plural by adding *-es.*

church—churches    bush—bushes    bus—buses
dress—dresses      box—boxes      buzz—buzzes

(4) Most nouns ending with an *o* which follows a vowel are changed to the plural form by adding *-s.*

trio—trios    ratio—ratios

(5) Most nouns ending with an *o* which follows a consonant are changed to the plural form by adding *-es.*

tomato—tomatoes

*Exception:* Nouns which refer to music are made plural by adding only -*s* after the final *o*.

solo—solos     piano—pianos     alto—altos

(6) Nouns ending with a *y* which follows a consonant are changed to the plural form by changing the *y* to *i* and adding -*es*.

sky—skies     country—countries

**A.5b.**

(7) Nouns ending with a *y* which follows a vowel are made plural by adding -*s*.

donkey—donkeys     monkey—monkeys

(8) Some nouns ending with *f* or *fe* are made plural by changing the *f* or *fe* to *v* and adding -*es*.

calf—calves     wife—wives     wolf—wolves

(9) Others with the same ending are made plural by adding only -*s*.

proof—proofs     safe—safes     roof—roofs

(10) Some nouns are made plural by changing the vowel or vowels in the word.

man—men     foot—feet     tooth—teeth

(11) Nouns ending in -*ful* are made plural by adding -*s* at the end.

spoonful—spoonfuls (not spoonsful)

(12) Collective nouns are singular or plural according to the meaning of the sentence in which they are used.

> The *company* is noted for *its* integrity. (*Company* intended as one unit. Notice that the singular verb, *is*, and the singular pronoun, *it*, agree in number with the singular subject, *company*.)

> The *group* were presented their gifts of appreciation. (The individual members of the group are being referred to. Notice that the plural verb, *were*, and pronoun, *their*, agree with plural subject.)

> It is best to consult a dictionary when forming the plural of a *compound* noun. There is no one rule that applies to all of these.

(13) Some nouns do not change form but are the same for singular

and plural.

> sheep, deer

# 6.

# Case

*Case* indicates how a noun or pronoun is used in the sentence in relation to other words. There are three cases: *nominative, objective,* and *possessive.*

### 6a.

*Nominative case* (or subjective case) *nouns* are used as subjects in sentences in situations such as the following.

> SUBJECT OF A VERB: *Saul* was king.
> PREDICATE NOMINATIVE (sometimes called subjective complement): The king was *Saul.*
> DIRECT ADDRESS: *Saul,* you have sinned.
> EXCLAMATION: *Saul!*
> NOMINATIVE ABSOLUTE: *Saul* having sinned, David became king.
> COMPLEMENT OF THE INFINITIVE *TO BE* WITHOUT A SUBJECT: He was taken to be *Saul.*
> APPOSITIVE TO ANOTHER WORD IN THE NOMINATIVE CASE: They, *Saul* and Samuel, met after the battle.

### 6b.

*Objective case nouns* serve as objects in the sentence.

> DIRECT OBJECT OF VERB: I saw *June.*
> OBJECTIVE COMPLEMENT: They named Fred *sponsor.*
> INDIRECT OBJECT: She gave *Billy* her coat.
> OBJECT OF PREPOSITION: They worked in the *kitchen.*
> OBJECT OF AN INFINITIVE: Henry decided to help *Dan.*
> OBJECT OF A GERUND: Encouraging *Elmer* was his desire.
> OBJECT OF A PARTICIPLE: Finding *Phoebe* in the kitchen, *Mother* returned to her work on the porch.
> APPOSITIVE TO ANOTHER WORD IN THE OBJECTIVE CASE: Jesus comforted the sisters, *Mary* and *Martha.*
> SUBJECT OF AN INFINITIVE: The teacher asked *Mark* to read.

*Exception:* Though *Mark* is the *subject* of the infinitive, the entire phrase is the *object* of the verb *asked.*

*6c.*

*Possessive case nouns* always express ownership.

(1) Most nouns in the possessive case were formed by adding -'s to the noun.

> *Paul's* Bible is worn.
> Do you know my brother *Albert's* wife?

(2) Some singular nouns which end in *s* are difficult to pronounce if another *s* is added to form the possessive. In this case the apostrophe is added after the word without another *s*.

> For *Jesus'* sake we helped the man. (not *Jesus's*)
> The *waitress'* words were sympathetic. (not *waitress's*)

(3) When a plural noun ends in *s*, the possessive form of the word is made by adding only an apostrophe after the word.

> The *boys'* bicycles were neatly parked.
> The *ministers'* lunches were served first.

(4) Nouns in the possessive case are modifiers and in diagraming are placed as adjectives.

# 7.

## Inflections

Changing the form of a word when its use in the sentence changes is called *inflection.* (See "Declension of Personal Pronouns," section 11d.) Notice that *case, gender, number,* and *person* are shown by changing the form of the noun.

# 8.

## Usage

*8a.*

Be consistent with the use of plural and singular nouns within the sentence. They should always agree in meaning.

*8b.*

To show separate ownership, add -'s to both nouns.

**Mildred's and Margaret's rooms were neat.**

*8c.*

To show joint ownership, add -'s to only the last noun.

**Keener and Sensenig's Lawn Care.**

*8d.*

Inanimate things do not usually have a possessive form unless the noun is personified.

A.8b.

> **the roof of the house (not "the house's roof")**
> **the feel of the breeze (not "the breeze's feel")**
> *but:* **Wisdom's ways, Autumn's glory (personification)**

**Some common exceptions are:**

**the earth's surface, a day's wages, a stone's throw**

*8e.*

A noun used as a modifier before a gerund should be in the possessive case.

**Paul's (not Paul) going to Jerusalem brought sorrow to his friends.**

**Do not confuse this with the *nominative absolute*, which has no direct relation to the rest of the sentence. It is not in the possessive case.**

**The *night* being cold, we dressed warmly.**

# 9.

## Substantives

*Substantive* is another word for noun. Any word, phrase, or clause that is used as a noun—to name something—is called a substantive. Substantives usually consist of nouns and pronouns. However, any word that usually is another part of speech may also be a substantive if it is used as a noun in the sentence.

> ADJECTIVE: *Beautiful* was the first word on the spelling test.
> ADVERB: We came from *there.*

GERUND: The *living* are responsible for their deeds.

GERUND PHRASE: *Sledding on the road* is dangerous.

INFINITIVE: *To delay* takes courage sometimes.

INFINITIVE PHRASE: *To chase the cat under the porch* was our collie's chief delight.

QUOTATION: God said, *"Let there be light."*

CLAUSE: He did not know *who I was.*

# B. PRONOUNS

## 10.

### Definition

A pronoun is a word used in place of a noun to avoid repetition.

John saw John in the mirror. (repetitious)
John saw *himself* in the mirror. (pronoun used instead)

*10a.*
Many pronouns have an antecedent—a noun used previously, to which the pronoun refers.

*David* forgot *his* Bible. (*David* is the antecedent to which the pronoun, *his*, refers.)

*10b.*
Some pronouns, like some nouns, have gender, person, number, and case. Every pronoun should agree with its antecedent in gender, person, and number. *His* in the sentence above is masculine, third person, singular, agreeing with *David*, which also is masculine, third person, and singular.

The case of a pronoun depends on how it is used in the sentence. *His* is in the possessive case.

Pronouns are classified as *personal, demonstrative, relative, interrogative,* and *indefinite.*

## 11.

### Personal Pronouns

Personal pronouns are the most commonly used pronouns. They indicate either:

THE PERSON SPEAKING: I, me, us, we;
THE PERSON SPOKEN TO: you, yours;
OR THE PERSON (OR THING) SPOKEN OF: he, she, it.

Personal pronouns have many inflections, and the form used should always agree with its antecedent in gender, person, and number.

*11a.*

*Case:* The case of a personal pronoun depends on how the pronoun is used in the sentence. Pronouns occur in the same cases as nouns do.

(1) *Nominative, or subjective case:* A pronoun is in the nominative case when it acts as a subject.

> *I* will sing of the mercies of the Lord. (subject of the verb)
> I am *he*. (predicate nominative, renames the subject)
> *You*, brethren, remain steadfast. (direct address)
> Not *you*! (exclamation)
> *They* having come, we did not stay longer. (nominative absolute)
> They, Silas and *he*, were cast into prison. (appositive of another word, *they*, which is in the nominative case)

(2) *Objective case*: A pronoun is in the objective case when it serves as an object in the sentence. (Note one exception below.)

> John saw *him* first. (direct object of the verb, *saw*)
> Jesus gave *them* bread and fish to eat. (indirect object)
> Bring the book to *me*. (object of the preposition)

*Exception:* Mother wanted *me* to come. (*me* is the *subject* of the infinitive; but the entire phrase is the *object* of the verb, *wanted*.)

> Jairus asked Jesus to help *him*. (object of the infinitive)
> Helping *her* was Janet's pleasure. (object of the gerund)
> Peter, recognizing *Him*, leaped into the water and swam to the shore. (object of the participle)
> The boys thought the teacher to be *him*. (complement of the infinitive, *to be*, with subject)
> Father gave us, Robert and *me*, some work to do. (appositive to another word in the objective case)

Note that pronouns are not used as objective complements.

(3) *Possessive case*: Pronouns in the possessive case usually modify nouns and thus function as adjectives. Possessive pronouns are also called possessive adjectives, adjective pronouns, and pronominal adjectives.

> *my* dog            *their* home
> *your* smile       *his* essay
> *its* speed        *her* cooking
> *our* bike         *its* universal joint

(a) Absolute possessive pronouns do not modify nouns. They stand alone, representing both the possessor and the thing possessed.

mine    This is *mine.*
yours   I knew it was *yours* as soon as I saw it.
ours    *Ours* is not as pretty as yours.
theirs  I guess *theirs* has more sugar in it than ours.
his     I was ashamed of mine when I saw how *his* looked.
hers    *Hers* died because she forgot to water it.

(b) Notice that possessive pronouns never use an apostrophe to show possession as nouns do. Remembering this fact will keep you from the common mistake of writing the contraction *it's* (it is) for the possessive pronoun *its.* The only time to use an apostrophe with a personal pronoun is to write a contraction.

**B.11b.**

I'll, we'll, you're

*11b.*

*Usage*

(1) A pronoun following *than* or *as* is in the nominative or objective case according to its use.

Jesus is greater than *he.* (Than *he* is great; *he* is the subject of the verb *is;* nominative case.)

She likes her more than *me.* (Than she likes *me; me* is the direct object of the verb *likes;* objective case.)

You are just as tall as *I.* (As *I* am tall; *I* is the subject of the verb *am;* nominative case.)

(2) When a pronoun is used as part of a compound, be especially careful to choose the correct case form. This will be easy if you read the sentence using only the pronoun.

Paul and *he* sang praises at midnight. (*He,* not *him,* sang praises; subject, nominative case.)

The travelers were John and *they.* (*They,* not *them,* were the travelers; predicate nominative, nominative case.)

Give it to Susan and *me.* (Give it to *me,* not *I;* object of the preposition, objective case.)

Mother fed the baby and *her.* (Mother fed *her,* not *she;* direct object, objective case.)

*He* and *I* will travel together. (*He,* not *him,* will travel; *I,* not *me,* will travel; subject of verb, nominative case.)

(3) Do not create a double subject by using both a noun and a pronoun, except in direct address.

> CORRECT: Lazarus (not "Lazarus, *he*") was dead four days.
> CORRECT: Harold, *you* may collect the songbooks.

(4) Use the correct case when you have a pronoun followed by an appositive. Here again, you can determine the correct case by omitting the noun when you read it.

> *We* girls read from the Psalms. (*We*, not *us*, read from the Psalms.)
> Mother told a story to *us* children. (Mother told a story to *us*, not *we*.)

### 11c.
### *Antecedents*

(1) A pronoun with a compound antecedent joined by *and* should be plural unless the compound part refers to only one person or thing.

> The teacher and janitor has finished *his* job. (The teacher and the janitor are the same person. Notice the singular verb, *has*, and the direct object, *job*.)
> The teacher and the janitor have finished *their* jobs. (The teacher and the janitor are two persons. Notice the plural verb, *have*, and the direct object, *jobs*.)

(2) If the antecedents of a pronoun are singular and are joined by *either . . . or* or *neither . . . nor*, the pronoun is to be singular. The compound parts are being considered separately.

> Either Anna or Jean will have *her* book along.

(3) If the antecedents are both plural, the pronoun is to be plural.

> Neither fathers nor mothers gave *their* consent.

(4) If one antecedent is singular and one is plural, the pronoun is to agree in number and gender with the antecedent nearer to it.

> Either they or Jason will give *his* help.
> Neither the teacher nor the pupils gave *their* word.

(5) Use a third-person pronoun with a third-person antecedent.

> If *anyone* plans to attend, *he* (not *you*) should let us know.

(6) If the antecedent names a group acting as a unit, the pronoun should be singular. If members of the group act individually, the pronoun should be plural.

> The church made *its* decision promptly.
> The class voiced *their* opinions.

### 11d.

*Declension of personal pronouns* includes gender, person, number, and case.

## Singular

| PERSON | NOMINATIVE | POSSESSIVE | OBJECTIVE | |
|--------|-----------|-----------|-----------|---|
| First | I | my, mine | me | |
| Second | you | your, yours | you | |
| | he | his | him | (masculine) |
| Third | she | her, hers | her | (feminine) |
| | it | its | it | (neuter) |

## Plural

| PERSON | NOMINATIVE | POSSESSIVE | OBJECTIVE | |
|--------|-----------|-----------|-----------|---|
| First | we | our, ours | us | (common gender as determined by antecedent) |
| Second | you | your, yours | you | |
| Third | they | their, theirs | them | (usually common gender unless antecedent shows otherwise) |

### 11e.

*Compound Pronouns*

(1) Personal pronouns with *-self* or *-selves* added are called *compound pronouns*. (Examples: myself, yourself, himself, herself, itself, ourselves, yourselves, themselves.) They are used in two ways.

(a) *Intensive pronouns* are used for emphasis.

> He *himself* admitted that he was wrong.
> We will finish the work *ourselves*.

(b) *Reflexive pronouns* show an action done by the subject to himself. The action "reflects" back to the subject.

> Nebuchadnezzar exalted *himself*.
> A house divided against *itself* cannot stand.

(2) Do not use a compound personal pronoun as the subject of a sentence.

> James and *I* (not *myself*) plan to be there.

(3) Do not use incorrect forms such as *hisself, ourself, themself,* or *theirselves*.

## 12.

### Demonstrative Pronouns

Demonstrative pronouns point out *particular* persons, places, or things. There are only four of this kind of pronoun. *This* and *these* point out things close at hand. *That* and *those* indicate things at a distance. *This* and *that* are singular. *These* and *those* are plural.

> *This* is the book I wanted to show you, not *that* one.
> *Those* were difficult days—more difficult than *these*.

*12a.*

The gender and person of a demonstrative pronoun automatically are the same as those of its antecedent. A demonstrative pronoun does not have inflections to show case. Its case depends on its use in the sentence.

> *That* was why I could not come. (nominative case)
> I did not expect the situation to come to *that*. (objective case)

*12b.*

Demonstrative pronouns are often used to modify nouns. As such they serve as adjectives.

> *Those* girls surely were a big help.
> *These* times are perilous.

*12c.*
When used alone, demonstrative pronouns are true pronouns.

> *That* was all I needed.
> He gave me *this*.

*12d.*
Do not use *them* where *these* or *those* should be used.

> *Those* (not *them*) apples were delicious.

*12e.*
Do not use *here* or *there* after a demonstrative pronoun.

B.12c.

> Please bring me *that* (not *that there*) book.
> Look at *this* (not *this here*) butterfly.

# 13.

## Relative Pronouns

These are called relative pronouns because they relate to their antecedents in the main clause. They have no inflections to show person or number or gender.

*13a.*
Relative pronouns introduce adjective clauses which modify the antecedent of the pronoun. They also serve as the subject or an object in the clause itself.

> *who, whom, whose, which, that, what*

(1) *Who, whom,* and *whose* should be used to refer to persons or personified animals or things. Occasionally, *whose* is used as the possessive of *who* when the phrase *of which* would be awkward.
(2) *Which, that,* and *what* refer to inanimate objects, but also sometimes to persons.

> There is the guard *that* told us we could park here.
> She picked curtains *which* were washable.

*13b.*
The case form of a relative pronoun depends upon its use in the clause it introduces.

> Martha was the one *who* prepared the food. (subject of the verb

*prepared,* nominative case)

Mary was the one *whom* Jesus taught. (Jesus taught *whom,* direct object of verb *taught,* objective case)

Jairus was the man *whose* daughter was sick. (indicates ownership of daughter, possessive case)

### 13c.

Compound relative pronouns are formed by adding *-ever* or *-soever* to certain relative pronouns. Instead of introducing adjective clauses, they introduce noun clauses which are often part of the basic sentence pattern.

**B.13c.**

Be careful to use the correct case form of these pronouns.

*Whosoever* will may come. (subject, nominative case)

Jesus showed love to *whomever* He met. (*Whomever* is the direct object: He met *whomever.* The whole clause is the object of the preposition, *to.* Objective case.)

He shows mercy to *whoever* comes to Him. (*Whoever* is the subject of the verb *comes.* Nominative case.)

## 14.

## Interrogative Pronouns

Interrogative pronouns are used in asking questions. Notice that these pronouns are the same words as relative pronouns. You can identify them only by how they are used in the sentence.

*who, whom, whose, which, what*

### 14a.

*Who, whom,* and *whose* refer to people. *Which* and *what* often ask questions about things or places, but in some cases they may also refer to people.

*Who* saw the comet last night?

*Whom* did Jesus call to follow Him?

*Whose* is this?

*What* did you see at the zoo?

*Which* is your brother?

*Which* is the middle verse in the Bible?

*14b.*

Interrogative pronouns have no inflections to show case or number. Case forms are the same as when these pronouns are used as relative pronouns.

*14c.*

Interrogative pronouns can also modify nouns, and are then considered adjectives. Like demonstrative pronouns, they also are called adjective pronouns or pronominal adjectives.

> *Which* verse are you reading?
> *Whose* kitten is that climbing up the screen door?
> *What* color rug would go best with this wallpaper?

B.14b.

*14d.*

Do not think that all "question words" are interrogative pronouns. *How, when, where,* and *why* also ask questions, but they are adverbs. When the answer to the "question word" is a noun—a person, place, or thing—then the word is an interrogative pronoun.

## 15.

### Indefinite Pronouns

Indefinite pronouns refer to no particular person, place, or thing. They often serve as antecedents in a sentence, just as nouns do.

> *Few* of the students brought their umbrellas.
> *Somebody* ought to befriend him.

*15a.*

The possessive of an indefinite pronoun is formed by adding *-'s.* Otherwise these pronouns have no inflections to show gender or case. They usually are in the third person.

*15b.*

*Singular* forms are *any, each, every, either, neither, everyone, anyone, someone, nobody, no one.*

> *Each* should bring *his* (not *their*) songbook.
> *Everyone* was hungry for *his* (not *their*) lunch.

*15c.*

*Plural* forms are *both, few, many, several.*

> "*Many* are called, but *few* are chosen."
> *Several* birds were singing *their* morning songs.

*15d.*

*All, none, some,* and *such* may be singular or plural. Let the meaning of the sentence help you decide which verb to use. Be sure to use the singular form of the verb when the meaning of the pronoun is singular, and a plural verb when the meaning is plural.

> *All* the candy *was* eaten. (singular)
> *All* the people *were* leaving. (plural)

*15e.*

Like demonstrative and interrogative pronouns, indefinite pronouns sometimes modify nouns, thus serving as adjectives in the sentence.

**B.15d.**

> *Many* had been called to the feast. (true pronoun)
> *Many* people refused to come. (adjective, modifying *people*)

# C. VERBS

## 16.

### Definition

A verb is a word that expresses action or shows a state of being. It may state a fact, ask a question, give a command, indicate ownership, or make an exclamation. The verb with its various forms makes the English language expressive. Different forms bring out various shades of meaning in a sentence. A group of words acting together as a verb is called a *verb phrase*.

C.16.

## 17.

### Classes

Verbs may be classed as *regular* or *irregular*.

*17a.*
**Regular verbs** are those whose tense is changed by adding *-d,* or *-ed* to the present-tense form.

> **hike—hike***d*
> **walk—walk***ed*

*17b.*
**Irregular verbs** are those whose tenses are not formed in the regular (above) way, but by one of the following ways or any other way.

> ADDING *-en:* **beat—beaten**
> CHANGING A VOWEL: **run—ran**
> CHANGING A VOWEL AND ADDING *-t:* **feel—felt**
> CHANGING A FINAL *d* TO *t:* **send—sent**
> CHANGING A NUMBER OF LETTERS: **bring—brought, teach—taught**
> CHANGING NO LETTERS: **read—read, spit—spit**

## 18.

### Kinds

Verbs are further classified as *action* or *state-of-being* verbs.

*18a.*
*Action Verbs*

> Janet *slept.* (states a fact)
> Did you *try?* (asks a question)
> Please *finish* your homework. (command)
> I *have* a book. (indicates ownership)
> *Run, run!* (exclamation)

*18b.*
*Verbs of Being or Condition*

**C.18a.**

> I *am* he.
> The weather *grew* cold.
> She *was* sick.
> The apples *taste* good.

## 19.

## Use

Verbs are also divided according to their use. They may be *transitive, intransitive,* or *auxiliary* (helping) verbs.

*19a.*
*Transitive verbs* are action verbs which require a receiver of the action. When this receiver is a direct object, the verb is in the *active* voice and the subject *performs* the action.

> The birds *ate* the suet. (transitive, active voice)

(1) When the subject *receives* the action instead of performing it, the verb is still transitive, but in the *passive* voice.

> The suet *was eaten* by the birds. (transitive, passive voice)

(2) A sentence using a passive verb may or may not name the doer of the action.

> The suet *was eaten.* (no doer named)

*19b.*
*Intransitive verbs* have no receiver of the action. They do not transmit action to a subject or to a direct object as transitive verbs do. Intransitive verbs may be *linking* or *complete.*

(1) *Linking verbs* link the subject of the sentence with a subject complement. The complement may be a *predicate adjective,* a *predicate noun,* or a *predicate pronoun.*

| | |
|---|---|
| The Lord *is* good to all. | (The linking verb, *is,* links the |
| The servant *is* worthy. | subject to the predicate adjective.) |
| She *was* a sweet girl. | (The linking verb, *was,* links the |
| God *was* a guide to him. | subject to the predicate noun.) |
| I *am* he. | (The linking verb, *am,* links the |
| | subject to the predicate pronoun.) |

C.19c.

*The verbs of being* are the most common linking verbs. *Appear, become, seem,* and the verbs pertaining to the senses—*look, smell, taste, sound,* and *feel*—are also linking verbs when followed by a predicate adjective.

She *seems* satisfied.
That *looks* unsafe.
The air *felt* warmer in the sunshine.

(2) *Complete verbs* make a complete statement without the help of a complement.

Horses *eat.*
Children *sing.*

If the verbs in the two sentences above were given direct objects, the verbs would then be transitive.

Horses eat *grain.*
Children sing *hymns.*

Note: A verb of being is sometimes used with the meaning "to exist." In that case, the verb is intransitive complete.
God *is.*

*19c.*
*Auxiliary verbs* are those which help other verbs. The main verb with its helpers is called a *verb phrase.* The most common auxiliary verbs are *shall, will, have, has, had, do, did, must,* and forms of *be—been, being, am, is, were, are, was.* These are used in forming the *future, perfect, emphatic,* and *progressive* tenses of verbs.

(1) Auxiliary verbs can be used in various combinations.

> I *should have been* watching more carefully.
> They *must have* gone long ago.

(2) Other auxiliary verbs are used to give special meaning to verbs.

(a) *May* and *might* show possibility.

> We *might* go.
> He *may* do better than we think.

(b) *Can* and *could* show ability.

> He *could* lift two hundred pounds over his head.
> "I *can* do all things through Christ."

(c) *Should* shows duty.

> You *should* consider the feelings of others first.

(d) *Would* shows a condition, determination, or uncertainty.

> I *would* milk the cows if I were certain I knew how.

(3) Sometimes another word, phrase, or clause (called an interrupter) separates an auxiliary from the main verb.

> Satan *could* not *get* Job to curse God. (*Not* interrupts.)
> You never *should*—so the directions say—*mix* Clorox and ammonia. (The clause between the dashes is the interrupter.)
> A Christian *will* never intentionally *hurt* anyone. (*Never intentionally* is the interrupter.)

## 20.

## Inflections

*Inflections* are changes in the verb form which show *voice, mood, tense, number,* and *person.*

*20a.*

*Voice* tells whether the subject of the sentence is the actor or whether it is acted upon. (See "Transitive verbs," section 19a.) Verbs can be in *active* or *passive* voice.

(1) *Active* voice shows the subject *doing* the action.

> Rufus *threw* the ball.
> Jesus *died* for me.

(2) *Passive* voice shows the subject *being acted upon.*

> Julia *was spoken to* by the teacher.
> The car *was pushed* by the jeep.

*20b.*

**Mood** indicates the manner of the action. It may be *indicative, imperative,* or *subjunctive.*

(1) *Indicative mood* indicates or states a fact or asks a question.

> Jesus *is* our friend.
> *Is* He a friend of sinners, too?

C.20b.

If a past condition is known to be fact, use the indicative mood (is, was), not the subjunctive (were).

> If James *was* sick, I certainly did not notice it.
> If he *is* such a wise man, why does he not accept counsel?

(2) *Imperative mood* gives a command or makes an entreaty.

> "*Take* up thy bed, and *walk.*"
> Please *leave* me alone.

(3) *Subjunctive mood,* though almost totally replaced by indicative or alternate structures, is used in formal English to express a wish or condition contrary to fact, and in "that" clauses of recommendation or request.

> I wish I *were* as sweet-voiced as she.
> If only it *weren't* so dark, we would make better time.
> If Jesus *had been* there, Lazarus *might have* lived.
> The teacher recommended *that* James *have* his eyes *checked.*
> I request *that* she *be allowed* to go along.

(a) Subjunctive mood verbs also follow *as if* and *as though* constructions. The correct verb is always *were.*

> We should not act *as though* we *were* in bondage.
> Bobby tried to look *as if* he *were* not involved in the prank.

(b) Use the *present* subjunctive form after words showing necessity or command, even when other verbs in the sentence are in *past* tense.

> The leader thought it necessary that the preaching *stop.*
> They commanded that the apostles *be arrested.* (or *should be*)

*20c.*

*Tense* shows whether the time of the action is *past, present,* or *future.* Each of these "times" has *simple* and *perfect* forms.

(1) *Simple tense* calls attention merely to the *time* of the action.

> I *wrote* a story. (simple past tense)
> I *write* stories. (simple present tense)
> I *shall write* a story. (simple future tense)

(2) *Perfect tense* places more emphasis on *perfected* or *completed* action. Perfect-tense verbs always use an auxiliary verb (*have, has,* or *had*) and the third principal part of the verb.

**C.20c.**

> I *had written* a story. (past perfect tense)
> I *have written* another story. (present perfect tense)
> Next month, the Lord willing, I *shall have written* several more stories. (future perfect tense)

(3) *Principal parts of verbs:* All verbs have three principal parts, or forms, which are used to show the six tenses explained above. Not all verbs change their form when showing a change in tense.

| | | | |
|---|---|---|---|
| FIRST PRINCIPAL PART: | weep | put | split |
| SECOND PRINCIPAL PART: | wept | put | split |
| THIRD PRINCIPAL PART: | wept | put | split |

(a) The *first principal part* of a verb is used for all *simple present* and *simple future* tenses. The future tense always requires a helping word.

> I *speak* softly. (simple present)
> I *will speak* softly. (simple future)

(b) The *second principal part* of a verb is used for all *simple past* action.

> I *spoke* yesterday. (simple past)

(c) The *third principal part* (or past participle) is used for all *perfect* tense verbs—past, present, and future.

> I *had spoken.* (past perfect tense)
> I *have spoken.* (present perfect tense)
> I *will have spoken.* (future perfect tense)

(d)

| PRESENT TENSE | PAST TENSE | PAST PARTICIPLE |
|---|---|---|
| abide | abode | abode |
| am *(be)* | was | been |
| arise | arose | arisen |
| awake | awoke<br>or awaked | awaked<br>or awoke |
| bear *(bring forth)* | bore | born |
| bear *(carry)* | bore | borne |
| beat | beat | beaten<br>or beat |
| become | became | become |
| begin | began | begun |
| behold | beheld | beheld |
| bend | bent | bent |
| beseech | besought<br>or beseeched | besought<br>or beseeched |
| bid *(command)* | bade | bidden |
| bid *(make an offer)* | bid | bid |
| bite | bit | bitten<br>or bit |
| bleed | bled | bled |
| blow | blew | blown |
| break | broke | broken |
| bring | brought | brought |
| build | built | built |
| burst | burst | burst |
| catch | caught | caught |

C.20c.

| PRESENT TENSE | PAST TENSE | PAST PARTICIPLE |
|---|---|---|
| choose | chose | chosen |
| come | came | come |
| cost | cost | cost |
| creep | crept | crept |
| deal | dealt | dealt |
| dig | dug | dug |
| dive | dived<br>or dove | dived |
| do | did | done |
| drag | dragged | dragged |
| draw | drew | drawn |
| drink | drank | drunk |
| drive | drove | driven |
| drown | drowned | drowned |
| dwell | dwelt<br>or dwelled | dwelt<br>or dwelled |
| eat | ate | eaten |
| fall | fell | fallen |
| feed | fed | fed |
| feel | felt | felt |
| fight | fought | fought |
| flee | fled | fled |
| flow | flowed | flowed |
| fly | flew | flown |
| forget | forgot | forgotten<br>or forgot |
| forsake | forsook | forsaken |

C.20c.

| PRESENT TENSE | PAST TENSE | PAST PARTICIPLE |
|---|---|---|
| freeze | froze | frozen |
| get | got | got or gotten |
| give | gave | given |
| go | went | gone |
| grow | grew | grown |
| hang (suspend) | hung | hung |
| hang (execute) | hanged | hanged |
| hear | heard | heard |
| hide | hid | hidden |
| hold | held | held |
| hurt | hurt | hurt |
| kneel | knelt or kneeled | knelt or kneeled |
| know | knew | known |
| lay | laid | laid |
| lead | led | led |
| leave | left | left |
| lend | lent | lent |
| let | let | let |
| lie (recline) | lay | lain |
| lie (deceive) | lied | lied |
| lose | lost | lost |
| mean | meant | meant |
| put | put | put |
| raise | raised | raised |

C.20c.

C.20c.

| PRESENT TENSE | PAST TENSE | PAST PARTICIPLE |
| --- | --- | --- |
| read | read | read |
| rid | rid | rid |
| ride | rode | ridden |
| ring | rang | rung |
| rise | rose | risen |
| run | ran | run |
| see | saw | seen |
| set | set | set |
| shake | shook | shaken |
| shine | shone or shined | shone or shined |
| show | showed | shown |
| shrink | shrank or shrunk | shrunk |
| sing | sang or sung | sung |
| sink | sank or sunk | sunk |
| sit | sat | sat |
| slay | slew | slain |
| slide | slid | slid |
| sling | slung | slung |
| slink | slunk | slunk |
| speak | spoke | spoken |
| spend | spent | spent |
| spit | spit or spat | spit or spat |
| spring | sprang or sprung | sprung |
| stand | stood | stood |

| PRESENT TENSE | PAST TENSE | PAST PARTICIPLE |
|---|---|---|
| steal | stole | stolen |
| sting | stung | stung |
| strike | struck | struck |
| strive | strove | striven |
| swear | swore | sworn |
| sweep | swept | swept |
| swim | swam | swum |
| swing | swung | swung |
| take | took | taken |
| teach | taught | taught |
| tear | tore | torn |
| think | thought | thought |
| throw | threw | thrown |
| thrust | thrust | thrust |
| tread | trod | trodden or trod |
| wake | woke or wake | waked |
| wear | wore | worn |
| weave | wove | woven |
| weep | wept | wept |
| wind | wound | wound |
| wring | wrung | wrung |

C.20c.

(4) *Progressive form:* Our language also has progressive verb forms which are verb phrases consisting of a form of *be (been, being, is, am, are, was, were)* plus an *-ing* verb. The progressive form is not a different tense, but a form that may be used with all six tenses. It expresses a *continuing* action. Notice that the *perfect* tenses require an additional helping word.

C.20c.

> He *is going.* (present progressive)
> He *was going.* (past progressive)
> He *will be going.* (future progressive)
> He *has been going.* (present perfect progressive)
> He *had been going.* (past perfect progressive)
> He *will have been going.* (future perfect progressive)

(5) *Emphatic form* gives emphasis by using *do, does,* or *did* with the verb.

> I *did* go, just like I promised.
> He *does* love his little sisters, though it is hard for him to express that love.
> She *did* close the gate. I saw her.

*Do, does,* and *did* are not emphatic forms when they are used as questions or in simple negative statements.

> *Did* you go along? (question; not emphatic)
> I *do* not expect them very early. (negative statement; not emphatic)
> She *does* not care for oysters. (negative statement; not emphatic)

(6) *Usage Guides for Correct Tenses*
(a) The tense of the verb in a subordinate clause should relate logically to the tense in the main clause. The earlier of the two past actions should be in the *past perfect* tense.

> I suddenly *realized* that I *had not finished* my lesson. (The unfinished lesson occurred first; then the realization.)
> I suddenly *realized* that I *did not finish* my lesson. (incorrect)

(b) Do not use two *would have* auxiliaries in the same sentence. Use *had* for the earlier action.

> If I *had* (not *would have*) started it sooner, I *would have* finished it long ago.

(c) A statement that expresses a general truth should be in the *present* tense (it is always currently true) regardless of the tense of other verbs in the sentence.

> Paul preached that Jesus *is* the Christ.
> By the time you have finished fifth grade geography you *will have learned* that the earth *is* not perfectly round.

(d) However, if a "truth" formerly established is now known to be false, the *past* tense is used.

> The Greeks taught that the sun *went* around the earth.

C.20d.

*20d.*

*Number* is the form of the verb which indicates whether the subject of the sentence is singular or plural. A verb must agree with its subject in number.

(1) *Singular verbs* are necessary when the subject is singular.

> One horse *kicks*. (*Kicks* is the singular verb which agrees with the singular subject, *horse*.)

(2) *Plural verbs* are used when the subject is plural.

> Many horses *kick*. (*Kick* is the plural verb which agrees in number with the plural subject, *horses*.)

*Note:* We add -*s* to many nouns to make them plural, but the opposite is true of verbs. *S* is the mark of a *singular* verb.

(3) *Usage Guides for Correct Number*

(a) Compound subjects joined by *and* call for a plural verb. This is true even if only one subject is actually expressed.

> Harold *and* David *enjoy* hiking together.
> A black *and* a white cow *were* in the cornfield.

(b) If, however, the compound subject refers to only one thing, the verb should be singular.

> My roommate and best friend *brings* me home every weekend.
> Bread and jam *makes* a good snack.

(c) Phrases beginning with *as well as, along with, in addition to, including,* or *together with* do not change the number of the subject. They simply provide additional information.

A *boy,* as well as a girl, *is* able to learn cooking. (boy is able)
The study *hall,* in addition to the classroom, *is* a place to learn. (study hall is a place)

(d) Two singular subjects joined by *or* or *nor* require a singular verb, since the sentence is meaning either *one* of them, not *both.*

An oak *or* a maple *is* a good shade tree.

(e) When one singular and one plural subject are joined by *or* or *nor,* the verb should agree with the nearer subject.

Neither the boys *or* Father *knows* where the hammer is.
Neither Father *nor* the boys *know* where the hammer is.

(f) When two plural subjects are joined by *or* or *nor,* a plural verb is needed.

Oaks *or* maples *are* excellent for lumber.

(g) Be especially careful to choose the right verb when it precedes the subject in the sentence.

*Doesn't* (not *don't*) he know what time it is? (he *does* know)
There *are* (not *is*) several rabbits in the garden. (rabbits *are*)

(h) The verb always agrees in number with its *subject,* never with the object of a preposition.

*One* of the pieces *is* missing. (not *"pieces are* missing")

(i) When the subject is a word like *more, most,* or *some,* as well as in expressions such as *plenty of, abundance of, half of, rest of, number of,* the verb can be singular or plural, depending on the context and meaning of the sentence.

Six inches fell today and *more is* expected tonight.
*More are* coming for the food than for the program.
*Plenty* of food *was* passed to the people.
*Plenty* of people *were* astonished at the sight.
A *number* of these men *were* determined to make Jesus king.
The *number* of men *was* five thousand.
*Half* the children *were* laughing.
*Half* of the apple *was* rotten.

*Note:* Though the object of the preposition usually agrees with the verb in number, it actually is not the determining factor. The prepositional phrase simply gives meaning to the subject and indicates whether it is plural or singular. The subject then calls for a singular or plural verb, depending on the meaning supplied by the prepositional phrase.

(j) A noun naming a group which acts as a unit requires a *singular* verb.

> The *brotherhood agrees* unanimously on this matter.
> The *class becomes* noisy when the teacher leaves.

(k) When members of a group act as individuals, a *plural* verb is used.

> The *class were* writing their essays.
> The *jury were* slow in coming to a decision.

(l) When a relative pronoun is the subject in a sentence, the verb agrees with the number of its antecedent.

> It is the lower-grade teacher *who* often *discovers* talents in the pupil. (The antecedent of *who* is *teacher,* which calls for a singular verb.)
> Vitamins and minerals are food supplements *that* often *are* necessary to our health. (*Supplements* is the plural antecedent of the relative pronoun, *that.* Therefore, a plural verb is needed.)

(m) Indefinite pronouns such as *anybody, anyone, each, either, everybody, neither, nobody, no one,* and *somebody* usually require a singular verb. Even though the meaning of the pronoun may be plural, the form is singular.

> *Either* of the boys *knows* how to do the chores.
> *Anybody* who does that *is* wise.

(n) Other indefinite pronouns such as *many, some, both,* and *all* may take a plural verb.

> *All were* saved though *many were* not able to swim.
> *Both like* strawberry ice cream better than vanilla.

(o) Plural numbers take a *singular* verb when they are used in a sentence to indicate a measurement, a sum, or a unit.

> Ten dollars *is* far too much to pay for that.

Four acres *is* the size of this field.
Thirty hours *is* a short workweek.

(p) Expressions in arithmetic usually take singular verbs, though sometimes either singular or plural is correct. The verb following numbers joined by *and* is always plural because *both* constitute the subject. Otherwise there is no specific rule and whichever sounds the best may be used.

C.20d.

Eight divided by four *is* two.
Two plus five *is* seven.
One-fourth of eight *is* two.
Five times eight *is* (or *are*) forty.
Two *and* five *are* seven.

(q) The title of a book, magazine, newspaper, or the like, takes a singular verb even though it contains plural words.

Romans *contains* much encouragement for Christians.
The *New York Times has* been published for many years.

(r) When a sentence is introduced by *there* or *here*, the verb agrees with the subject, which follows the verb.

Here *is* your coat. (coat *is*)
Here *are* the answers to the questions. (answers *are*)
There *is* only one day of salvation—today. (day *is*)
There *are* no opportunities for repentance after death. (opportunities *are*)

(s) When a sentence begins with the expletive *it*, the verb is always singular regardless of the number of the subject.

It *is* the minister and his wife.
It *is* one thing to know, another to do.

(t) Subjects which are plural in form but singular in meaning take singular verbs.

Mathematics *is* often easier for boys than for girls.
No news *is* good news.

(u) A subject which is a plural word used simply as a word calls for a singular verb.

*Idiosyncrasies is* hard to spell.

*Apples was* the only legible word on the memorandum.

*20e.*

*Person* is the form of a verb or pronoun which indicates whether a person is speaking, is spoken to, or is spoken about. When a personal pronoun is the subject of a sentence, the verb must agree with it in *person.*

(1) *First person*—the person speaking.

*I*—first-person *singular* pronoun calls for *am*, first-person *singular* verb.

C.20e.

I *am* always here on Wednesday morning.

*We*—first-person *plural* pronoun calls for *are*, first-person *plural* verb.

We *are* coming after dark.

(2) *Second person*—the person spoken to.

*You* is the singular and the plural form of the pronoun. The second-person verb that agrees with *you* is the same for singular and plural.

You *are* the only one here. (singular)
You *are* my favorite parents. (plural)

(3) *Third person*—the person spoken about.

(a) *He, she,* and *it* are the singular personal pronouns in third person. The *third-person singular* verb that agrees with these pronouns is *is.*

He *is* cold, and *she is* too; but I doubt if *it is* very cold outside.

(b) *They* is the third-person plural pronoun, which calls for *are*, the *third-person plural* verb.

They *are* wiser than we.

(4) *Usage Guides for Correct Person*

(a) *Plural* personal pronouns in the first, second, and third person which can be used as subjects (we, you, they) always take plural *third-*person verbs.

We *run*. We *work*. We *study*. (first-person plural pronouns with third-person plural verbs)

You *jump*. You *smile*. You *decide*. (second-person pronouns with third-person plural verbs)

They *explore*. They *wash*. They *operate*. (third-person pronouns with third-person plural verbs)

(b) When the subject is *first*- or *second*-person *singular* (I, you), use the *plural* of a *present-tense* verb. This is an exception, but it is the correct form of the verb to use.

I *go*. I *sing*. I *meditate*. (*Go, sing,* and *meditate* are present-tense plural verbs, while *I* is *singular*.)

You *bake*. You *sell*. You *save*. (*You* is second-person singular, while the verbs are present-tense *plural*.)

**C.21.**

## 21.

## Conjugations

A conjugation is a listing of all the forms of a verb according to *voice, mood, tense, number,* and *person*. Conjugation is helpful in the study of a language and shows how verbs agree with their subject in person and number.

*21a.*      Conjugation of the Verb *to Be*

**INDICATIVE MOOD**

| *Singular* | *Plural* |
|---|---|
| **PRESENT TENSE** | |
| 1. I am | 1. We are |
| 2. You are | 2. You are |
| 3. He is | 3. They are |
| **PAST TENSE** | |
| 1. I was | 1. We were |
| 2. You were | 2. You were |
| 3. He was | 3. They were |
| **FUTURE TENSE** | |
| 1. I shall be | 1. We shall be |
| 2. You will be | 2. You will be |
| 3. He will be | 3. They will be |

*Singular*                          *Plural*

## PRESENT PERFECT TENSE

1. I have been              1. We have been
2. You have been           2. You have been
3. He has been             3. They have been

## PAST PERFECT TENSE

1. I had been              1. We had been
2. You had been            2. You had been
3. He had been             3. They had been

## FUTURE PERFECT TENSE

1. I shall have been       1. We shall have been
2. You will have been      2. You will have been
3. He will have been       3. They will have been

### SUBJUNCTIVE MOOD

*Singular*                          *Plural*

## PRESENT TENSE

1. (If) I be               1. (If) We be
2. (If) You be             2. (If) You be
3. (If) He be              3. (If) They be

## PAST TENSE

1. (If) I were             1. (If) We were
2. (If) You were           2. (If) You were
3. (If) He were            3. (If) They were

*Singular*                          *Plural*

## PRESENT PERFECT TENSE

1. (If) I have been        1. (If) We have been
2. (If) You have been      2. (If) You have been
3. (If) He have been       3. (If) They have been

## PAST PERFECT TENSE

1. (If) I had been         1. (If) We had been
2. (If) You had been       2. (If) You had been
3. (If) He had been        3. (If) They had been

## IMPERATIVE MOOD

### PRESENT TENSE

| *Singular* | *Plural* |
|---|---|
| Be | Be |

|  | PRESENT | PAST | PERFECT |
|---|---|---|---|
| Infinitives | To be |  | To have been |
| Participles | Being | Been | Having been |
| Gerunds | Being |  | Having been |

**C.21b.**

*21b.*    Conjugation of the Verb *to Grow*

### *Active Voice*

#### INDICATIVE MOOD

| *Singular* | *Plural* |
|---|---|

##### PRESENT TENSE

| 1. I grow | 1. We grow |
|---|---|
| 2. You grow | 2. You grow |
| 3. He grows | 3. They grow |

##### PAST TENSE

| 1. I grew | 1. We grew |
|---|---|
| 2. You grew | 2. You grew |
| 3. He grew | 3. They grew |

##### FUTURE TENSE

| 1. I shall grow | 1. We shall grow |
|---|---|
| 2. You will grow | 2. You will grow |
| 3. He will grow | 3. They will grow |

| *Singular* | *Plural* |
|---|---|

##### PRESENT PERFECT TENSE

| 1. I have grown | 1. We have grown |
|---|---|
| 2. You have grown | 2. You have grown |
| 3. He has grown | 3. They have grown |

##### PAST PERFECT TENSE

| 1. I had grown | 1. We had grown |
|---|---|
| 2. You had grown | 2. You had grown |
| 3. He had grown | 3. They had grown |

FUTURE PERFECT TENSE

1. I shall have grown
2. You will have grown
3. He will have grown

1. We shall have grown
2. You will have grown
3. They will have grown

## SUBJUNCTIVE MOOD

*Singular*                                    *Plural*

PRESENT TENSE

1. (If) I grow
2. (If) You grow
3. (If) He grow

1. (If) We grow
2. (If) You grow
3. (If) They grow

PAST TENSE

1. (If) I grew
2. (If) You grew
3. (If) He grew

1. (If) We grew
2. (If) You grew
3. (If) They grew

*Singular*                                    *Plural*

PRESENT PERFECT TENSE

1. (If) I have grown
2. (If) You have grown
3. (If) He have grown

1. (If) We have grown
2. (If) You have grown
3. (If) They have grown

PAST PERFECT TENSE

1. (If) I had grown
2. (If) You had grown
3. (If) He had grown

1. (If) We had grown
2. (If) You had grown
3. (If) They had grown

## IMPERATIVE MOOD

PRESENT TENSE

*Singular*                    *Plural*
Grow                          Grow

|             | PRESENT | PAST  | PERFECT        |
|-------------|---------|-------|----------------|
| Infinitives | To grow |       | To have grown  |
| Participles | Growing | Grown | Having grown   |
| Gerunds     | Growing |       | Having grown   |

*21c.*    Conjugation of the Verb *to Be Grown*

### Passive Voice

#### INDICATIVE MOOD

| *Singular* | *Plural* |
|---|---|

##### PRESENT TENSE

1. I am grown
2. You are grown
3. He is grown

1. We are grown
2. You are grown
3. They are grown

##### PAST TENSE

1. I was grown
2. You were grown
3. He was grown

1. We were grown
2. You were grown
3. They were grown

##### FUTURE TENSE

1. I shall be grown
2. You will be grown
3. He will be grown

1. We shall be grown
2. You will be grown
3. They will be grown

| *Singular* | *Plural* |
|---|---|

##### PRESENT PERFECT TENSE

1. I have been grown
2. You have been grown
3. He has been grown

1. We have been grown
2. You have been grown
3. They have been grown

##### PAST PERFECT TENSE

1. I had been grown
2. You had been grown
3. He had been grown

1. We had been grown
2. You had been grown
3. They had been grown

##### FUTURE PERFECT TENSE

1. I shall have been grown
2. You will have been grown
3. He will have been grown

1. We shall have been grown
2. You will have been grown
3. They will have been grown

#### SUBJUNCTIVE MOOD

| *Singular* | *Plural* |
|---|---|

##### PRESENT TENSE

1. (If) I be grown
2. (If) You be grown
3. (If) He be grown

1. (If) We be grown
2. (If) You be grown
3. (If) They be grown

PAST TENSE

1. (If) I were grown
2. (If) You were grown
3. (If) He were grown

1. (If) We were grown
2. (If) You were grown
3. (If) They were grown

PRESENT PERFECT TENSE

1. (If) I have been grown
2. (If) You have been grown
3. (If) He have been grown

1. (If) We have been grown
2. (If) You have been grown
3. (If) They have been grown

PAST PERFECT TENSE

1. (If) I had been grown
2. (If) You had been grown
3. (If) He had been grown

1. (If) We had been grown
2. (If) You had been grown
3. (If) They had been grown

C.22.

IMPERATIVE MOOD

PRESENT TENSE

| *Singular* | *Plural* |
|---|---|
| Be grown | Be grown |

| | PRESENT | PAST | PERFECT |
|---|---|---|---|
| Infinitives | To be grown | | To have been grown |
| Participles | Being grown | Grown | Having been grown |
| Gerunds | Being grown | | Having been grown |

## 22.

## Verbals

A verbal is a verb form used as some other part of speech. There are three kinds of verbals—*infinitives, gerunds,* and *participles.*

*22a.*

*Infinitive:* This is the first principal part of any verb preceded by the word *to* (*to go, to sing, to brag*). It can be used as a noun, an adjective, and an adverb.

> *To steal* is wrong. (noun, subject of the sentence)
> His desire was *to learn.* (predicate noun)
> She wanted *to stay.* (noun, direct object)
> His one desire, *to be rich,* led him into evil. (appositive)
> We have many lessons *to learn.* (adjective describing *lessons*)
> The men went outside *to work.* (adverb modifying *went*)

*Note: To* plus a *noun* or *pronoun* is merely a prepositional phrase, not an infinitive.

(1) *Infinitive phrases* consist of an infinitive together with its complements and modifiers. The phrase can serve as a noun, an adjective, or an adverb.

> *To tease a child constantly* is cruel. (The entire phrase is the subject of the sentence. *Child* is the object of the infinitive, *to tease*. *Constantly* modifies the infinitive, *to tease*.)
>
> He is the teacher *to see about the assignment*. (The whole phrase serves as an adjective modifying *teacher*. *About the assignment* is a prepositional phrase which modifies the infinitive, *to see*, and hence is an adverbial phrase.)
>
> Grandma was glad *to see the new baby*. (The infinitive phrase is used as an adverb to modify the predicate adjective, *glad*. *Baby* is the direct object of the infinitive, *to see*.)

C.22a.

Infinitives can have a subject and an object.

> The fire siren made the dog (to) *howl*. (*Dog* is the subject of the infinitive, *to howl*.)
>
> She begged *to ring* the bell. (*Bell* is the direct object of the infinitive, *to ring*.)

(2) *Infinitive clauses* consist of the infinitive, its subject, its complements, and its modifiers.

> Irvin wanted *Jack to help* him *with the plowing*. (*Jack* is the subject of the infinitive, *to help*, and *him* is the complement. *With the plowing* is a prepositional-phrase modifier.)

(3) *Usage Guides for Infinitives*

(a) Infinitives without the *to* frequently occur with verbs such as *see, hear, feel, watch, help, know, dare, need, make, let*, and *please*.

> We had Ellie *make* the doughnuts. (to make)
> I want you to come and *see* me. (to see)

(b) *Split* infinitives occur when other words come between the *to* and the verb. This usually sounds awkward and should be avoided. Sometimes, however, it sounds awkward *not* to split the infinitive. There is nothing grammatically wrong with a split infinitive if it sounds best.

> He was told *to not waste* any time. (awkward split)
> He was told not *to waste* any time. (correct)

It is impossible *to* always *know* exactly what to do. (Split sounds better.)

It is impossible *to know* always exactly what to do. (not split, but awkward)

(c) The *present* infinitive may be used with any verb tense if it refers to both actions occurring at the same time.

I hope *to come* soon.
I hoped *to come* soon. (not *to have come*)
I was hoping *to come* soon.
I had hoped *to come* soon.

C.22b.

(d) Use the *perfect* infinitive in cases where the *present* form leaves a question. Such instances usually occur after verbs of desire, hope, or duty.

I *hoped* to visit him. (does not tell whether or not the visit was made)

I hoped *to have visited* him. (shows that the visit was not made)

(e) The *perfect* infinitive after verbs such as *know*, *think*, and *seem* shows that its action was completed before the action of the main verb in the sentence. Do not use a *present* infinitive in such cases.

Naboth was thought *to have blasphemed*. (not *to blaspheme*)
Ahab seemed *to have gotten* away with his crime. (not "*to get away*")

(f) *Dangling* infinitives are not very common, but they need to be recognized and avoided.

*To trust* in God, our own wisdom must be cast aside. (dangling)
*To trust* in God, *we* must cast aside our own wisdom. (correct)

**22b.**
*Gerund:* A gerund is an *-ing* form of a verb which is used as a *noun.*

*Singing* is worthwhile. (subject of the sentence)
A favorite worship activity is *singing*. (predicate noun)
We enjoy *singing*. (direct object)
Do you have enthusiasm for *singing*? (object of preposition)
This subject, *singing*, has been well discussed. (appositive)

Gerunds may take objects, complements, or modifiers.

Building *bridges* is his livelihood. (*Bridges* is object of the gerund, *building*.)

Jogging is a favorite *exercise* of many people. (*Exercise* complements the gerund, *jogging*.)

Reading *carefully* will help you find the answer. (*Carefully* modifies the gerund, *reading*.)

A gerund with its objects and modifiers is called a gerund phrase.

*Loving God and man sincerely in this life* is a prerequisite for entering heaven. (This gerund phrase has two objects, *God* and *man*. *Sincerely* is an adverb. The adverbial phrase modifies the gerund.)

*Usage Guides for Gerunds*

(1) Do not confuse a gerund, the *name* of an action, with a participle that simply replaces a noun.

*Living* right is important. (true gerund)

We pray for the *living*, not for the dead. (Here, *living* is a participle which stands for *living people*.)

(2) Use the *possessive* form of a noun or pronoun before a gerund, as you would before any other noun (*his* assignment, *cat's* dish).

*His* mentioning the resurrection brought mockery to Paul. (not "*him* or *he* mentioning")

The *puppy's* dying brought sadness to the boy. (not "the *puppy* dying")

(3) Beware of dangling gerunds.

Before *beginning* the meeting, prayer should be offered. (Dangling: *Beginning* does not modify any word in the sentence.)

Before beginning the meeting, *we* should offer prayer. (correct)

We should offer prayer before beginning the meeting. (correct)

After *putting* a worm on my hook, the fish began to bite. (dangling gerund)

After putting a worm on my hook, *I* noticed the fish began to bite. (correct)

*22c.*

*Participles:* A participle is a form of a verb that is used as an *adjective*. It is part verb and part adjective.

(1) The *present participle* ends in *-ing*.

The boys, *running* as hard as they could, reached the school before the girls did. (The participle, *running*, describes *boys*.)

(2) The *past participle* ends in *-d, -ed, -t, -n, -en*, or changes a vowel in the present form of the verb.

die—died—d
fill—filled—ed
deal—dealt—t
see—seen—n
be—been—en
wring—wrung—changes vowel

C.22c.

(3) A *participial phrase* consists of the participle and its related parts, such as modifiers and complements. The entire phrase acts as an adjective in the sentence.

*Eluding the yapping puppies*, the cat reached the tree. (Participle with a direct object, *puppies*, describes *cat. Puppies* completes the meaning of the participle *eluding*.)

*Laughing helplessly*, we tried to stuff the feathers back into the pillow. (*Laughing* is a participle with a modifying adverb, *helplessly*.)

*Tripping unexpectedly over a rug*, Grandmother fell and broke her wrist. (*Unexpectedly* is an adverb modifying the participle, *tripping. Over a rug* is a prepositional phrase that modifies the participle, *tripping*.)

(4) According to its use in the sentence, a participle is *attributive, appositive*, or *predicate*.

The *rushing* water made me dizzy. (Attributive: *Rushing* precedes and attributes a quality to the noun, *water*.)

The children, *talking* excitedly, hurried home to begin their projects. (appositive, immediately following subject)

The book seemed *lost* forever. (participle in the predicate)

(5) *Usage Guides for Participles*

(a) Use the *present* participle if its action occurs at the same time as that of the main verb of the sentence. Otherwise use the *present perfect* form.

*Being* grieved, Paul cast the evil spirit out of the girl. (Paul was grieved at the same time he cast out the spirit.)

*Beating* the missionaries severely, the magistrates threw them into prison. (This *incorrect* form of the participle, *beating*, indicates that the beating occurred at the same time the missionaries were cast into prison.)

*Having beaten* the missionaries severely, the magistrates cast them into prison. (This *present perfect* form of the participle correctly places the time of the beating before the casting into prison.)

**C.23.**

(b)  Avoid dangling participles. A participle or other modifier is said to dangle when there is no logical word for it to modify. Participles should be placed in such a position in the sentence that there is no question about which word they modify.

*Looking* at the stars, a meteor flashed across the sky. (Dangling: The meteor was not looking at the stars.)

*Looking* at the stars, I saw a meteor flash across the sky. (Correct: *Looking* modifies *I*.)

*Running* down the alley, a wall suddenly blocked his path. (Dangling: The wall was not running down the alley.)

*Running* down the alley, he suddenly found his path blocked by a wall. (Correct: The participle modifies *he*.)

*Huddled* on the bank, the rushing water frightened the sheep. (Dangling: The water was not huddled on the bank.)

The rushing water frightened the sheep *huddled* on the bank. (Correct: *Huddled* modifies *sheep*.)

## 23.

## Troublesome Verbs

Some verbs are similar enough in form and meaning to cause mistakes in their usage. Following are some of the most common ones.

### 23a.

#### *Lie* and *Lay*

(1)  *Lie* means "to rest in or get into a reclining position." It is always intransitive, without an object. Its forms are *lie, lay, lain,* and *lying.*

You may *lie* down if you feel sick.
He *lay* on the couch.

He *was lying* there when his wife came home.
He *had lain* there so long that he was stiff.

(2) *Lay.* Though this is spelled the same way as the past tense of *lie,* it is the *present* tense of a word that means "to put or place." *Lay* is a transitive verb requiring a direct object to complete its meaning. Its forms are *lay, laid,* and *laying.* Some forms require auxiliary verbs to indicate the correct tense. Notice the object of each of these verbs in the following examples.

C.23b.

*Lay* your books on the table. (lay books)
The blocks were *laid* well. (laid blocks)
He always *has laid* his hat on the bookcase. (laid hat)
They *are laying* their pictures on that wet table. (laying pictures)

*Exception:* When *lay* means "to produce eggs," it may be intransitive.

Our hens *are laying* well. (no object)

### 23b.
#### Rise and Raise

(1) *Rise* means "to go up, or get up." It is always intransitive, not requiring an object. Its forms are *rise, rose, risen,* and *rising,* used with and without auxiliary verbs to indicate various tenses.

We *rose* at six o'clock.
The sun *had risen* by then.
The Bible says we *should rise* in the presence of older folks.

(2) *Raise* means "to *cause* to go up or to grow up." It is always a transitive verb having an object. Its forms are *raise, raised,* and *raising,* used with and without auxiliary verbs to indicate the various tenses. Notice the object of each verb in the sentences below.

They *raise* cattle for a living.
Competition *has raised* the quality of many goods.
Next January they *will have been raising* chickens for twenty years.

### 23c.
#### Sit and Set

(1) *Sit* means "to be at rest" or "to occupy a seat." It is always intransitive, without an object. Its forms are *sit, sat,* and *sitting,* with various auxiliary verbs to indicate various tenses.

Please *sit* down.
They *have sat* through many such meetings.
We *have been sitting* here since noon.

(2) *Set* means "to put or place," and in this sense it is always transitive, having an object. Its forms are *set* and *setting*, with helping words to indicate the different tenses. Notice the objects and helping words in the examples below.

C.23d.

*Set* your lunch box on the table.
Yesterday he *set* his lunch box here.
I *have set* the table.
Paul *was setting* things in order.

(3) *Set* may also be *intransitive* in several common idioms. In these cases it does not require an object.

The sun *was setting.*
The hen *set* for three weeks.
The concrete *would* not *set* properly.

*23d.*

*Let* and *Leave*

(1) *Let* means "to allow or permit." *Let* is always transitive, with an object to complete its meaning. It usually is followed by an infinitive without the *to,* or some other elliptical expression. Its forms are *let* and *letting*, with auxiliary verbs to indicate some of the tenses.

Mother *is letting* him go along.
She *will let* the others go later.

(2) *Leave* has two meanings. The forms for both are *leave, left,* and *leaving.* One meaning is "to depart." In this sense it is intransitive, not requiring an object.

We *will leave* immediately.
We *left* on time.
We *will be leaving* before the children arrive.

(3) *Leave* also means "to cause to remain behind." In this sense it is transitive, requiring an object.

Jesus *left* the temple.
We *leave* Rufus in the washhouse.
She *was leaving* two hams with Grandpa.

In the following common sentence either *leave* or *let* is correct, depending on the meaning desired. *Let* requires the infinitive *be*.

> We *leave* him alone. (We cause him to remain behind alone.)
> We *let* him alone. (We allow him *to be* alone.)

*23e.*

*Learn* and *Teach*

(1) *Learn* means "to gain knowledge." It may be either transitive or intransitive. Its forms are *learn, learned,* and *learning.* Various helping words are employed to complete various meanings.

> We *learn* in school. (intransitive, no object)
> We *learn* Spanish. (transitive, object *Spanish*)

(2) *Teach* means "to impart knowledge." This also may be transitive or intransitive. Its forms are *teach, taught,* and *teaching,* with different auxiliary verbs.

> Sister Mabel *teaches* in our school. (intransitive)
> She *taught* the lower grades last year. (transitive, object *grades*)
> She *will be teaching* again next year. (intransitive)

*23f.*

*Can* and *May*

(1) *Can* means "to have the ability, the right, or the knowledge to do something."

Its forms are *can* and *could,* and it is used as an auxiliary verb followed by a present-tense verb either expressed or implied.

> Carelessness *can* cause an accident. (ability)
> I *can* drive as well as anyone who has a license. (ability)
> I *could* come another day. (ability expressed)
> I *can.* (Ability is implied for doing whatever the context referred to.)

(2) *May* means "possibility or permission." Its forms are *may* and *might.* It also is an auxiliary verb followed by a present-tense verb expressed or implied.

> *May* I read this book?
> She *might* come. (Verb expressed)
> She really *might.* (A verb is implied.)
> Carelessness *may* cause an accident. (possibility)

In informal usage *can* is commonly used to imply both ability and permission. In most formal writing, the above distinctions are still observed.

*23g.*
*Forms of go, see, come, and do* are often used incorrectly. The mistakes are usually made in the second and third principal parts.

> The boys *had gone* (not *had went*) fishing.
> They *saw* (not *seen*) several deer in the woods.
> They *came* (not *come*) running to tell us.
> The deer *did* (not *done*) a good job of hiding.

# D. ADJECTIVES

## 24.

### Definition

Adjectives are words that describe or limit nouns or pronouns. They answer the questions:

What kind? *purple* clouds, *crippled* children
Which one? *that* nurse, *any* day
How many or how much? *full* glass, *four* dogs, *a* box

D.24.

Skillful choice of adjectives improves the quality of writing and speaking.

Flowers grew along the garden. (simple statement)
*The* brilliant, *orange* marigolds along *the* edge of *the* garden accented *the bushy* rows of beans and *the tall, straight* stalks of corn growing behind them. (*Orange, bushy, tall,* and *straight* provide a more vivid picture of the flower-bordered garden.)

## 25.

### Single-Word Adjectives

Adjectives may be single words like *orange, bushy, tall,* and *straight* in the sentence above. These adjectives usually precede the noun or pronoun which they modify. Single-word adjectives may occur in a series. Commas generally separate them.

A *soft, fluffy, blue, woolen* blanket lined the crib.

Single-word adjectives also include hyphenated constructions.

*Spur-of-the-moment* decisions often are unwise.

## 26.

### Adjective Phrases

Phrases can serve as adjectives in a sentence. They may be prepositional phrases, participial phrases, or infinitive phrases.

The man *with a bald head* was Elisha. (prepositional phrase)
The children, *mocking him,* were disrespectful. (participial phrase)
The One *to take care of things* was God. (infinitive phrase)

## 27.

### Adjective Clauses

Any clause which modifies a noun or a pronoun is an adjective clause.

### 27a.

Adjective clauses usually follow the noun they modify. They are most frequently introduced by a relative pronoun.

> This is the man *who built our house.*
> The valley *which stretched to the opposite mountain* was blanketed by fog.

**D.27.**

### 27b.

Adjective clauses also begin with words such as *where, why,* or *when.*

> The Isle of Patmos, *where John was exiled,* is in the Aegean Sea.
> His wife's illness was the reason *why he could not go.*
> This is the time *when all men should pray.*

### 27c.

The relative pronoun in an adjective clause may be omitted if it is not the subject of the clause.

> He is a teen-ager I admire. (*whom* I admire)

## 28.

### Position According to Use

### 28a.

*Attributive:* The attributive adjective is a direct modifier which *precedes* a noun.

> "He leadeth me beside the *still* waters."

Sometimes other words come between the adjective and its noun.

> *Gentle* but *firm* with children, she made a good teacher.

### 28b.

*Appositive:* An appositive adjective *follows* the noun or pronoun in the position of an appositive, and is usually set off by commas.

The trees, *tall* and *strong,* withstood the storm.
Jesus, *seeing the multitudes,* went up into a mountain.

*28c.*
*Predicate:* Predicate adjectives occur in the predicate, completing the meaning of the verb by describing the subject.

> The Lord is *merciful* and *gracious.* (The adjectives describe *Lord.*)

An adjective in the predicate may also be an objective complement after a direct object.

**D.28c.**

> Frost turned the leaves *brown.* (*Brown* completes the meaning of the direct object, *leaves.*)

## 29.

## Kinds

There are two kinds of adjectives—*descriptive* and *limiting.*

*29a.*
*Descriptive adjectives* name some quality of a noun or pronoun.

> *The winding* road made me dizzy.
> *Spicy* odors filled the kitchen.
> Everyone is inspired by *courageous young* people.

(2) When descriptive adjectives are derived from proper nouns, they are called proper adjectives and are always capitalized.

> The *Indian* woman smiled broadly.
> The *Philistine* soldiers fled in all directions.
> On a tossed salad, *Italian* dressing is my favorite.

*29b.*
*Limiting adjectives* restrict the meaning of a noun or pronoun to a particular object, a certain number, or a specific quantity. They answer the questions, Which one? How many? or How much?
(1) *Articles:* The articles *a, an,* and *the* are the most frequently used adjectives in our language. *A* and *an* are *indefinite* articles because they refer to *any* one of a general group.

*A* woman swept the glass away.
Mother gave Jack *an* orange.

(a) *An* is used before words that begin with a *vowel sound.*

She was *an* honest person. (*Honest* begins with an *o* sound.)
*An* indigo bunting flitted to the fence post.

(b) *A* is used before words that begin with a *consonant sound.*

A unique advertisement caught his eye. (*Unique* begins with a *y* sound.)
What *a* great splash it made!

(c) *The* is a definite article, indicating a *definite* noun or pronoun.

*The* fox easily outran *the* hounds.
She could hardly wait to see *the* picture.

(2) *Demonstrative adjectives* point to a *particular* noun or pronoun. They are the only adjectives that have inflections to indicate number.

*This* pen writes nicely. (singular)
*These* pens write well too. (plural)
*That* house needs paint. (singular)
*Those* barns also need paint. (plural)

Notice that these demonstrative adjectives are the same words as demonstrative pronouns. (See section 12.) The difference is in their function in the sentence. When used alone, they are pronouns. When used as modifiers, they are adjectives.

(3) *Indefinite adjectives* indicate *any unspecified* object.

*Most* houses cannot escape having *some* mice in them.
*Few* drivers realize the *many* risks they take when traveling above the speed limit.

(4) *Interrogative adjectives* are relative pronouns used in the capacity of adjectives in asking questions.

*Whose* land is this?
*Which* one do you prefer?
*What* incident was she referring to?

(5) *Numerical adjectives* indicate numbers and chronological order.

He dashed for *third* base.
*Seven* dogs were chasing *one* little cat.

(6) *Possessive adjectives* are possessive nouns or pronouns used as modifiers.

*Our* ears should be tuned to the voice of God as *Samuel's* ears were.
*My* advice is unreliable unless it is supported by Scripture.

(7) *Relative adjectives* introduce adjective clauses which describe a noun in the sentence.

The little boy, *whose* father was preaching, sat quietly on the front bench.
The excuse *that* had been used before was not acceptable this time.

## 30.

## Degrees

Descriptive adjectives and a few limiting adjectives change form to indicate to what degree a certain quality is intended in the sentence. This change is called *comparison*. The English language contains three degrees of comparison.

*30a.*
*Positive degree* simply states a quality without comparing it to anything.

Roger is *courteous*.
Those are *delicate* leaves.

*30b.*
*Comparative degree* is the form used to make a comparison between two persons or things. It shows that the quality of one is more or less than that of the other.

My knife is *sharper* than yours.
It is the *sharper* of the two.
This flock of sheep is *less contented* than that flock.

*30c.*
*Superlative degree* is the lowest or highest degree of comparison. It

always involves at least three objects.

> This knife is the *sharpest* of all three.
> The raccoon scrambled to the *lowest* branch.

## 31.
## Rules for Forming Comparisons

*31a.*
*Regular comparisons* of most adjectives of one syllable are formed by adding *-er* or *-est* to the positive form.

| POSITIVE | COMPARATIVE | SUPERLATIVE |
|----------|-------------|-------------|
| dark | darker | darkest |
| kind | kinder | kindest |
| sweet | sweeter | sweetest |

The different degrees of longer adjectives are formed by using *more, most, less,* or *least* with the positive degree.

| POSITIVE | COMPARATIVE | SUPERLATIVE |
|----------|-------------|-------------|
| beautiful | more beautiful | most beautiful |
| energetic | less energetic | least energetic |

*31b.*
*Irregular comparisons* are formed in ways other than by adding *-er* and *-est* to the positive degree. When in doubt about any form of comparison, consult a dictionary. Below are some common irregular comparisons.

| POSITIVE | COMPARATIVE | SUPERLATIVE |
|----------|-------------|-------------|
| bad | worse | worst |
| good | better | best |
| many or much | more | most |

When the positive degree of a *regular* adjective ends in *y*, change the *y* to *i* and add *-er* or *-est* to form the other degrees.

| POSITIVE | COMPARATIVE | SUPERLATIVE |
|----------|-------------|-------------|
| happy | happier | happiest |
| jolly | jollier | jolliest |
| funny | funnier | funniest |

## 32.

## Usage Guidelines for Adjectives

*32a.*

Adjectives that express absolute qualities, such as *dead, unique, perfect, square, straight, fatal,* or *waterproof,* cannot logically show comparison. Either a test paper is perfect or it is not; a cover is waterproof or it leaks; a tree is dead or alive. A line cannot be straight*er* than straight, nor something fatal*er* than fatal.

However, in informal usage, writers and speakers often use the adverb *nearly* or *more nearly* to indicate a condition not quite absolute.

D.32.

> This block is *more nearly square* than that one. (but not *squarer*)
> The rosebush was *nearly* dead. (but not *deader* or *less* dead)

*32b.*

In using comparative adjectives, adding the word *other* can change the meaning of the sentence.

> John is *shorter* than any *other* ninth grader. (*Other* shows that John is a ninth grader himself.)
> John is shorter than any ninth grader. (John might be a tenth or eleventh grader.)

*32c.*

When using *first* or *last* with a number, place it before the number word for clearer meaning.

> You may spend the *last ten* minutes cleaning the room. (not "the *ten last* minutes")
> The *first two* girls may hold the doors open. (not "the *two first* girls")

*32d.*

Use *less* to indicate *quantity,* and *fewer* when referring to *number.*

> There will be *less* time for studying tomorrow.
> *Fewer* people attended the meeting this month.

*32e.*

Use an article with every noun in a sentence.

> *A* blue and brown rug was on the floor. (One article indicates one rug.)

*A* blue and *a* brown rug were on the floor. (Two rugs are shown by the use of two articles though *rug* is used only once.)

*The* writer and publisher of this book will speak. (There is one article, so the writer and publisher are the same person.)

*The* writer and *the* publisher of this book will speak. (Two articles indicate two different people will speak.)

*32f.*

Other determiners (words that signal nouns) need not be repeated unless necessary for clarity, or to show that the nouns are considered as individuals, not as a unit.

*My* father and mother were waiting. (There are clearly two people, so *my* need not be repeated before *mother.*)

*My* teacher and father taught me to enjoy history. (Are the teacher and father different people? This is not clear.)

The teacher talked with all *the* boys and girls. (one group, one article)

The teacher talked with all *the* boys and all *the* girls. (Individual groups call for a repetition of the article.)

*32g.*

Do not use articles unnecessarily.

What kind of wrench do you need? (not "kind of *a* wrench")
James was sick with measles. (not "with *the* measles")

# E. ADVERBS

## 33.

### Definition

An adverb is a word that modifies a verb, an adjective, another adverb, or a verbal.

> He can run *fast*. (The adverb, *fast*, modifies the **verb, can run**.)
> The western sky looked *oddly* green. (The adverb, *oddly*, modifies the **adjective green**.)
> She dresses *quite* modestly. (The adverb *quite* modifies the **adverb modestly**.)
> To forgive *freely* is possible only to the Christian. (The adverb *freely* modifies the **verbal to forgive**.)

Adverbs make the meaning of a sentence more clear. Compare the following sentences.

> We are disappointed.
> We *usually* are disappointed *too easily*.

## 34.

### Single-Word Adverbs

Single-word adverbs are divided into classes—adverbs of *manner, time, place, condition or reason*, and *extent*.

*Simple* one-word adverbs make a statement. *Interrogative* adverbs ask a question.

#### 34a.

*Adverbs of manner* tell or ask *how* an action occurred.

> He peered *cautiously* around the door.

#### 34b.

*Adverbs of time* tell or ask *when* an action occurred.

> I want you to come *now*.
> *When* do you plan to stop for lunch?

#### 34c.

*Adverbs of place* tell or ask *where* an action occurred.

> We are going *home*.
> *Where* was Jesus born?

*34d.*

*Adverbs of condition or reason* tell or ask *under what condition* or for what *reason* an action occurred.

> God always forgives *if we repent of our sins.*
> *If I go,* will you come too?
> The seeds did not sprout *because it was too cold.*
> *Why* did Harry think he could run as fast as the wagon?

*34e.*

*Adverbs of extent* tell or ask *how much, how often,* and *to what extent* or *degree* an action occurred.

> She sang *twice.*
> Was it *entirely* burned?

*34f.*

*Sentence Parts Modified by Single Adverbs*

Single-word adverbs can modify another word, a phrase, a clause, or the entire remainder of the sentence.

> *Come* quietly. (*Quietly* modifies one word, *come.*)
> He was nearly *out of breath.* (*Nearly* modifies the phrase, *out of breath.*)
> They arrived soon *after we did.* (*Soon* modifies the clause *after we did.*)
> Naturally, *we did not tell the boys anything about it.* (*Naturally* modifies the rest of the sentence.)

## 35.

## Verbals Modified by Adverbs

Although verbals serve as nouns or adjectives in a sentence, their verb characteristics require an adverb for a modifier.

> Answering *softly* turns away the wrath of others. (*Softly* modifies the **gerund,** *answering,* although the verbal is a noun, the subject of the sentence.)
> Paul was taught to work *hard.* (*Hard* modifies the **infinitive,** *to work,* which is the direct object of the verb, *taught.*)
> The dog, barking *crossly,* could not be trusted. (*Crossly* modifies the **participle,** *barking.*)

## 36.

## Adverb Phrases

Phrases can be used as adverbs to modify verbs, adjectives, or other adverbs. Adverbial phrases are either *prepositional* or *infinitive* phrases.

*36a.*
*Prepositional Phrases*

We meet *at church.* (The adverbial phrase modifies the *verb, meet.*)

*All over the steep, forested mountain side* roamed the cattle. (The prepositional phrase modifies the *verb, roamed*)

I will call you early *in the morning.* (The adverbial phrase modifies the *adverb, early.*)

He was delighted *with the invitation.* (The adverbial phrase modifies the *adjective, delighted.*)

*36b.*
*Infinitive Phrases*

We come *to worship God.* (The infinitive phrase modifies the *verb, come.*)

*"To be sure,* you may go along," declared Mother. (The adverbial phrase modifies the *verb phrase, may go.*)

## 37.

## Adverb Clauses

An adverb clause is a subordinate clause which modifies a verb, an adjective, or another adverb.

*Before the rain started,* we managed to plant the corn. (The adverbial clause modifies the *verb, managed.*)

She was delighted *that they were going along.* (The adverbial clause modifies the *adjective, delighted.*)

The cat sleeps later *than the birds do.* (The adverbial clause modifies the *adverb, later.*)

Adverbs used to connect or relate main clauses are called *conjunctive adverbs.* They may be words generally used as prepositions, or words such as *however, therefore, thus, accordingly, nevertheless, henceforth, unless, anyhow, furthermore, consequently, meanwhile, likewise, otherwise, besides,* and *moreover.*

## 38.

## Adverb Degrees

There are three degrees to show comparison of adverbs, just as there are for adjectives—*positive, comparative,* and *superlative.*

*38a.*

*Positive degree* is the simple form of the adverb. It shows no comparison at all.

> The girls laughed *merrily.*
> Jeffrey skated *fast.*

*38b.*

*Comparative degree* is used to compare two things. One is *more* or *less* than the other.

(1) Adverbs that end in *-ly* are compared by putting *more* or *less* before the positive form.

> The boys laughed *more merrily* than the girls.

(2) Adverbs that do not end in *-ly* usually add *-er* to show the comparative degree.

> Jeffrey skated fast, but John Mark skated *faster.*

*38c.*

*Superlative degree* indicates the *most* or the *least* among more than two things.

(1) The superlative form of adverbs ending in *-ly* is made by putting *most* or *least* before the positive form.

> The parents laughed *most merrily* of all.

(2) Adverbs which do not end in *-ly* indicate the superlative degree by adding *-est* to the positive form.

> Curtis skated *fastest* of all.

(3) Adding *more, most, less, least, -er,* and *-est* to adverbs is called making *regular* comparisons. When adverbs are compared in ways other than these, they are called *irregular* comparisons.

(a) *Regular*

| POSITIVE | COMPARATIVE | SUPERLATIVE |
|---|---|---|
| sweetly | more sweetly | most sweetly |
| near | nearer | nearest |
| kindly | less kindly | least kindly |

(b) *Irregular*

| POSITIVE | COMPARATIVE | SUPERLATIVE |
|---|---|---|
| ill, badly | worse | worst |
| well | better | best |

(4) Avoid using extravagant superlatives. Writers and speakers become less effective and convincing if they use superlatives without substantiating their statements.

"Safe in the Arms of Jesus" is Fanny Crosby's *most* touching hymn. (Who can prove this? It is merely an opinion.)

## 39.

## Position of Adverbs in the Sentence

*39a.*

An important characteristic of adverbs is that they can be placed in different positions in a sentence. This makes possible an interesting variety of sentence forms.

(1) Adverbs can come before the words they modify.

He *often* thought about his mother's warning.

(2) Adverbs can follow the words they modify.

She laughed *unexpectedly* when the dish broke.

(3) When an adverb modifies a phrase, it may come in the middle of the phrase.

Daffodils are *sometimes* seen blooming above snow.

(4) For emphasis or variety, an adverb may be placed at the beginning of the sentence and separated from the word it modifies by another part of the sentence.

*Eventually*, after months of trustful waiting, her prayer was answered.

(5) Adverbial phrases may be placed at the beginning or at the end of a sentence.

> *Behind the barn* stood the remains of our first Model T.
> Christians are safe *in the shelter of His wings.*

(6) Clauses, too, may be placed at the beginning or at the end of a sentence.

> *At the moment the clock began to strike,* Jerry fainted.
> Father picked up the hitchhiker *because night was falling and the rain had turned to sleet.*

(7) Adverbs can come in the middle of a sentence.

> A mockingbird trilled ecstatically *in the lilac bush,* convincing all of us that spring had indeed arrived.

### 39b.

Adverbs can usually be placed in various positions in a sentence without changing the meaning. Be careful, however, with adverbs such as *only, almost,* and *not.* Wrong placement of these can change the meaning entirely. Compare the meanings below.

> Satan *almost* destroyed all of Job's possessions.
> Satan destroyed *almost* all of Job's possessions. (*Almost destroyed* carries a different meaning than *almost all.*)

> Everyone who reads the Bible is *not* saved.
> *Not* everyone who reads the Bible is saved. (*Not saved* is different from *not everyone.*)

> I *only* ate five cookies. (This common misplacement of *only* means that I did not *see* the cookies. I did not *touch, smell, taste,* or do anything else to them but *eat* them.)
> I ate *only* five cookies. (Obviously this is the correct meaning.)

### 39c.

Avoid awkward placement of adverbs even if the meaning is not incorrect.

> We should learn to *correctly place* modifiers. (awkward)
> We should learn to *place* modifiers *correctly.* (better)

# 40.

## Usage Guidelines for Adverbs

*40a.*
Use *from* after the adverb *differently* instead of *than.*

> After his conversion, Saul lived *differently from* the way he had lived before.

*40b.*
Certain modifiers, especially when used in imperative sentences, can be used as adverbs *or* adjectives.

> Drive *slow* (or *slowly*) through residential districts. (*Slow* and *slowly* both are adverbs.)
> This bus is *slow.* (*Slow* is an adjective.)

> Hold the rope *tight* (or *tightly*). (Both are adverbs.)
> *Tight* shoes are uncomfortable. (adjective)

*40c.*
Do not confuse adjectives with adverbs. It is important in writing and speaking to use the correct modifier.

> John can read *well.* (Not *good: Well* is an adverb that modifies *can read.*)
> The meat smells *good.* (*Good* is an adjective modifying the *noun, meat.*)

> He *surely* enjoys company. *Surely* is an adverb that modifies the verb, *enjoys.*)
> The man was *sure* that the moneymaking scheme was a *sure* thing. (*Sure,* in both places, is an adjective. It modifies *man* and *thing.*)

*Note:* In informal speech *sure* is used for *surely* or *certainly.*

*40d.*
The adverbs *very* and *too* should be accompanied by another adverb when modifying past participles.

> I am not *too greatly* surprised by the verdict. (not *too surprised*)

*40e.*
*Very* is an overworked adverb and should be replaced with more

explicit modifiers or omitted entirely.

> He was *very* much pleased with the assignment. (overworked)
>
> Replace with:
> > He was pleased . . .
> > He was much pleased . . .
> > He was exceedingly pleased . . .

*40f.*

The following are not considered correct adverbs: *anywheres, nowheres near, illy, muchly, somewheres, nohow.*

**E.40f.**

*40g.*

The *-ly* ending is used to change most adjectives to adverbs. There are, however, some exceptions to this, so consult a dictionary for spelling if there is any question.

> *sudden* turn (adjective and noun)
> *suddenly* turning (adverb and verb)
>
> *natural* action (adjective and noun)
> acting *naturally* (verb and adverb)
>
> an *accidental* drowning (adjective and noun)
> drowning *accidentally* (verb and adverb)

*40h.*

Do not use adverbs unnecessarily.

> The robbers had beaten the traveler. (not "beaten *up*")
> When will they connect the lights? (not "connect *up*")
> The children continued singing despite the noise. (not "continued *on* singing")

*40i.*

Do not use *kind of* or *sort of* for *rather* or *somewhat.*

> We felt *rather* tired. (not "*kind of* tired")
> This tastes *somewhat* like coconut. (not "*sort of* like")

*40j.*

Do not use two negatives. One cancels the other, and the statement becomes positive. *No, none, nothing, nobody,* and *never* should not be used with the adverbs *not, scarcely,* or *hardly,* which are negative in meaning.

The children did *not* have *no* crayons. (incorrect)
The children had *no* crayons. (correct)
The children did *not* have any crayons. (correct)

I *can't hardly* see the road. (incorrect)
I can *hardly* see the road. (correct)
I *can't* see the road. (correct)

We *haven't scarcely* enough money for the rent. (incorrect)
We *haven't* enough money for the rent. (correct)
We have *scarcely* enough money for rent. (correct)

*40k.*

*But* is also negative in meaning sometimes.

We *haven't but* three minutes left. (incorrect)
We *have but* three minutes left. (correct)

*40l.*

*Not* is nearly always used as an adverb. When *not* is part of a contraction, the *n't* is still an adverb, not part of the verb.

*40m.*

In certain situations a double negative is acceptable for educated usage for an affirmative statement.

Grandfather's voice was *not unkind* as he talked with the thief.
I am *not unwilling* to go.

Notice that these sentences are intended to be positive, whereas the common incorrect use of two negatives is in a statement that is meant to be negative.

*40n.*

Though most adverbs end in *-ly*, this is not a reliable clue, because some *adjectives* end in *-ly* also. In addition, not all adverbs end in *-ly*. The only sure way to identify an adverb is by its use in the sentence.

They went *happily* to bed. (adverb ending in *-ly*)
He was a *manly* little fellow. (adjective ending in *-ly*)
They sailed *straight* into the cove. (adverb not ending in *-ly*)

# F. PREPOSITIONS

## 41.

### Definition

A preposition is a word that shows the relationship between a noun or pronoun and another word in the sentence.

Prepositions do not have different forms as nouns, pronouns, verbs, adverbs, and adjectives do. That is why they do not belong to the *form* class of words, but are called *function* or *structure* words. Prepositions always have an object, which is usually a noun or pronoun.

**F.41.**

Prepositions can be one word or several words.

## 42.

### One-Word Prepositions

*42a.*

The following are some of the more common prepositions.

| | | | |
|---|---|---|---|
| aboard | behind | from | throughout |
| about | below | in | to |
| above | beneath | into | toward |
| across | beside | like | under |
| after | between | of | underneath |
| against | beyond | off | until |
| along | by | on | up |
| among | down | over | upon |
| around | during | past | with |
| at | except | since | within |
| before | for | through | without |

*42b.*

Most of these prepositions show relationship of *time* or *place*.

(1) *TIME.*

| | |
|---|---|
| *during* the storm | *until* the storm |
| *after* the storm | *since* the storm |
| *before* the storm | *throughout* the storm |

(2) *PLACE.*

| | |
|---|---|
| *past* the tree | *toward* the tree |
| *in* the tree | *beside* the tree |
| *behind* the tree | *above* the tree |
| *under* the tree | *against* the tree |
| *across* the tree | *at* the tree |

All the prepositions in the above list can be used with one-word objects.

# 43.

## Two- or Three-Word Prepositions

The following are prepositions that include more than one word.

| | |
|---|---|
| because of | with regard to |
| instead of | in spite of |
| from among | on account of |
| outside of | in reference to |

# 44.

## Prepositional Phrases

In simple terms, a preposition with its object and modifiers is called a prepositional phrase. The preposition is the first word of the phrase, and a noun or pronoun is the last word. These phrases make your writing more clear, exact, and interesting.

### 44a.
### Adjective Phrases

(1) A prepositional phrase that serves as an adjective modifies a noun or pronoun just as a single adjective does. It usually tells *which one* or *what kind.*

> *Bring the cup with the cracked handle.* (which one)
> In heaven there are streets *of gold.* (what kind)

(2) An adjective prepositional phrase sometimes follows another adjective phrase with both phrases modifying the same noun.

> She bought a book *of short poems by Laurel Wood.*

(3) An adjective prepositional phrase which is part of an adverb phrase

modifies a noun in the adverb phrase.

> The plane landed *on the beach of black sand.* (The adjective phrase, *of black sand*, modifies the noun *beach*, which is the object of the preposition *on*. *On a beach of black sand* is an adverb phrase modifying the verb, *landed*.)

(4) An adjective phrase which is part of a larger adjective phrase modifies a noun in the larger adjective phrase.

> Most *of the students in ninth grade* went along. (*In ninth grade* modifies the noun *students*. *Students* is the object of the first preposition in the adjective phrase *of the students in ninth grade*.)

### 44b.
#### Adverb Phrases

(1) A prepositional phrase that serves as an adverb modifies a verb, an adjective, or an adverb, just as a single adverb does. It answers the questions *how, when, where, to what extent*, and *why*.

> He sings *like his brothers.* (how)
> He sings *during his devotions.* (when)
> He sings *at church.* (where)
> He sings *for hours.* (to what extent)
> He sings *for many reasons.* (why)

(2) Two adverb phrases may occur in a series, both modifying the same verb.

> The sale will be held *on Wednesday at ten o'clock.*

### 44c.
#### Noun Phrases

A phrase that begins with a preposition and serves as the subject of the sentence is a prepositional noun phrase.

> *Before sunrise* is a delightful time to get up in summer.
> *Through the window* was the quickest way to get out of the burning house.

## 45.

## Position of Prepositions in the Sentence

### 45a.

One-word prepositions usually precede their objects.

We got up *at dawn*.

No one wanted to talk *about* the *accident*.

*45b.*

They may also correctly follow their object, appearing at the end of the sentence.

The Bible is *what* we live *by*.

There are three patterns *which* you may choose *from*.

*45c.*

Prepositional phrases can be placed in the beginning, in the middle, or at the end of a sentence. This flexibility makes possible interesting variety in sentence forms.

**F.45b.**

(1) An adjective phrase normally follows the noun or pronoun it modifies.

A glass *of iced mint tea* was served each helper.

The white-haired gentleman *in the first row* is my father.

(2) Adverb phrases can be placed almost anywhere in the sentence.

*In my opinion,* camel meat would not be good to eat.

He closed his book *with a bang* that woke the baby.

The hail roared on the roof *for an hour*.

# 46.

## Usage Guidelines for Prepositions

*46a.*

Use the correct preposition to show exact meanings.

(1) *At* or *To*

(a) *At* shows position *in* or *by* or *near* something.

We were *at* home by dark. (not "*to* home")

(b) *To* means "in the direction of."

We ran *to* the mailbox.

(2) *In* or *into*

(a) Use *in* when the meaning is *within*.

She is *in* the store.

(b) Use *into* to express movement from one place to another.

> She ran *into* the store.
> We counted fifty bats flying *into* the cave, so we know there are at least several dozen *in* there.

(3) *Between* or *Among*

(a) Use *between* when referring to *two* people or things.

> They divided the work *between* Sally and Joan.

(b) Use *among* when referring to *more* than two.

> Violets grew *among* the trees.

**46b.**

A word that is a preposition in one sentence may be an adverb in another.

> The ball rolled *off* the table. (preposition, has an object)
> The ball rolled *off*. (adverb, modifying *rolled*)
> The children ran *around* the house and dashed *inside* the garage. (Both prepositions have objects, *house* and *garage*.)
> The girls walked *around* for a while, then went *inside*. (These adverbs modify the verbs, *walked* and *went*. They have no objects.)

**46c.**

If two verbs require different prepositions, do not omit the first one.

> Such a small amount of garlic does not detract or add *to* the flavor. (incorrect)
> Such a small amount of garlic does not detract *from* or add *to* the flavor. (correct)

**46d.**

Prepositions may be used effectively in parallel structures.

> Happiness does not lie *in* man's wealth, *in* his social success, *in* his physical health, but *in* his relationship with the Lord.
> The money was not *in* the book, *on* the book, or *under* the book.

**46e.**

Prepositions may have more than one object.

> The letter *to Bob* and *Betty* made them happy.

*46f.*
Short introductory prepositional phrases usually are not followed by a comma unless they are distinctly parenthetical.

> *Before going home* they sang "The Lord's Prayer." (comma not needed)
> *For example*, think of the prodigal son. (comma needed)

*46g.*
Do not use prepositions unnecessarily.

> The widow used all the oil (not "all *of* the oil")
> When the argument was over, no one had changed his mind. (not "over *with*")
> We are going to Julia's house to practice. (not "*over* to")
> Where is the service to be held? (not "held *at*")
> Put a slab of cheese between the bread slices. (not "*in* between")
> Where does this path lead? (not "lead *to*")

Other phrases in which prepositions are used unnecessarily.

continue *on*     remember *of*
off *of*          where *at*
plan *on*         where *to*
Use *behind* instead of *in back of.*

*46h.*
The word *to* may introduce a prepositional phrase or an infinitive phrase. The indentifying feature of each is that a prepositional phrase beginning with *to* always ends with a *noun* or a *pronoun*, while an infinitive phrase has a *verb* following the *to*.

> She enjoys going *to school.* (The prepositional phrase ends with a *noun, school.*)
> She goes there *to learn.* (The infinitive phrase ends with a *verb, learn.*)

*46i.*
Use *arrive in* when referring to a general area, and *arrive at* when referring to a specific point.

> They arrived *in* the United States in 1846.
> After six hours of driving, we arrived *at* the border.

# G. CONJUNCTIONS

## 47.

### Definition

A conjunction is a word that joins words, phrases, or clauses in a sentence. A conjunction is often called a connector because it connects various sentence elements.

## 48.

### Coordinate Conjunctions

A coordinate conjunction connects words, phrases, or clauses of *equal* rank in the sentence. The construction is *parallel*.

> He left Judea *and* departed again into Galilee. (The conjunction *and* joins *left* and *departed*, which are equal—both are verbs. They also are parallel—both are single words.)
>
> I am sure it is in the drawer *or* on the table. (The conjunction, *or*, joins *in the drawer* and *on the table*, which are equal—both are modifiers. They are parallel—both are prepositional phrases.)
>
> "He must increase, *but* I must decrease." (The conjunction, *but*, joins two equal, independent clauses.)

*48a.*
*Main Coordinate Conjunctions*
The main coordinate conjunctions are *and, or, but, nor,* and *for. Yet* is also a simple conjunction when used in the sense of *but*. When *so* is used to mean *therefore*, it also is a main simple coordinating conjunction.

Main coordinate conjunctions may be used to show three relationships.

(1) *Addition* or *Continuing Thought*

> Malinda did not think much of the plan, *nor* was she slow in letting us know how she felt.
>
> Rhonda *and* Jeffrey brought the ice cream.

(2) *Contrast*

> A cold, wet snow was falling, *but* the men were warm and dry in the chicken house.

G.47.

He looked completely bedraggled, *yet* he smiled engagingly.

(3) *Result* or *Consequence*

A shower was coming up in the west, *so* we took umbrellas.
Drop the letter in the box now, *or* the mailman may go.

*48b.*
*Conjunctive adverbs* are adverbs used to connect main clauses in a
sentence. They also are used to show three relationships.

(1) *Addition* or *Continuing Thought*

We ran out of gas; *also* we had a flat tire.
We didn't ask for any money; *indeed,* we never expected to be
paid for helping a stranger in trouble.

(2) *Contrast*

The teacher did not scold; *instead* he praised Roy.
Libby Ann told the truth; *nevertheless* it sounded like a made-
up story.

(3) *Result* or *Consequence*

Randolph did not listen to the instructions; *consequently* he
made numerous mistakes.
Betsy knew she had done her work well; *therefore* her conscience
was at peace.

*48c.*
*Correlative conjunctions* are connectives used in pairs. They express
a choice between one idea and another and usually connect parallel
structures.

The Bible gives us facts on *both* the past *and* the future.
Mother said she could *neither* decide that quickly *nor* get ready
that fast.

# 49.

## Subordinate Conjunctions

Subordinate conjunctions connect two clauses of *unequal* rank.
They do not join words or phrases, but connect a subordinate clause
to the main clause.

These conjunctions are sometimes called subordinate-clause

markers because they indicate the beginning of a subordinate clause. They can express four relationships between the main clause and the subordinate clause.

*49a.*

*Time* (after, before, since, until, when, whenever, while)

> I will reply to the letter *after* I hear from you.
> *Until* you realize your lost condition, you can never appreciate Christ's sacrifice on the cross.

**G.49a.** *49b.*

*Cause* or *Reason* (as, because, inasmuch as, whereas)

> *Because* he had arthritis, he avoided shaking hands.
> They thought she was snobbish, *whereas* she was only shy.

*49c.*

*Purpose* or *Result* (that, in order that, so that)

> Mother cut the pie *in order that* we all could have some.
> We opened the barn door *so that* the horses could get out.

*49d.*

*Condition* (although, provided, unless, if, even though)

> *Even though* it was pouring rain, they went hiking.
> You may use the car, *provided* you fill it with gas.

## 50.

## Usage Guidelines for Conjunctions

*50a.*

Some subordinate conjunctions may be used as prepositions. Others are essentially adverbs while they serve as connectors. The conjunction *that* is also a relative pronoun.

*50b.*

Do not use the preposition *like* for the conjunction *as* or *as if.*

> He drives as a Christian should. (not *"like* a Christian")
> She smiled *as if* she were highly pleased. (not *"like* she were pleased")

*50c.*
Do not use *because* instead of *that*.

> The reason I was late was *that* I had car trouble. (not *"because I had car trouble"*)

*50d.*
The following conjunctive adverbs are usually preceded by a semicolon: *besides, likewise, furthermore, moreover, however, nevertheless, otherwise, consequently, therefore,* and *accordingly.*
(1) The use of a comma after them is frequently a matter of taste.
(2) When the following conjunctions are used to join coordinate clauses, they usually are preceded by a comma: *or, nor, for, and, yet, so,* and *but.*

G.50c.

### COORDINATE CONJUNCTIONS

| Simple | Correlative | Conjunctive Adverbs | |
|---|---|---|---|
| and | both . . . and | accordingly | instead |
| but | either . . . or | also | likewise |
| for | neither . . . nor | anyhow | meanwhile |
| nor | not only . . . but also | besides | moreover |
| or | whether . . . or | consequently | namely |
| so | | furthermore | nevertheless |
| yet | | hence | otherwise |
| | | henceforth | still |
| | | however | then |
| | | indeed | therefore |
| | | | thus |

### SUBORDINATE CONJUNCTIONS

| | | | |
|---|---|---|---|
| after | because | provided | until |
| although | before | since | when |
| as | even if | so that | whenever |
| as if | even though | than | where |
| as long as | how | that | wherever |
| as much as | if | though | whether |
| as soon as | inasmuch as | till | while |
| as though | in order that | unless | why |

# H. INTERJECTIONS

## 51.

### Definition

An interjection is a word that expresses emotion.

*51a.*
It may be part of the sentence.

**H.51**

> *Oh, well,* it really doesn't matter that much.

*51b.*
An interjection may be separate from the sentence.

> **Help! My car's on fire!**

*51c.*
Interjections are usually single words used to express feelings such as anger, sorrow, disgust, joy, pain, surprise, or excitement. They have no grammatical relation to the rest of the sentence and are not included in diagrams.

*51d.*
Some imitated sounds are classed as interjections.

> **gr-r-r-r, bang, cluck, drip-drop, ba-a-a**

*51e.*
Words spoken to animals often are interjections.

> **whoa, gee, haw, steady there**

*51f.*
Any word when used as an independent exclamation can be an interjection.

> *Ice cream!* I don't even want to see it after that dinner we just ate.
> *Beautiful!* You always had a knack with flower arrangements.
> *What!* That's certainly not the way I heard it.
> *Imagine!* They asked me to go along to Europe.

*51g.*
Single words of profanity, minced oaths, and bywords are classed as

interjections.

## 52.

## Usage Guidelines for Interjections

*52a.*

Mild interjections are followed by commas, while exclamation marks indicate more emphatic ones. The sentence following an emphatic interjection should begin with a capital letter.

> *My,* how you have grown.
> *Ouch!* That hurts.

H.52.

*52b.*

If the whole sentence shows strong feeling, a comma may be placed after the interjection and an exclamation mark at the end of the sentence.

> *Oh,* what a horrible wreck!

# II. Word Origins

## A BRIEF STUDY
## OF THE ENGLISH LANGUAGE

The study of origins of words shows that the English language of today is composed largely of other languages. The *derivation* of a word, given in most dictionaries, tells its background. For example, *period* is derived from Old French *periode*, based on the Latin word *periodus,* which in turn was borrowed from the Greek *periodos.* The Greek term is compound: *peri* means "around" and *hodos* means "way." *Period,* therefore, meant "a way around" or "a going around; a cycle."

The reason for the mixture of all these languages is that English is such a new language compared with many others (Hebrew, for example). A brief survey of the history of English will readily explain why so many older languages went into the making of our language.

The earliest speakers of an ancestral form of English were the Indo-Europeans who lived in central Europe. They had migrated into this area shortly before the birth of Christ; several centuries later they contributed to the fall of the Roman Empire. But even these Teutons did not speak a uniform language; because of lack of communications, they gradually developed three dialects: East Teutonic, North Teutonic, and West Teutonic. This group of languages is called the Germanic group because it was located in the general area of Germany.

East Teutonic (Gothic) is today extinct. The North Teutonic group moved to Scandinavia, and their language survives today as Danish, Swedish, and Norwegian. But most of the West Teutonic group remained in Germany and the Netherlands, where they developed the German and Dutch languages through later centuries.

How did England become involved? In A.D. 550, three groups of West Teutons, the Angles, the Saxons, and the Jutes, crossed the North Sea and occupied England (the name means Angle-land). The Celts who had lived there were simply driven back; their language survives today as Welsh and Irish. These West Teutonic conquerors spoke Anglo-Saxon (Old English), a complicated, highly inflected language that we would barely recognize today as being a form of English.

For the next several centuries, the language of the Anglo-Saxons changed slowly, about the only outside influence being Danish invasions during the 800s. But the Norman Conquest in 1066 brought a major change to England. At that time the victorious Normans (from Normandy, France) made French the language of the nobles, holding themselves aloof from the English-speaking common people whom they ruled. As the years rolled on, however, the nobles and the common people intermingled more and more until, in the 1300s, they had a language that was neither Old English nor French. It was Middle English, now vastly changed by the French influence.

Middle English continued to change steadily for the next three centuries, losing more and more of the cumbersome inflections and changing gradually in pronunciation. By the 1600s it was again substantially different. The English of that period is called Elizabethan English (in honor of Queen Elizabeth I), and it is the language of the King James Bible. Elizabethan English was the beginning of the Modern English which we use today.

But why did Middle English change so much from 1300 to 1600, as compared with the little change in Modern English from 1600 to today? After all, the King James Version was finished in 1611, and more than 350 years later we have very little difficulty understanding its language. The answer is the widespread use of the printing press. Whereas individual copyists of earlier times could change spelling, inflection, and punctuation at their leisure, the printing press "froze" one style of English throughout a run. Thus many more people were influenced by the particular style of one printer than by that of one copyist, and gradually a standard style was worked out for all writers of English.

English has yet been changing, despite standardization. One reason has been the many discoveries and inventions of the Renaissance (new awakening of learning), the Protestant Reformation, the New World explorations, and the Industrial Revolution. Greek and Latin terms were borrowed to form new words for new developments. With the enlargement of the English language, some terms were also eliminated, such as the familiar pronouns *thou* and *ye* (called familiar because they were used in addressing family members).

Because of its rich heritage, the English language of today has an especially broad vocabulary, making possible an almost endless variety in shades of meaning. Let us use it to the best of our ability, and to the glory of God.

# III. Usage

**A. ENGLISH USAGE**

**B. CURRENT USAGE**

**C. LEVELS OF USAGE**

**D. GLOSSARY OF USAGE**

# III. Usage

## A. ENGLISH USAGE

Usage refers to what is considered correct or incorrect in the expression of a language. The standard for English usage is largely determined by established custom. Those who study the English language decide which expressions are generally approved and understood, and which are not. They record their conclusions in dictionaries and other books of language. And if our writing is to be respected and understood by the majority of people, it must conform to the standards which these authorities have established.

This idea carries even more weight when we consider the far-reaching and long-lasting influence of the printed page. The spoken word reaches only several hundred people in a limited area at best, and it is valuable only as long as the hearers remember it. Therefore we can make some allowance for expressions that are not always considered standard. But the printed page is often read by thousands of people over widely scattered territories. It is often stored by one generation for following generations to read. And if the message is forgotten, it can easily be reviewed.

Imagine for a moment what would happen if no one bothered to follow the rules of standard English. If you lived in the North and bought a book printed in the South, you probably could not even read it. If you found a letter written a hundred years ago by your great-grandfather, you would get as much satisfaction from reading it as you would if it were written in French. And if you grew to be a grandfather yourself, you would have some trouble understanding your grandchildren. In fact, this is one reason that there are so many languages today. Without a standard, the West Germanic language became Dutch, German, and English within a period of only five hundred years.

But we do have a standard for English, and we do desire to keep it as consistent as possible. Though there is no such thing as perfect English, we are thankful for the rules of standard English which keep our language reasonably stable.

## B. CURRENT USAGE

Along with a knowledge of standard usage, we need a knowledge of current usage because language is constantly changing. For example, *pious* formerly had only a good meaning, denoting true devotion to God. But current usage also gives it a bad connotation, suggesting a false show of religion. If we completely ignore the current usage of words such as this one, we could easily offend someone.

We need a balance. While we do need an understanding of current usage, we must also be careful not to adopt every new fad of expression that comes along. Only when a standard dictionary approves an expression should we even consider using it for standard writing.

## C. LEVELS OF USAGE

Most words are acceptable without question. Such words are *formal* and usually are not labeled. In our writing we prefer the *formal* use to the more informal style currently being used. Dictionaries mark the questionable expressions with entries such as these below:

*Slang:* Unconventional terms, frequently not suitable for Christians, such as *grub* for food.

*Colloquial:* Used in conversations only.

*Obsolete:* Terms out-of-date.

*Archaic:* Old forms such as *thee* and *thou.*

*Informal: Phone* for *telephone, jam* for *predicament*—acceptable for everyday speaking or writing but not for formal writing.

*Illiterate:* Nonstandard terms, including *ain't* (also called vulgarisms).

*Provincial:* Terms characteristic of certain geographic boundaries, such as *fetch* for *bring.*

## D. GLOSSARY OF USAGE

The following glossary brings to your attention many unpreferred terms. Use it to refer to questionable terms before you use them in writing.

A, an—Use *a* before a consonant sound, *an* before a vowel sound.

*a* boy, *a* gift, *an* hour, *an* uncle

Ability, capacity—*Ability* refers to one's power to *do* something; *capacity* means "power to receive."

> He served to the best of his *ability*. (not *capacity*)
> He has a great *capacity* for learning.

Above—Do not use for *preceding* or *foregoing*, except in legal business writing. *Above* may be used as an adverb or as a preposition.

> LEGAL: The *above* information is confidential.
> BETTER: The *foregoing* information is confidential.
> STANDARD: The information *above* is confidential.

Accept, except—*Accept* means "to receive"; *except* (hardly ever used as a verb) means "to exclude." As a preposition it means "not including."

> Please *accept* the mail in my stead.
> The teacher *excepted* John from playing tag. (verb)
> Everyone played *except* John. (preposition)

Accompany— Use *accompanied by* for persons, *accompanied with* for things.

> I was *accompanied by* my sister.
> Riches are *accompanied with* many temptations.

Ad— Informal. Write out the full word in formal writing.

> The *advertisement* indicated a price reduction.

Adapt, adopt—*Adapt* means "to make suitable." *Adopt* means "to make one's own."

> The song was *adapted* to fit the occasion.
> Paul *adopted* the Christian faith as his own.

Advice, advise—*Advice* is a noun meaning *counsel. Advise* is a verb meaning "to give counsel." *Advise* should not be used for *inform*.

Affect, effect—*Affect* means "to influence"; *effect* means "to bring to pass." *Effect* is also a noun meaning "result."

> Does the new law *affect* farmers?
> The sewing circle *effected* a plan to include young mothers.
> The article in the paper had a good *effect*.

After—Needless with a perfect participle.

> WORDY: *After having* eaten lunch, Samuel read the book.
> IMPROVED: *Having eaten* lunch, Samuel read the book.

Aggravate—Means "to make worse" or "to intensify." Its colloquial use is "to exasperate" or "to arouse to anger."

> COLLOQUIAL: His bad table manners *aggravate* his sister.
> FORMAL: Wading in the creek *aggravated* Mary's cough.

Agree to, agree with—*Agree to* a plan; *agree with* a person.

> We have *agreed to* build a churchhouse.
> I *agree with* you.

Ain't—Considered illiterate. Use *am not, are not, is not.*

> ILLITERATE: I *ain't* helping very much.
> STANDARD: I *am not* helping very much.

All of—*Of* is not needed with nouns.

> STANDARD: I ate *all of* it. *All of* us were there.
> INFORMAL: This is *all of* the apples.
> FORMAL: This is *all* the apples.

All the farther, all the faster—Do not use for *as far as* and *as fast as.*

> STANDARD: This is *as far as* we shall read.
> STANDARD: Is that *as fast as* you can add?

Allude, elude—*Allude* means "to refer to indirectly; hint." *Elude* means "to escape notice by evading or avoiding."

> Jesus often *alluded* to the sins of the Pharisees in His parables.
> Jeroboam's wife disguised herself to *elude* the detection of the prophet.

Allude, refer—*Allude* means "to refer to indirectly." *Refer* means "to mention specifically."

> When Jesus mentioned self-righteousness, often He *alluded* to the Pharisees.
> When He told His disciples to "tell that fox," He *referred* to Herod.

Allusion, illusion—*Allusion* means "an indirect reference." *Illusion* means "a false image or idea."

> The minister began his topic on "The Home" with an *allusion* to the Garden of Eden.
> On the highway ahead appeared an *illusion* of a lake.

Almost, most—*Almost* as an adverb means "nearly, but not altogether." Do not use the adjective *most*, meaning "the majority of," incorrectly for *almost*.

> Singing is enjoyed by *almost* everyone. (not *most*)

Almost, quite—*Quite* means "completely."

> ILLITERATE: The tree is *quite almost* bare of leaves.
> STANDARD: The tree is *quite* bare of leaves.

A lot—Often misspelled as *alot*.

**D.**

Already, all ready—*Already* means "before a certain time." *All ready* means "completely prepared."

> "But that which ye have *already* hold fast till I come" (Revelation 2:25).
> The meal is *all ready* to be served.

Alright—*All right* is considered to be the correct spelling.

> INCORRECT: Are you *alright*?
> STANDARD: I am *all right*.

Although, though—Generally mean the same, and can be used interchangeably. *Though* can be an adverb.

Altogether, all together—*Altogether* means "totally, thoroughly." *All together* means "in a group."

> Shopping on Sunday is *altogether* unnecessary.
> The class was *all together* for supper.

A.M., P.M.—Use only with figures.

Among, between—*Among* implies "more than two," and *between* implies "two." However, *between* is often used with "three" when each is considered individually.

Divide the pie *among* the four boys.
Can you see any difference *between* the three chairs?
The competition is great *between* the two brothers.

**Amount, number**—*Amount* relates to "quantity." *Number* relates to objects that can be counted.

Success requires a large *amount* of diligent *labor.*
The barn was raised by a large *number* of strong *men.*

**And etc.**—*And* is unnecessary with *etc.* However, *and so forth* is preferred to *etc.*

Myers will sell towels, linens, *etc.* (or *and so forth*)

**And/or**—Should not be used in standard writing.

**D.**   **And which (who), but which (who)**—Should be preceded by another *which (who)* clause.

**Angry at**—*Angry with* is the proper term to use with persons.

COLLOQUIAL: Never be *angry at* your friend.
STANDARD: Never be *angry with* your friend.
STANDARD: The man was *angry at* the insult. (or *about*)

**Anxious, eager**—*Anxious* implies "dread" or "worry." *Eager* implies "a pleasant desire."

Mrs. Miller was *anxious* about her son's late return.
Her son was *eager* to reach home.

**Anymore**—Colloquial in affirmative context.

COLLOQUIAL: *Anymore,* people live very loosely.
STANDARD: People do not live very strictly *anymore.*

**Anyone**—Written as one word unless emphasis is needed on the *one.*

*Anyone* should know John 3:16 by memory.
There is not *any one* who does not have a depraved nature.

**Anyplace**—Do not use for *anywhere.*

COLLOQUIAL: The book does not seem to be *anyplace.*
STANDARD: The book does not seem to be *anywhere.*

Anyway, anywhere—Say *anyway* and *anywhere*, not *anyways* or *anywheres.*

> NONSTANDARD: I am not going *anyways.*
> STANDARD: I am not going *anyway.*

Apt—Refers to "ability." Should not be used for *likely.*

> INFORMAL: She is *apt* to tell the untruth.
> CORRECT: She is *likely* to tell the untruth.
> CORRECT: She is an *apt* student.

Around—Do not use for *about* or *nearly.* Also see **Round.**

Arrive—One *arrives in* large areas, but *at* specific points.

> He finally *arrived in* New York City.
> He finally *arrived at* Central Park.

As—Avoid using *as* instead of *whether* or *that.*

> NONSTANDARD: I do not know *as* I saw the dog.
> STANDARD: I do not know *that* I saw the dog.

As, like—*As* is a conjunction; *like* is a preposition.

> Do it *as* I do.
> Do it *like* me.

As, so—Formal English uses *so* after "negatives" and *as* with "positives."

> He is not *so* nimble as he used to be.
> He is *as* nimble as Father.

At—Do not finish a question with *at.*

> ILLITERATE: Where is my book *at?*
> STANDARD: Where is my book?

At about—Illogical. Use *at* for exact reference and *about* for approximate reference.

Attackted—Incorrect for *attacked.*

Auto—Use *automobile* in standard writing.

**Awful**— *Awful* denotes "inspiring with awe and wonder" or "filling with terror." It should not be used to mean "disagreeable" but is acceptable when used to denote "intensity."

> STANDARD: "Before Jehovah's *awful* throne, / Ye nations, bow with sacred joy" (Isaac Watts).

> ACCEPTED: Did you hear about the *awful* accident?
> PREFERRED: Did you hear about the *serious* accident?
> NONSTANDARD: The baby acts *awful* today.

**Awhile, a while**— Do not confuse the adverb *awhile* with the prepositional phrase *for a while*.

**Back of**— Do not use for *behind*.

**Bad, badly**— *Bad* is an adjective. *Badly* is an adverb used after most verbs, except *want* or *need*.

> STANDARD: John feels *bad* about breaking the cup.
> NONSTANDARD: I need a new purse *badly*. (*very much* is better.)
> STANDARD: Miss Carper hears *badly*.

**Balance**— Do not use for *remainder*.

> COLLOQUIAL: We had no more trouble for the *balance* of the journey.
> STANDARD: We had no more trouble for the *rest* of the journey. (or *remainder*)

**Bank on, take stock in**— It is better to say *rely on* or *trust in*.

> COLLOQUIAL: I cannot *bank on* getting the goods tomorrow.
> STANDARD: I cannot *rely on* getting the goods tomorrow.
> COLLOQUIAL: I do *not take stock* in such ideas.
> STANDARD: I do not *trust in* such ideas.

**Because**— Do not use *because* to introduce a noun clause.

> INCORRECT: The reason he fell was *because* he was too bold.
> CORRECT: The reason he fell was *that* he was too bold.

**Beg**— Unnecessary in business letter expressions such as "I beg leave to. . . ." Simply say "I request."

**Being as, being that**— Do not substitute for *because* or *since*.

**Beside, besides**— Beside means "by the side of." Besides means "in addition to."

**Better**— Nonstandard term for the idiomatic expression *had better*.

> STANDARD: You *had better* run.
> NONSTANDARD: You *better* run.

**Bring, take**— *Bring* means "to convey toward" and *take* means "to convey away from."

**Bug**— *Informal* noun used for "a germ or defect." Slang used instead of verb *annoy* or *nag*.

> INFORMAL: Even the teacher must have caught the *bug*.
> BETTER: Even the teacher must have a *cold*.
> SLANG: You are immature if you *bug* your parents for money.
> BETTER: You are immature if you *nag* your parents for money.

**Bunch**— Do not use to refer to "a group of people."

> CORRECT: I bought a *bunch* of carrots.
> COLLOQUIAL: We saw a *bunch* of people standing at the corner.
> CORRECT: We saw a *group* of people standing at the corner.

**Burst, bursted, busted**— The correct term is *burst*, and the principle parts are *burst, burst, burst* (not *bursted*). *Bursted* and *busted* are illiterate expressions.

> INCORRECT: The water pipes *bursted*. The water pipes *busted*.
> CORRECT: The water pipes *burst*.

**But what, but that**— Do not use after negatives. Use *whether* or *that*, or revise the sentence.

> POOR: You do not know *but what* he may do better than you.
> CORRECT: You do not know *whether* he may do better than you.
> REVISED: How do you know that he will not do better than you?

**Can, may**— *Can* denotes "ability"; *may* denotes "permission."

> INFORMAL: *Can* I borrow your tools?
> FORMAL: *May* I borrow your tools?

**Cannot help but**— *But* is unnecessary after *cannot help*.

> COLLOQUIAL: I *cannot help but* speak up.

STANDARD: I *cannot help* speaking up.

Can't hardly—Double negative. Say *can't* or *can hardly*.

Can't seem to—Nonstandard expression for *seem unable to*.

> NONSTANDARD: I *can't seem to* find the missing sock.
> STANDARD: I *seem unable to* find the missing sock.

Case—Often used in wordy expressions such as *in the case of*. Revise.

> WORDY: *In most cases* Jesus condemned the scribes, but *in one case* He commended one of them.
> REVISED: Jesus *usually* condemned the scribes, but once He commended one of them.

Cause of—Do not say the *cause of* something was *on account of* something.

> NONSTANDARD: The *cause of* the accident was *on account of* drunkenness.
> PREFERRED: The *cause* of the accident was drunkenness.

Censure, criticize—*Censure* means "to reprove or condemn," usually without any just reason. *Criticize* means "to judge or evaluate," with either a good or a poor motive.

Common, mutual—*Common* means "shared by several persons," usually referring to something other than the persons themselves. *Mutual* refers to feelings which two persons share toward each other.

> The early church had all things in *common*.
> There was a *mutual* feeling of distrust between Jacob and Laban.

Company—Denotes "a group of people" or "an association." It can be used in informal writing to mean "visitors."

> CORRECT: "And there went up with him both chariots and horsemen: and it was a very great *company*" (Genesis 50:9).
> CORRECT: Keep *company* with those who help you to know God.
> INFORMAL: We plan to have *company* on Sunday.
> PREFERRED: We plan to have *guests* on Sunday.

Compare with, in contrast, compare to—*Compare with* is used to show a relative value, likenesses, or differences. *Contrast* is used only to show differences. *Compare to* is used only to show likenesses.

The Christian home is often *compared with* heaven.
Heaven's joys are immeasurable *in contrast* to earth's sorrows.
Jesus *contrasted* the proud with the humble in Luke 18.
We should often *compare* our life *to* a pilgrimage.

Complected—Used in some regions instead of *complexioned*.

PROVINCIAL: John Martin's children are all dark-*complected*.
STANDARD: John Martin's children are all dark-*complexioned*.

Complement(ary), compliment(ary)—A *complement* completes something. A *compliment* is an expression of praise.

Considerable—To be used as an adjective and not as a noun or adverb.

POOR: He gained *considerable* during their stay here.
CORRECT: He gained *considerable* weight during their stay here.
POOR: He was grieved *considerable*.
CORRECT: He was grieved *considerably*.

Contact—Overworked term for more exact verbs such as *ask, inform, consult, talk with*.

Continual(ly), continuous(ly)—*Continual* means "occurring steadily, rapidly, or often, but not in unbroken succession." *Continuous* means "without stopping."

Her *continual* coming wearied him.
The *continuous* blessings of God are because of His mercy to us.

Continue on—*On* is unnecessary.

POOR: *Continue on* in the work you are doing.
PREFERRED: *Continue* in the work you are doing.

Contrast from—It is better to say *contrast to*.

POOR: This rose is quite a *contrast from* that one.
PREFERRED: This rose is quite a *contrast to* that one.

Correspond with—It is better to say *correspond to*, except when referring to letter writing.

POOR: How does this *correspond with* what you said before?

PREFERRED: How does this *correspond to* what you said before?

Could of— Incorrectly used instead of *could have*.

CORRECT: He *could have* done better.

Couple— A noun meaning "two people or things considered as a unit." Its colloquial use is acceptable when used as an adjective meaning "two or an indefinite small number."

CORRECT: The *couple* was married in 1925 by Brother Hurst, a late bishop.

ACCEPTED: We were gone a *couple* days. (meaning "two or three")

PREFERRED: We were gone a *few* days.

PREFERRED: We were gone *two* days.

D. Credible, credulous— *Credible* refers to *things* which are "correct or worthy of believing"; *credulous* refers to *people* who are "too easily convinced."

It is a *credible* fact that Jesus rose from the dead.
Brother Mark is not a *credulous* teacher.

Cute— Informal. Use *pretty* or *attractive*.

Data— Plural form of Latin *datum*. *Data* may have a singular or plural verb form in good English usage.

Date— Used informally to mean "appointment."

ACCEPTED: We made a *date* for them to come.
PREFERRED: We made an *appointment* for them to come.

Deal— Used informally for *transaction, purchase, sale, bargain.*

ACCEPTED: The *deal* on the car is nearly finished.
PREFERRED: The *transaction* on the car is nearly finished.

Die with— Say *die of*.

POOR: He *died with* cancer.
CORRECT: He *died of* cancer.

Different than— Say *different from*.

POOR: Apple leaves are *different than* peach leaves.

CORRECT: Apple leaves are *different from* peach leaves.

**Differ from, differ with**— *Differ from* means "to be unlike"; *differ with* means *"to disagree."*

In Ohio, January weather *differs from* June weather.
I love you although I *differ with* your opinion.

**Discover, invent**— *Discover* means "to find," referring to something already existing. *Invent* means "to make for the first time."

Columbus *discovered* America.
Newton *discovered* the laws of motion.
Edison *invented* the light bulb.

**Disinterested**— Means "impartial" but is used informally for *uninterested*, which means "indifferent."

**Disregardless**— Incorrect for *regardless*.

**Done**— Correct as an adjective and as a past participle of the verb *do*. Do not use as an adverb or instead of *did*.

POOR: Who *done* the job so well?
CORRECT: Who *did* the job so well?
POOR: The work was *done* finished this afternoon.
CORRECT: The work was *done* by four o'clock.

**Don't**— Often wrongly used in a singular position instead of the contraction *doesn't*.

POOR: He *don't* go away from home often.
CORRECT: He *doesn't* go away from home often.
CORRECT: They *don't* go away often.

**Doubt whether, doubt that**— Formal English uses *whether* when the verb expresses positive doubtfulness, and *that* when the construction is negative. *But* is unnecessary in *doubt but that*.

The preacher *doubts whether* the lady was saved.
No one today should *doubt that* Christian schools are commanded. (not *doubt but that*)

**Dove**— Informal past tense of *dive*. Use *dived* in standard writing.

Drownded—Incorrect for *drowned.*

> POOR: Eddie put the duckling in a tub and it *drownded.*
> CORRECT: Eddie put the duckling in a tub and it *drowned.*

Drug—Incorrect for *dragged.*

> POOR: She *drug* the rug behind her.
> CORRECT: She *dragged* the rug behind her.

Due to—It is generally better to say *because of. Due to,* if it is used, always follows a verb of being.

> POOR: He was absent *due to* illness.
> CORRECT: He was absent *because of* illness.
> CORRECT: His absence was *due to* illness.

Each and every—Wordy.

> POOR: I want *each and every* student to examine the specimen.
> CORRECT: I want *each* student to examine the specimen.

Easy—Be sure to use as an adjective. *Easily* is the adverb form.

> We can *easily* finish by noon. (not *easy*)

Either, neither—Both are singular terms.

> *Neither* of the girls is ready to leave.
> *Either* the cake or the pie will serve as dessert.

Emigrate, immigrate—*Emigrate* means "to leave a country to take up residence in another." *Immigrate* means "to enter a country for residence."

Eminent, imminent, immanent—*Eminent* means "prominent"; *imminent* means "about to happen"; *immanent* means "indwelling."

> He was an *eminent* church leader in his time.
> We believe the Lord's return to be *imminent.*
> Our lives should speak of the *immanent* Holy Spirit.

Enthuse, enthused—Informal terms for *enthusiastic.*

> POOR: The idea does not *enthuse* us at all.
> POOR: Carl was surely *enthused* about the spinach.

PREFERRED: We are all *enthusiastic* about the idea.

Equally as good, equally as bad—Wordy. Say *equal to* or *as good as*.

> POOR: This brand is *equally as good* as that brand.
> CORRECT: This brand is *equal to* that brand. (or *as good as*)

Etc.—*And so forth* is preferred in standard writing.

Every—Do not use with these expressions: every *now and then*, every *once in a while*, every *which way*, every *so often*.

> POOR: I see my brother from California *every now and then*.
> CORRECT: I see my brother from California *now and then*.
> POOR: The marbles rolled *every which way*.
> CORRECT: The marbles rolled *every direction*.

Every bit—Informal expression of comparison. Use a better word or omit entirely.

> POOR: Mary is *every bit* as tall as her mother.
> CORRECT: Mary is as tall as her mother.

Everyplace—Do not use for *everywhere*.

Everywheres—Incorrect for *everywhere*.

Exam—Use *examination* in standard writing.

Expect—Means "anticipate." Colloquial expression for *suppose* or *think*.

> POOR: I *expect* James brought the supplies for art class.
> CORRECT: I *suppose* James brought the supplies for art class.
> CORRECT: I *expect* James to be in art class.

Fabulous—Derived from the word *fable*, it means "imaginary or astounding," and should not be used to mean "very good or pleasing."

> POOR: They have a *fabulous* yard.
> CORRECT: The story of Jonah sounds *fabulous* to many.

Farther, further—These words are often used interchangeably to express *distance*. *Farther* is considered correct to express "distance" and *further* expresses "additional."

West Liberty is six miles *farther* south than Greenville.
Does anyone have any *further* comments?

Faze—Do not use for *daunt* or *affect.*

> POOR: The bright light did not *faze* him.
> CORRECT: The bright light did not *affect* him.

Feel of—*Of* is unnecessary.

> Let me *feel* the material. (not *feel of*)

Fellow—Means a "comrade, partner, or associate." It is also acceptable to use for *man* or *boy.*

> PREFERRED: Let us encourage each other as *fellow* travelers to heaven.
> ACCEPTED: The *fellows* went for a walk through the woods.

**D.** Fewer, less—*Fewer* refers to "number"; *less* refers to "value, amount, or degree."

> *Fewer* people attended the second session than the first.
> We seem to have *less* time for visiting in spite of modern conveniences.

Figure—Provincial for *think, suppose,* or *plan.*

Fine—Informal term for *good* or *excellent.*

> The house is in *fine* condition. (*excellent* condition)

First-rate—Usually a colloquial term. Use *excellent* or *very good* instead.

Fix—Means "to make firm or stable." Also acceptable when used to mean "arrange, repair, predicament."

> CORRECT: "He shall not be afraid. . . : his heart is *fixed,* trusting in the Lord" (Psalm 112:7).
> ACCEPTABLE: He *fixed* the chair. (*Repaired* is preferred.)
> ACCEPTABLE: George was in a *fix* without a spare tire. (*Predicament* is preferred.)

Flunk—Slang for *fail.*

> POOR: Ray did not expect to *flunk* the driver's test.
> CORRECT: Ray did not expect to *fail* the driver's test.

Folks—Means "people." Informally used to mean "parents" or "relatives."

> CORRECT: Sick *folks* were brought to Jesus.
> ACCEPTED: Have you heard from your *folks*?
> PREFERRED: Have you heard from your *parents*?

Former—Use to refer to the first of two items mentioned before.

> Judas and Peter both sinned; however, the *former* did not seek forgiveness.

Free of—Say *free from*.

> He is *free from* pain. (not *free of*)

Funny—Means "amusing." Informally used for *strange*.

> CORRECT: The story was so *funny* that we had to laugh.
> POOR: It is *funny* that John is so late.
> PREFERRED: It is *strange* that John is so late.

Get—The verb *get* is used informally in many ways. The varied expressions serve varied needs, but should never be used carelessly in formal writing or speaking.

| | | |
|---|---|---|
| get at the work | get by with it | get hurt |
| get to go | get on to it | get moving |
| get behind | get around it | get it across |

Good, well—*Good* is an adjective; *well*, an adverb unless it refers to "a state of health or condition."

> CORRECT: The story about Dr. Mayer is *good*.
> CORRECT: It is *well* with my soul.
> CORRECT: The car runs *well* today.

Growed—Do not use for *grew*.

> The weeds *grew* (not *growed*) so tall we could hardly see the beets.

Guess—Means "to form an opinion with little evidence." It can mean "suppose" or "think."

> CORRECT: Try to *guess* who is coming to our house.
> ACCEPTED: I *guess* I will finish tomorrow.

Guy—Informally used to mean "man." Does not imply godliness and should be avoided in the Christian's use.

Gym—Use *gymnasium* in standard writing, except in phrases such as *gym suit*.

Hadn't ought, had ought—Say *ought* or *ought not*, or *should* or *should not*.

> POOR: He *hadn't ought* to have sworn. He *had ought* to know better.
> CORRECT: He *ought not* to have sworn. He *should* know better.

Had of—Say *had*.

> POOR: I wish I *had of* gone along.
> CORRECT: I wish I *had* gone along.

**D.** Hain't—Never a good term. Say *haven't*.

Half a—Use only one *a*.

> POOR: I have *a half a* dollar.
> CORRECT: I have *half a* dollar. Or I have *a half* dollar.

Hanged, hung—*Hanged* means "executed." *Hung* means "suspended."

Hardly—Do not use with negatives.

> POOR: He *couldn't hardly* walk on his sore foot.
> CORRECT: He *could hardly* walk on his sore foot.

Have got—*Got* is unnecessary.

> POOR: How many dollars *have* you *got*? I *have got* five.
> CORRECT: How many dollars *have* you? I *have* five.

Haven't but, haven't only—Double negatives. Say *have but* or *have only*.

Healthy, healthful—*Healthy* means "being in sound state" or "having health." *Heathful* means "giving health."

> God kept the children of Israel *healthy* in the wilderness. Manna was a *healthful* food.

Heaps of—Colloquial for *an abundance of* or *much.*

> We have *much* work to do. (not *heaps of*)

Hear to—Do not use for *allow.*

> We offered to furnish food, but Grandmother would not *allow* it. (not *hear to*)

Help but—Do not use for *avoid* in formal writing.

> INFORMAL: He could not *help but* run over the rabbit.
> FORMAL: He could not *avoid* running over the rabbit.

Himself—See **Myself.**

Hisself—Never use for *himself.*

How come—Say *why.*

> POOR: *How come* these apples are here?
> CORRECT: *Why* are these apples here?

If, whether—*If* denotes "a sign of condition"; *whether* means "which of two things."

> "Ye are my friends, *if* ye do whatsoever I command you" (John 15:14).
> "Christ shall be magnified in my body, *whether* it be by life, or by death" (Philippians 1:20).

In, into—*In* means "to be within"; *into* means "direction toward a place within."

> I heard Joe walk *in* the house. (He must have entered previously.)
> I heard Joe step *into* the house. (He just got there now.)

In back of, in between—Say *behind* or *between.*

Incredible, incredulous—*Incredible* means "not believable." *Incredulous* means "not believing," referring only to people.

> Father was *incredulous* when he heard the *incredible* story.

Infer, imply—*Infer* means to "reach a conclusion by reasoning, from evidence." *Imply* means "to suggest indirectly." A reader or listener *infers,* whereas a writer or speaker *implies.*

> From what you said, I *infer* that the man was not in his right mind.
>
> I did not mean to *imply* that you are lazy.

Inferior—Use *inferior to,* not *inferior than.*

Ingenious, ingenuous—*Ingenious* means "clever, skillful"; *ingenuous* means "open, frank, fair."

> Vernon is an *ingenious* mechanic.
>
> Pearl is easy to talk with because she is so *ingenuous.*

In regards to—Say *in regard to* or *as regards.*

Inside, inside of—Do not use to mean "within" or "into."

> POOR: Come back *inside* an hour.
> CORRECT: Come back *within* an hour.
> POOR: He climbed *inside of* the box.
> CORRECT: He climbed *into* the box.

Invite—Do not use as a noun.

> We received an *invitation* to the wedding. (not *invite*)

Irregardless—Incorrect for *regardless.*

Its, it's—*Its* is a possessive pronoun and does not require an apostrophe. *It's* is a contraction meaning "it is."

> The little kitten missed *its* mother.
>
> *It's* wise to listen more than to speak.

Just—*Just* means "fair, righteous, and exactly" when used as an adjective, and "exactly, only, and barely" when used as an adverb. Avoid using colloquially as *quite.*

> CORRECT: God is *just* and will do *just* as He has promised.
> CORRECT: He *just* missed the train by a few minutes.
> QUESTIONED: It is *just* terrible to show disrespect. (*quite* terrible)

Just exactly—Both mean the same. Use one or the other.

Kind, kinds—Be sure to use *this* and *that* with *kind,* and *these* and *those* with *kinds.*

> POOR: These *kind* of faults should be overcome.
> CORRECT: This *kind* of fault should be overcome.
> CORRECT: These *kinds* of faults should be overcome.

Kind of a, sort of a—*A* is unnecessary.

> POOR: What *kind of a* book are you reading?
> CORRECT: What *kind of* book are you reading?

Later, latter—*Later* refers to "time"; *latter* refers to "the second when two are named." If more than two are named, use *last.*

> Come *later* and I'll listen to your story.
> James Smith and Simon Jones are here. The *latter* is my second cousin.
> James, John, and Peter were Jesus' close disciples. The *last* denied Him thrice.

Later on—*On* is unnecessary.

> They will come *later* in the day. (not *later on*)

Lay, lie—*Lay* is a transitive verb meaning "to place something." *Lie* is an intransitive verb meaning "to recline or rest."

> When did you *lay* the money on the desk?
> I was glad to *lie* down a few minutes.

Learn, teach—*Learn* means "to gain knowledge or skill"; *teach* means "to impart knowledge or instruct."

> We *learn* lessons by experience as well as by studying.
> Jesus tried to *teach* the disciples about His kingdom.

Leave, let—*Leave* means "to depart from" or "to allow to remain behind"; *let* means "to permit."

> We plan to *leave* tomorrow noon.
> He will *let* us depart tomorrow noon. (not *leave*)
> *Leave* the water in the basin. (not *let*)
> *Let* the water remain in the basin. (not *leave*)

Let's us, let's we—Illogical. Say *let us*. However, appositives may follow if used correctly.

> *Let's* you and me (not I) visit her.

Like—Do not use *like* in the place of *as, as if,* or *as though* as a conjunction to introduce an adverbial clause making a comparison.

> POOR: He sings *like* he means it.
> CORRECT: He sings *as though* he means it.

Likely, liable—Do not use *liable* where *likely* or *probably* is correct. *Liable* means "probability of harm" or "legally responsible."

> The apples are *likely* to be ready next week.
> If you are not careful, you are *liable* to hurt yourself.

Line—Often used in wordy expressions. Revise.

**D.**

> WORDY: He said something *along that line*.
> REVISED: He said something *like that*.

Loan, lend—Both are verbs, and *loan* can also be a noun. *Loan* refers chiefly to money, but *lend* refers to anything borrowed.

Locate—Colloquial for *settle* or *take up residence*.

> The pioneers decided to *settle* farther west. (not *locate*)

Lose, loose, loosen—*Lose* means "to suffer loss." *Loose* (adjective) and *loosen* (verb) refer to "laxity" or "unattachment."

> Do not *lose* faith.
> The *loose* tooth has been *loosened* by a fall.

Lose out on—*Out on* is unnecessary.

> If he refuses, he will *lose* some blessings. (not *lose out on*)

Lots, lots of—Informally used to mean "much, many," and so forth.

> ACCEPTED: We have *lots of* fruit this year.
> PREFERRED: We have *an abundance* of fruit this year.

Loud—May be used either as an adjective or as an adverb. However, *loudly* is the preferred adverb form.

Mad—Means "insane, crazy." It is also used informally to mean "angry."

CORRECT: The *mad* dog had to be shot.
ACCEPTED: The man became *mad* when he was cheated.
PREFERRED: The man became *angry* when he was cheated.

May, might—See **Can.**

May be, maybe—Do not confuse. *May be* is a verb phrase. *Maybe* means "possibly, perhaps."

May of, might of—A fast, careless way to say *may have, might have.*

I *may have* forgotten the details. (not *may of*)

Mean—Colloquial for *ill-tempered* or *cruel.* Use only in the sense of "lowly" in standard writing.

Memo—Use *memorandum* in standard writing.

Mighty—Means "powerful, great in size, extraordinary." Informal for "very."

CORRECT: Jesus did many *mighty* works.
POOR: I am *mighty* glad you got here.

Miss out on—*Out on* is unnecessary.

They will *miss* the meetings. (not *miss out on*)

Moral, morale, mortal—*Moral* means "lesson" or "virtue." *Morale* refers to "mental state." *Mortal* means "subject to death."

This story has an excellent *moral.*
Joshua's *morale* was low because of the defeat.
Man is a *mortal* creature.

Muchly—Unpreferred term for *much.*

Must of—Say *must have.*

You *must have* heard the answer before I did. (not *must of*)

Myself, himself, herself, yourself—Do not use for the personal pronouns *I, me, he, him,* or *you.* Properly used as intensive or reflexive pronouns.

There will be six people, including *me,* for dinner. (not *myself*)
Joe must find the answer for *himself.*

**Negatives**—Use only one negative to express a negative thought.

> INCORRECT: He *can't hardly* wait.
> CORRECT: He *can hardly* wait.

**Nice**—Overworked and vague. Use a more specific word such as *thoughtful, kind,* or *pretty.*

**No account, no good**—Informally used for the words *worthless* or *of no value.*

> POOR: This stove is *of no account.*
> CORRECT: This stove is *worthless.*

**Nohow**—Nonstandard expression for *not at all.*

> POOR: George was not interested in the job *nohow.*
> CORRECT: George was *not at all* interested in the job.

**D.**

**No other but**—Incorrect for *no other than.*

**Notable, famous, notorious**—*Notable* and *famous* apply to "a good reputation"; *notorious* applies to a "bad reputation."

> Barabbas was a *notorious* robber.
> Abraham Lincoln was a *notable* president. (certainly not *notorious*)

**Nowhere near**—Colloquial for *not nearly.*

> POOR: We are *nowhere near* finished.
> CORRECT: We are *not nearly* finished.

**Nowheres**—Incorrect for *nowhere.*

**O, oh**—*O* is not followed by a punctuation mark. It is usually used to call attention to what is to follow. *Oh* is an interjection used to express "grief, surprise, or longing," and it is followed by a comma or an exclamation mark.

> "*O* taste and see that the Lord is good" (Psalm 34:8).
> "*Oh,* this people have sinned a great sin" (Exodus 32:31).

**Off of**—*Of* is unnecessary.

> He fell *off* the roof. (not *off of*)

**OK, okay**—Either spelling of this colloquial expression is correct. However, *all right* or *in good condition* are preferred.

**One, one's**—These terms are often vague, and sometimes awkward. Revise with more definite pronouns.

> POOR: *One* should be careful about the influence *one* leaves on *one's* children.
> PREFERRED: *We* should be careful about the influence *we* leave on *our* children.

**Ought to of**—Replace with *ought to have* or *should have.*

**Out loud**—Say *aloud.*

> He talked *aloud* in his sleep. (not *out loud*)

**Out of**—A correct idiom when it means "from the inside to the outside of."

> He went *out of* Ur.

**Outside of**—*Of* is unnecessary. Neither should this expression be used for *except* or *besides.*

> Don't let the horse *outside* the gate.
> No one was there *besides* our family. (not *outside of*)

**Overly**—Informal for *excessively.*

> POOR: John tends to talk *overly* much.
> BETTER: John tends to talk *too* much.

**Over with**—*With* is unnecessary.

> The family relaxed when the storm was *over.* (not *over with*)

**Part**—One parts *from* people, and parts *with* things.

> Paul *parted from* the elders at Ephesus.
> Lot found it difficult to *part with* his possessions.

**Party**—Do not use for *person* except in legal papers.

> Do you know the *person* who advertised the car for sale?

**Pass out**—Informal for *faint.*

**Pep**—Informal for *energy* or *vigor.*

**Persecute, prosecute**—*Persecute* means "to annoy or punish for religious beliefs." *Prosecute* means "to take legal action against."

Paul was *persecuted* by the Jews.
The violator was *prosecuted* in court.

**Phone**—Informal for *telephone*.

**Photo**—Informal for *photograph*.

**Piece**—Provincial for *distance*.

We went a short *distance* down the road. (not *piece*)

**Plan on going**—Say *plan to go*.

**Plenty**—Do not use for *quite* or *very*.

POOR: This meal is *plenty good enough*.
CORRECT: This meal is *quite good enough*. (or *good enough*)

**Plus**—A preposition, not a substitute for *and* or *as well as*.

**Poorly**—Informal for *poor health*.

ACCEPTED: Grandmother is *poorly* this winter.
PREFERRED: Grandmother is *in poor health* this winter.

**Posted**—Do not use for *informed*.

He is well *informed* on his father's business. (not *posted*)

**Pretty**—Informal for *quite* or *considerably*.

ACCEPTED: The weeds are *pretty* tall already.
PREFERRED: The weeds are *quite* tall already.

**Principal, principle**—*Principal* means "most important." *Principle* means "law; truth."

Wisdom is the *principal* thing.
The law of gravity is an important *principle*.

**Propose, purpose**—To *propose* is to suggest. To *purpose* is to determine.

What solution to the problem do you *propose*?
Daniel *purposed* not to defile himself.

Providing—Do not use for *provided*.

I will be there, *provided* things work out. (not *providing*)

Put in—Do not use for *spend*.

He *spent* three hours weeding the garden. (not *put in*)

Quite—Means "*completely*." Do not use for *rather* or *somewhat*.

Raise, rise—*Raise* is transitive and requires an object. It means "to lift up or cause to go up or grow up. "*Rise* is intransitive and means "to ascend, extend upward, or increase."

He *raised* the window to let in fresh air.
He *rose* from his chair and walked away.

Rarely ever, seldom ever—*Ever* is unnecessary.

Real, really—Means "actual or true." Is used informally for *very*.

CORRECT: This is a *real* lily.
ACCEPTED: I am *real* happy to see you.
ACCEPTED: It is *really* warm today.

Reason (was) because—Incorrect for "reason . . . that."

The *reason* I am late *is that* the car would not start. (not *is because*)

Receipt, recipe—*Receipt* is the noun form of receive. *Recipe* means "formula" or "method."

I have a *receipt* for that bill.
Follow the *recipe* carefully when you bake a cake.

Reckon—Provincial for *think, suppose, guess*.

ACCEPTED: I *reckon* you are right.
CORRECT: I *think* you are right.

Refer back—Illogical except in special cases where *refer* means "*send.*"

The minister *referred* to a previous point. (not *referred back*)
The decision was *referred back* to the board.

Remember of—*Of* is unnecessary.

**Repeat again**—*Again* is unnecessary.

**Respectful, respective, respectable**—*Respectful* means "courteous." *Respective* means "in the order given." *Respectable* means "worthy of respect."

> Jesus wants us to be *respectful* to everyone.
> As the teacher called the names of the pupils, each went to his *respective* position.
> Our ungodly neighbor is not very *respectable*.

**Right**—Provincial for *very*.

> John's story was *very* funny. (not *right*)

**Right along**—Informal for *continuously*, *steadily*, or *without interruption*.

> POOR: The students have been advancing *right along* in English class.
> BETTER: The students have been advancing in English class *without interruption*.

**Round**—Do not use for *around*.

> The pup ran *around* and *around* the yard. (not *round* and *round*)

**Rumpus**—Informal for *disturbance*.

**Said, same, such**—The Bible often uses *same* instead of pronouns. "The *same* came to Jesus by night." However, when such expressions appear in other writing, they often sound stilted and unnatural.

> POOR: I received your letter and will try to answer *the same*.
> BETTER: I received your letter and will try to answer *it*.
> POOR: *The said* three men were traveling together.
> BETTER: *These* three men were traveling together.

**Says, said**—Be sure to use *says* for present tense and *said* for past tense.

> Jim *says* to George, "We can finish the work before seven."
> George *said* to Jim, "We can't finish the work before eight."

**Scarcely**—Do not use with negatives.

**Second-handed**—Incorrect for *secondhand*.

Seldom ever—Do not use for *seldom, seldom if ever,* or *hardly ever.*

Shall, will—Only the most formal writing requires the use of *shall* for first person and *will* for second and third person. Standard writing allows *will* to be used with all three persons to express future tense.

Shape—Informally used to mean "condition."

> The house is in poor *condition.* (not *shape*)

Should of—Replace with *should have.*

Show up—Informally used to mean "appear" or "arrive."

> I wonder when they will *arrive.* (not *show up*)

Sight—Colloquial to mean "something strange to see" or "large amount." Use preferred terms.

> The basement was *filthy* after the flood. (not *a sight*)
> I have *much* work to do. (not *a sight of*)

Sign up (for, with)—Colloquial to mean "employ" or "join." *Up* is unnecessary when *sign* is used.

> The rebellious young man *joined* the army. (not *signed up with*)
> I *signed* for a three-year subscription. (not *signed up*)

Sit, set—*Sit* is an intransitive verb meaning "to be in a sitting position." *Set* is a transitive verb needing a direct object and means "to place."

> Please *sit* down and visit awhile.
> Do not *set* the dishes near the edge.

*Note:* There are idiomatic uses of *set:* The sun is *setting.* The salad is *set.* He *set* to work with a will. They *set* out for Kansas.

Slow—May be used either as an adjective or as an adverb. However, *slowly* is the preferred adverb form.

So—*So* should be followed by *that* when followed by a clause that tells *why.*

> We should be ready *so that* we can go with Him. (not *so*)

So, such—Informally used as an intensives.

> POOR: I was *so* tired when I finished weeding the garden. It was *such* a warm day.
>
> CORRECT: I was *very* tired when I finished weeding the garden. It was *really* a warm day.

Some—Do not use for *somewhat*.

> Grandmother feels *somewhat* better today. (not *some*)

Someplace—Informal for *somewhere*.

Somewheres—Do not use for *somewhere*.

Stationary, stationery—*Stationary* means "in a fixed position." *Stationery* is writing material.

> The wheel revolves on a *stationary* post.
> She wrote a letter on pink *stationery*.

Statue, stature, statute—A *statue* is an image. *Stature* refers to a person's height. A *statute* is a law.

> We saw the *Statue* of Liberty.
> No one can add a cubit to his *stature*.
> David loved the *statutes* of God.

Such—When *such* is followed by a clause that shows result, *that* should follow *such*.

> The heat from the fire was *such that* it melted the windowpanes.

Superior than—Incorrect for *superior to*.

Suppose—In phrases such as *was supposed to, suppose* is always in past tense.

Sure, surely—*Sure* is an adjective; *surely* an adverb.

> We are *surely* grateful for what you have done for us. (not *sure*)

Sure and—Say *sure to*.

> *Be sure to* finish your work. (not *sure and*)

Suspicion, suspect—*Suspicion* is a noun. *Suspect* is a noun or verb.

> The incident raised *suspicion.* (noun)
> The officers had reason to *suspect* the man. (verb)
> The *suspect* was held in custody. (noun)

Swell—A slang expression for "desirable" things.

> POOR: We had a *swell* time picking blueberries.
> CORRECT: We had an *enjoyable* time picking blueberries.

Take in—Incorrect when used for *attend.*

> We plan to *attend* the wedding while we are in Virginia. (not *take in*)

Taste of, smell of—*Of* is unnecessary.

> Let me *taste* the soup. (not *taste of*)

Tasty—Informal for *delicious* or *savory.*

> INFORMAL: We had a *tasty* dinner.
> STANDARD: We had a *delicious* dinner.

Teach, learn—See **Learn, teach.**

Than—Do not use for *when* or *that* after *hardly* or *scarcely. Than* may, however, be used after *no sooner.*

> I had *hardly* begun working *when* it began to rain. (not *than*)
> *No sooner* had I begun working *than* it began to rain.

Than, then—*Than* is a conjunction used after comparatives. *Then* means "at that time"; sometimes it means "therefore."

> Goliath was much taller *than* David was.
> Jesus died for us; let us *then* live for Him.

Their, there, they're—*Their* means "belonging to them." *There* means "at that place." *They're* is a contraction for *they are.*

> *Their* house is *there.*
> *They're* not at home.

Theirselves—Incorrect for *themselves.*

> They promised *themselves* a treat after the work was done. (not

*theirselves*)

**Them**—Do not use as an adjective.

*Those* apples are too green to eat. (not *them*)

**This here, that there**—*Here* and *there* are unnecessary.

*That* book is very edifying. (not *that there*)
*This* is good handwriting. (not *this here*)

**Through**—Informal for *finished.*

ACCEPTED: I am *through* with my mathematics already.
PREFERRED: I have *finished* my mathematics already.

**D.** **To, too, two**—*To* is a preposition or part of an infinitive. *Too* is an intensive adverb, or it can mean "also." *Two* is a number.

David walked *to* school. (preposition)
I hope *to* be there. (infinitive)
That box is *too* big to fit into the trunk *too*. (intensifier; also)

**Transpired**—Means "leaked out." Do not use for *happened, occurred,* or *passed.*

The secret has finally *transpired.*
Many things have *happened* since those days. (not *transpired*)

**Try and**—Incorrect for *try to.*

We will *try to* be there at seven-thirty. (not *try and*)

**Until, till**—Do not use for *when* or *that* after *scarcely, barely, no sooner,* or *already.*

We had *barely* been seated *when* the singing began. (not *until*)

**Up**—Often used unnecessarily such as *opened up, swept up, ate up, cleaned up.*

Mabel *cleaned* the kitchen after the children made jelly. (not *cleaned up*)

**Used to**—Remember to add the *-d* in expressions such as "I *used to* live there."

**Used to could**—Incorrect for *used to be able.*

She *used to be able* to sing better than she does now.

Very—Avoid using *very* to modify a past participle. *Very much* is the preferred usage.

> She seemed *very much* worried about the outcome. (not *very*)

Wait on—Informally used for *wait for;* acceptable when used as *serve.*

> POOR: Henry had to *wait on* his sister while she mended her dress.
> CORRECT: Henry had to *wait for* his sister while she mended her dress.
> CORRECT: Old Joe *waited on* his invalid wife day and night.

Want in, want through, want off—Colloquial for *want to get in, want to get through,* and so forth. Include the infinitive, or revise the sentence.

Want that—Incorrect in expressions such as "I want that he should. . . ." Revise to "I want him to. . . ."

Ways—Colloquial for *way* or *distance.*

Where—Used incorrectly for *that.* (See "Conjunctions," section I. G., and also "Clauses," section 58c.)

> POOR: I read *where* Job was covered with boils.
> CORRECT: I read *that* Job was covered with boils.

Whereas, while—Use *whereas* to refer to contrary ideas and *while* for parallel ideas.

> Father straightened the living room *while* Mother washed the dishes.
> Peter denied Jesus three times, *whereas* he had boasted that he would die for Him.

Where . . . at, where . . . to—*At* and *to* are unnecessary.

> POOR: *Where* is Mother *at*? *Where* did she go *to*?
> CORRECT: *Where* is Mother? *Where* did she go?

Where, when—(after *is* in giving a definition)—restructure the sentence, deleting *where* or *when.*

> NONSTANDARD: Atonement is *where* man is reconciled to God.
> STANDARD: Atonement is being reconciled to God.
> NONSTANDARD: Grace is *when* God helps us to do what we

should.

STANDARD: Grace is God's help to do what we should.

Which, who—Use *which* to refer to things (except in "*which* person," and so forth), and *who* to refer to people. *Which* should not be used to refer to a clause (*see* "Usage Guidelines for Conjunctions," section 50).

> Jonah was the prophet *who* tried to run away from God." (not *which*)

While—*While* is usually used as a conjunction that refers to time. It may occasionally be used as a substitute for *and* or *but* if not ambiguous.

Who, whom—*Who* is nominative case; *whom* is objective. Their use in the adjective clause determines their case. *Whoever* and *whomever* follow the same rule.

> Cain was the one *who* slew his brother. (*who* slew—subject)
> Abel was the one *whom* he slew. (he slew *whom*—direct object)
> Give this to *whoever* needs it. (*whoever* needs—subject)
> Give this to *whomever* you choose. (you choose *whomever*—direct object)

Who's, whose—*Who's* is a contraction for *who is*. *Whose* means "belonging to whom."

> *Who's* at the door?
> Jairus was the man *whose* daughter was sick.

Widow woman—*Woman* is unnecessary. All those who are widows are women.

Win out—*Out* is unnecessary.

> Righteousness will *win* in the end. (not *win out*)

Wire—Do not use for *telegraph*. Do not use the expression *live wire* to refer to a person.

Worst way—Do not use for *very much*.

> Mrs. Jones wanted a new house *very much*. (not *in the worst way*)

Would of—Incorrect for *would have*.

Year of—*Of* is unnecessary.

Lincoln was born in the *year* (not *year of)* 1809.

You—Do not use as an indefinite pronoun.

POOR: When a person neglects prayer time, *you* will become weak spiritually.

BETTER: A person who neglects prayer time will become weak spiritually.

You all—Provincial for *you.*

We plan to visit *you* this summer. (not *you all*)

Yourself—See **Myself.**

You was—Never substitute for *you were.*

I saw that you *were* on the tractor last evening. (never *was*)

# WRITER'S GUIDE

# IV. The Sentence

## A. SENTENCE STRUCTURE

53. Definition of the Sentence
54. Basic Sentence Parts
    a. Skeleton
        (1) Finding the Subject
        (2) Finding the Predicate
    b. Complements
    c. Independent Elements
55. Sentence Classes
    a. Simple Sentence
    b. Compound Sentence
    c. Complex Sentence
    d. Compound-Complex Sentence
56. Sentence Kinds
    a. Declarative
    b. Interrogative
    c. Imperative
    d. Exclamatory
57. Sentence Order
    a. Natural Order
    b. Inverted Order
    c. Split Order
58. Sentence Parts
    a. Words
    b. Phrases
    c. Clauses
59. Sentence Analysis
    a. Analyzing
    b. Diagraming
60. Variety for Emphasis
    a. Arrangement of Sentences
    b. Variety of Modifiers
    c. Sentence Length
    d. Variety of Classes
    e. Figures of Speech
    f. Conciseness
    g. Passive Voice
    h. Order of Climax
61. Avoiding Faulty Sentences

IV

## B. SENTENCE MECHANICS
62. Capitalization
   a. Beginning Words
   b. Words in Titles
   c. Proper Nouns
63. Punctuation
   a. Period
   b. Question Mark
   c. Exclamation Mark
   d. Comma
   e. Colon
   f. Semicolon
   g. Quotation Marks
   h. Apostrophe
   i. Dash
   j. Parentheses
   k. Brackets
   l. Hyphen
64. Abbreviations
65. Italics
66. Numbers
67. Spelling and Syllabication
68. Penmanship
   a. Habits for Good Handwriting
   b. Model Letters

IV

## C. SENTENCE EFFECTIVENESS
69. Completeness
   a. Grammatically Complete Sentence
   b. Elliptical Sentence
   c. Incomplete Sentence
70. Unity
   a. Unrelated Ideas
   b. Comma Fault
   c. Run-on Sentence
   d. Period Fault
71. Coherence
   a. Ambiguous Pronouns
   b. Unclear Antecedents
   c. Misplaced Modifiers
   d. Misplaced or Dangling Phrases and Clauses

e. Elliptical Adverb Clauses
f. Careless Separating of Closely Related Parts
72. Parallelism
   a. Shifted Constructions
   b. Other Unparallel Constructions
73. Emphasis
   a. Sentence Style
   b. Sentence Length and Word Order
   c. Voice
   d. Quotations
   e. Repetition
74. Variety
   a. Length
   b. Beginning
   c. Basic Pattern
   d. Structure
   e. Use
75. Vocabulary (Exactness)
   a. Dictionary Use
   b. Denotation, Connotation
   c. Euphemisms
   d. Synonyms
   e. Prefixes and Suffixes
   f. Exact Words
   g. Idioms
   h. Similar Words
   i. Reading
76. Conciseness (versus Wordiness)
   a. Deadwood
   b. Redundancy
   c. Wordy Expressions
   d. Pretentious Writing
   e. Trite Expressions
77. Figurative Language
   a. Kinds of Figurative Language
   b. Trite Figures
   c. Mixed Figures
   d. Inappropriate Figures

IV

# IV. The Sentence

## A. SENTENCE STRUCTURE

### 53.

### Definition of the Sentence

Language is a gift of God which makes communication with others possible. When we analyze language, we find that it has order just like everything else God planned. Part of this order is the group of words called a sentence. In order for a group of words to be a sentence, they must express a complete thought and must have both a subject and a predicate.

### 54.

### Basic Sentence Parts

*54a.*

*Skeleton:* The most basic part of the sentence, called the skeleton, is composed of the *simple subject* and the *simple predicate*.

A.53.

(1) *Finding the Subject*

The *subject* of the sentence is usually the first part. It tells *who* or *what* the sentence is about. The noun or pronoun that names *who* or *what* is the simple subject. The simple subject, together with its modifiers, is called the complete subject.

Simple Subject
↑
Devout *men*     carried Stephen to his burial.
⌄
Complete Subject

Sometimes the subject is not stated in the sentence because it is understood or implied, as in sentences of command.

Close the door quietly. (The subject *you* is understood.)

A sentence may also have a compound subject, which means two or more simple subjects.

*Grass* and *weeds* grew along the fence.

The subject is never found in a modifying phrase.

A *flock* of geese flew overhead. (The subject is *flock*, not *geese*.)

To find the subject of a sentence not in natural word order, first change it to natural word order.

Where are you? You are where? (*You* is the subject.)
Down came the rain. The rain came down. (*Rain* is the subject.)

(2) *Finding the Predicate*

The *predicate* of a sentence, nearly always the last part, tells what the subject is, does, or has. The simple predicate is a verb; the complete predicate includes the verb and everything else not contained in the subject.

Simple Predicate
↑
Devout men    car̄ried Stephen to his burial.
Complete Predicate

The predicate may contain two or more verbs and is then called a compound predicate.

A.54b.

The children *shouted* merrily and *ran* to the orchard.

Sometimes a modifier of the verb is found at the beginning of the sentence. It is still part of the predicate. The complete predicate of this sentence is italicized.

*Suddenly* rain *began to fall.*

54b.

*Complements:* Many verbs need one or more additional words to complete their meanings. These additional words are called complements, and together with the skeleton they form the three basic sentence parts: *subject, verb, complement.*

(1) *Object complements* receive the action of the verb. (For complements used with verbals, see "Verbals," section 22.) There are three kinds: direct object, indirect object, and objective complement.

(2) *Direct objects* receive action directly. *Indirect objects* receive action indirectly, telling to whom or for whom something is done. An indirect object always comes between the verb and the direct object.

Indirect Object    Direct Object

Mark brought *Father* the *hammer.*

Sometimes a sentence in the passive voice keeps (retains) an object from the active voice. Notice that either the direct object or the indirect object may be a *retained object.*

ACTIVE: Philip taught the *eunuch* the *Gospel.*
PASSIVE: The eunuch was taught the *Gospel* by Philip. (retained direct object)
PASSIVE: The Gospel was taught the *eunuch* by Philip. (retained indirect object)

A direct object with a meaning similar to that of the verb is called a cognate object.

"Thou . . . hast *professed* a good *profession.*"
We shall *sing* a new *song.*

(3) *Objective complements* (distinguish carefully from object complements) are nouns or adjectives that follow direct objects and rename or modify the direct object. An objective complement performs the peculiar job of complementing another complement!

A.54b.

The church ordained Stephen *deacon.* (objective complement, noun)
David's popularity made Saul *jealous.* (objective complement, adjective)

Not all direct objects can have objective complements. Only direct objects of verbs meaning "to make" or "to consider" can have them.

She colored the picture blue. (She *made* it blue.)
He thought the lesson hard. (He *considered* it hard.)

(4) *Subjective complements* do not receive action. Rather, they follow linking verbs and relate to the subject of the sentence. There are two kinds: predicate adjective and predicate nominative.

PREDICATE ADJECTIVE: The sky is *blue.* (modifies *sky*)
The boy looked *unhappy.* (modifies *boy*)
PREDICATE NOMINATIVE: My teacher is *Brother John.* (renames *teacher*)
They were *fishermen.* (renames *they*)

*54c.*

*Independent elements* are not grammatically related to a sentence. Though related in thought, they do not function as subjects, verbs, modifiers, complements, or connectors. Therefore the sentence would be grammatically complete without them.

There are several kinds of independent elements. They are usually set off by commas.

(1) Response of *yes* or *no:*

> *Yes,* we plan to be there.

(2) Words of direct address:

> *John,* you may collect the papers.

(3) Parenthetical expressions. These are words such as

> *I think, we know, for example, on the other hand,* and *I pray.* Jonah was more inclined to obey, *we must believe,* after his encounter with the fish.

(4) Expletives. Though seemingly built into the sentence, expletives merely point forward to the subject. The sentence is quite complete without them.

**A.54c.**

> *There* was a bird in the attic. (A bird was in the attic.)
> *It* was hard to catch him. (To catch him was hard.)

Do not confuse these uses with cases where *there* and *it* do function as sentence parts.

> *There* it is. (tells *where*)
> *It* was a bird. (subject)

(5) Interjections:

> *Ouch!* I burned my finger.
> *Well,* be more careful.

(6) Exclamations:

> *The poor horse!* He looks thin and tired.
> *Good!* Here they come.

(7) Nominative absolutes. These are introductory phrases made of a noun and a participle. Often they can readily be changed to subordinate clauses.

*The car being low in oil,* we watched for a service station. (Since the car was low in oil, we watched for a service station.)

(8) Repeated words. This method is often used (especially in the Bible) for emphasis or for a poetical effect. Sometimes it is called *pheonasm.*

"*A woman that feareth the Lord,* she shall be praised."
"*The Lord,* he is the God."
"*Thy rod and thy staff* they comfort me."

# 55.

## Sentence Classes

Sentences are classified according to their structure: *simple, compound, complex,* and the less common *compound-complex.*

### 55a.

*Simple sentence:* A simple sentence consists of a subject and a predicate. It is called an independent clause, and it contains no other clauses.

The young ruler had great riches.

A simple sentence may have a compound subject or compound predicate as well as any number of phrases.

*Paul and Silas* sang praises *at midnight.*
    ↓                    ↓
compound subject    prepositional phrase

The children *visited* their uncle last summer and *did* some sightseeing in that vicinity. (compound predicate with complements, yet a simple sentence)

### 55b.

*Compound sentence:* A compound sentence consists of two or more simple sentences connected by conjunctions or by punctuation. Each part is known as an independent clause.

Hagar had no water, *and* Ishmael became weak.
Hagar had no water; Ishmael became weak.

### 55c.

*Complex sentence:* A complex sentence is one which contains one *independent clause* and one or more *dependent clauses.* These clauses may also be called the *main clause* and *subordinate clauses.*

*When Elijah saw the cloud,* **he believed** *that rain would come.*
     ↓             ↓          ↓
dependent         independent     dependent

**Ahab did not want to believe** *that God reigns.*
        ↓                  ↓
independent           dependent

*55d.*

*Compound-complex sentence:* If either of the clauses in a compound sentence contains a dependent clause within it, the sentence is known as compound-complex. It could also be said that a compound-complex sentence has at least two *independent clauses* and at least one *dependent clause.*

> *When Stephen's life was threatened,* **he looked toward heaven; and he asked God to forgive his enemies.**

# 56.

## Sentence Kinds

There are four kinds of sentences according to use: *declarative, interrogative, imperative,* and *exclamatory.*

*56a.*

A **declarative** sentence makes a statement and ends with a period.

> **Jesus was born in Bethlehem.**

*56b.*

An **interrogative** sentence asks a question and ends with a question mark.

> "Who shall ascend into the hill of the Lord?"

*56c.*

An **imperative** sentence gives a command or expresses an entreaty and ends with a period. The subject *you* is often not expressed.

> **(You) Be ready for the Lord's return.**

*56d.*

The **exclamatory** sentence expresses strong feelings and is punctuated with an exclamation mark.

How I would have liked to be there!

*Note:* Sentences such as these are declarative. The kind of quotation does not change the kind of sentence.

"What a sight!" he exclaimed.
"Let's go closer," she urged.

# 57.

## Sentence Order

*57a.*
The *natural order* of a sentence is for the subject to precede the predicate.

**Jesus passed under the sycamore tree.**

*57b.*
When all the predicate comes first in a sentence, the sentence is in *inverted order.*

**Under the sycamore tree stood the crowd.**

*57c.*
When part of the predicate comes before the subject and part comes after, the sentence is in *split order.*

**A.57.**

**Under the sycamore tree the crowd stood.**

# 58.

## Sentence Parts

Sentences are made up of *words, phrases,* and *clauses.*

*58a.*
*Words* are simply the eight parts of speech and have been discussed in section I, "Parts of Speech."

*58b.*
*Phrases* are groups of words used as a unit in a sentence; they have no subject or predicate. They can be used as substantives, adjectives, and adverbs.

(1) A *noun phrase* is used as a regular noun.

*The road* wound through the mountains.
*Jesus of Nazareth* rose from the dead.

(2) A *gerund phrase* is always used as a noun. An *infinitive phrase* is frequently used as a noun.

*Writing stories* requires time and effort. (gerund phrase)
*To write a book* is a task. (infinitive phrase)

(3) An *adjective phrase* is used as an adjective. An *infinitive phrase* is sometimes used as an adjective. A *participial phrase* is used as an adjective.

The girl *with the book* is my sister. (prepositional phrase used to modify *girl*)
She had a new song *to teach us.* (infinitive phrase used to modify *song*)
The girl *wearing a pink dress* enjoys singing, too. (participial phrase used to modify *girl*)

(4) An *adverb phrase* is used as an *adverb*. An *infinitive phrase* is sometimes used as an adverb.

John worked *inside the barn* while it rained. (prepositional phrase used to modify *worked*)
John came *to paint the fence.* (infinitive phrase used to modify *came*)

*58c.*

*Clauses:* A *clause* is a group of words which contains a subject and a predicate. It is considered a *part of a sentence.*

(1) An *independent clause* can stand alone without the remainder of the sentence. It could, in essence, be a simple sentence.

*Mary wrote a poem* which we will print on the front page of the paper.

(2) A *dependent clause* does not complete a thought when standing alone.

Mary wrote a poem *which we will print on the front page of the paper.*

The dependent (or subordinate) clause can be used as a noun or a modifier.

(3) *Noun Clauses*

SUBJECT: *How you do such fine sewing* is a puzzle to me.

DELAYED SUBJECT: It is a puzzle to me *how you do such fine sewing.*

OBJECT OF PREPOSITION: Give this coat to *whoever needs it.*

PREDICATE NOUN: The accident is *what we expected.*

APPOSTIVE: The fact *that Jesus died and rose again* is important to us.

DIRECT OBJECT: I understand *what you mean.*

OBJECT OF INFINITIVE: Do you want to hear *what we heard?*

OBJECT OF A GERUND: Do you mind repeating *what you said?*

INDEPENDENT ELEMENT: I did, *I confess,* take the wrong hammer.

(4) *Adjective Clauses*

(a) *Adjective clauses* are introduced by relative pronouns or relative adverbs.

Jesus is the one *whom* we love. (pronoun)
Gethsemane was the garden *where* He prayed. (adverb)

(See also "Relative Pronouns," section 13.)

(b) A *restrictive adjective clause* is necessary to complete the meaning of the sentence. It identifies the word it modifies.

A.58c.

I sleep better in a bed *that has a firm mattress.* (The sentence is not complete without the adjective clause.)

(c) A *nonrestrictive adjective clause* is not necessary to complete the meaning of the sentence. It only adds information, and is set off by commas to show that it is parenthetical.

This vase, *which I have had a long time,* is from Aunt Polly.

To decide whether a clause is restrictive or nonrestrictive, read the sentence without it. If the clause is restrictive, the sentence will then have a different meaning.

(5) *Adverb Clauses*

An *adverb clause* is used to modify a verb, an adjective, or an adverb; however, its most common use is to modify verbs. Adverb clauses answer the same questions that any other adverbs do.

I read the article *while I waited.* (tells when)

Put the medicine *where the children cannot reach it.* (tells where)

The boy ran *as if he were late.* (tells how)

We will watch from the window *because we don't want to miss the eclipse.* (tells why)

John may go along *if he hurries.* (conditional)

I promised, *although I would rather not have done so.* (makes an acknowledgment)

Adverb clauses modifying adjectives and other adverbs are used to tell *to what degree.*

Satan was so subtle *that Eve yielded* to his temptation.

You are later *than you usually are.*

## 59.

## Sentence Analysis

We have noted that sentences are made of words, phrases, and clauses; and they make a general pattern of subject-predicate order. It is possible to name the part of speech of every word, phrase, or clause by recognizing its use in a sentence.

**A.59.**

*59a.*

*Analyzing:* The two most common methods of studying the structure of a sentence are *analyzing* and *diagraming.* Analyzing is naming the sentence parts, and their relation to each other. To analyze a sentence, we should be able to answer the following questions.

1. Is the sentence declarative, imperative, interrogative, or exclamatory?
2. What is the complete subject and what is the complete predicate?
3. What are the phrases and clauses, and how are they used?
4. Is the sentence simple, compound, complex, or compound-complex?
5. Is the sentence in natural or inverted order?

*Example of sentence analysis:* The people of Nineveh believed God.

A simple declarative sentence in natural order.

SIMPLE SUBJECT: *people*

COMPLETE SUBJECT: *The people of Nineveh—of Nineveh* is a prepositional phrase modifying *people.*

SIMPLE PREDICATE: *believed*

COMPLETE PREDICATE: *believed God*—*God* is the object of the verb *believed*.

*Example*: Are you on a good diet, or are you starving spiritually?

A compound, interrogative sentence in split order.

FIRST CLAUSE: *are you on a good diet*
SIMPLE AND COMPLETE SUBJECT: *you*
SIMPLE PREDICATE: *are*
COMPLETE PREDICATE: *are on a good diet*
MODIFIERS: *On a good diet* is an adverb phrase modifying *are*. *Diet* is the object of the preposition *on;* *a* and *good* modify *diet*.
SECOND CLAUSE: *are you starving spiritually*
SIMPLE AND COMPLETE SUBJECT: *you*
SIMPLE PREDICATE: *are starving*
COMPLETE PREDICATE: *are starving spiritually*
MODIFIER: *Spiritually* is an adverb modifying *are starving*.

### 59b.

*Diagraming* is the most thorough study of sentences because it gives a picture of word relationships. Analyzing is included in correct diagraming.

In diagraming, the parts of the sentence are set in their places to show their relationship to each other. The complete subject is written on the lines before the vertical line that crosses the base line. The complete predicate is written on lines after the vertical line that crosses the base line.

The simple subject and the simple predicate are diagramed on the horizontal base line.

Adjectives and adverbs used as modifiers are placed on slanted lines below the words they modify.

Prepositions are placed on slanted lines, with their objects on connected horizontal lines, under the words that they modify.

Conjunctions are placed on broken lines, either horizontal, vertical, or slanting, according to the words they connect.

Following are examples of various types of sentences diagramed to show their parts.

### (1) Simple Sentences

*Complements* are diagramed on the horizontal line directly after the verb, except for indirect objects.

Direct object:

The wise men saw the *star.*

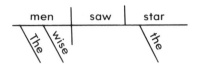

Indirect object:

They gave *Jesus* gifts.

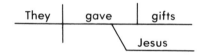

*Note:* Indirect objects are considered by some as being in a class of their own, not as the object of some "omitted preposition." Thus some English textbooks show a sentence like the one above diagramed in this way:

**A.59b.**

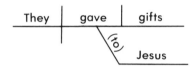

Object complement:

The Lord appointed Moses *leader* of Israel.

Notice how the line before the objective complement slants back toward the direct object, just as the line before a predicate nominative leans back toward the subject. We prefer this diagram rather than an alternate method shown in some older English textbooks.

Predicate nominative:

Moses was a good *leader.*

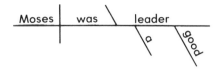

Predicate adjective:

Moses was *meek.*

*Note:* Sometimes it is hard to tell whether a predicate word is a part of the verb phrase or is a predicate adjective. In such a case ask: Does this word express *action* which the subject does or receives? If so, it is a verb. Does this word express a *quality* or a *condition* that could also be expressed by a pure adjective of similar meaning? If so, it is an adjective. Consult a dictionary if you are still in doubt; unless the form is listed as an adjective, diagram it as part of the main verb.

This book is interesting. (*Interesting* does not express an action which the subject does or receives. It could be replaced by *good;* therefore, it is a predicate adjective.)

The cow is grazing. (*Grazing* expresses an action which the subject does. It cannot be replaced by an adjective; therefore, it is a verb.)

*Compound parts* are diagramed with the conjunction on a broken line between the parts. Several types are illustrated here.

Compound subject and compound verb:

*Mary* and *Martha sorrowed* and *wept.*

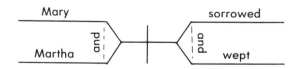

Compound objects of a preposition:

The Lord reigns over *earth* and *heaven*.

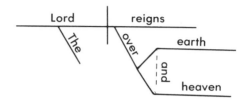

Compound modifiers:

A Holstein is a *black* and *white* cow.

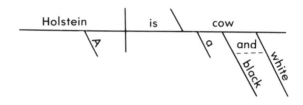

**A.59b.** **(2)** *Compound Sentences*

*Compound sentences* follow the same rules that simple sentences do. The two main clauses are diagramed side by side with the coordinating conjunction on a broken line between them.

Fierce winds swept the soil across the prairie, *and* this caused much damage to their crops.

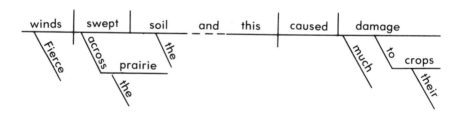

**(3)** *Complex Sentences*

*Modifying clauses* are diagramed on a separate base line beneath the main clause. A slanting broken line connects the two clauses.

*Adjective clauses* are usually introduced by relative pronouns. The broken line connects the pronoun with its antecedent.

Adjective clause with relative pronoun used as the subject:

Our neighbor is a man *who* studies the Bible daily.

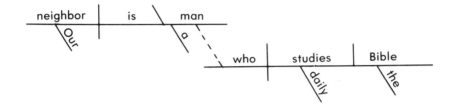

Adjective clause with relative pronoun used as the object of a preposition:

He was the one to *whom* I spoke.

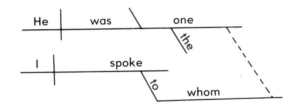

A.59b.

Adjective clause with relative pronoun used as a direct object:

This is the man *whom* I met yesterday.

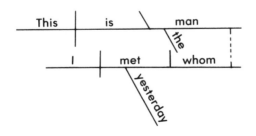

Adjective clause introduced by relative adverb:

This is the place *where* we met.

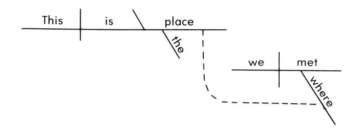

Adjective clause with relative pronoun used as a modifier:

This was the man *whose* eyes had been opened.

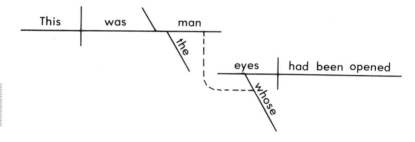

**A.59b.**

*Adverb clauses* are introduced by subordinating conjunctions. These conjunctions are placed on the slanting broken line between the two clauses. The top of the broken line is connected to the word which the clause modifies. The bottom is connected to the verb of the subordinate clause.

We will call you *when* we need you.

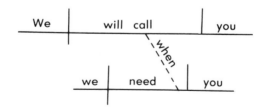

Germs are so small *that* they are invisible.

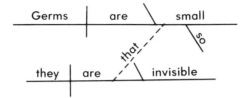

*Noun clauses* are diagramed on a stand connected to the position they fill. Several uses are illustrated here.

**Subject:**

*What he wanted* **was not available.**

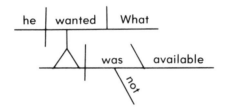

A.59b.

**Direct object:**

**Ellen knew** *that she had given the right answer.*

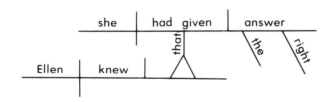

(When a word such as *that* merely introduces the noun clause, it is placed on the stem.)

Appositive:

The fact *that the earth is round* has been well established.

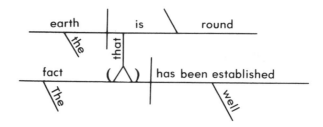

### (4) *Compound-Complex Sentences*

*Compound-complex sentences* are diagramed according to the rules for both compound and complex sentences. The subordinate clauses are connected to the main clauses of which they are part.

Paul preached to whoever would listen, whereas Peter preached mostly to Jews.

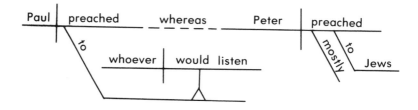

### (5) *Independent Elements*

*Independent elements* are diagramed on a line separate from the main diagram. Only a few kinds are illustrated here.

Words of direct address:

*Holy God,* we praise Thy name.

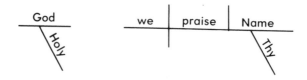

Parenthetical expression:

Jesus, *we know*, was also tempted.

Expletive:

*There* were three men with Jesus.

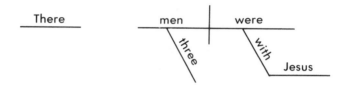

Exclamation:

*The children!* We cannot find them.

Nominative absolute:

*The children having been found,* we could relax.

Repeated words:

"*Thy rod and thy staff* they comfort me."

### (6) *Verbals*

All types of *verbals* are diagramed across the angle of a slanting and a horizontal line. Complements of verbals are placed on the horizontal line after them.

Infinitive phrase used as a noun:

Sue likes *to read true stories.*

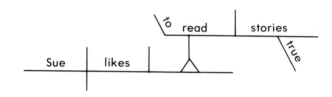

Infinitive used as a modifier:

I found a good book *to read.*

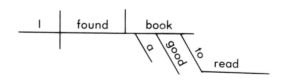

Gerund phrase used as a subject:

*Paul's going to Jerusalem* brought tears.

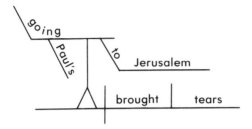

(Adjective modifiers of a gerund are placed to the *left* of the stem, and adverb modifiers to the *right*.)

Gerund used as a predicate nominative:

His work is *farming.*

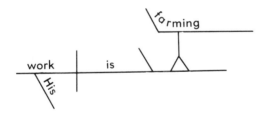

Gerund used as the object of a preposition:

Christians are opposed to *fighting.*

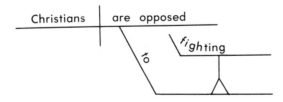

Participial phrases modifying the subject:

*Praising God* and *leaping for joy,* the healed man entered the temple.

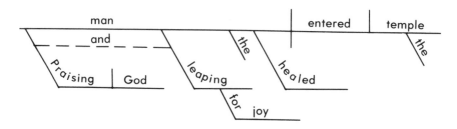

*Note:* Be careful not to confuse adjectives that look like verbs (*wicked, cunning*) with true participles (*bent, walking*). When one of the regular forms of a verb is used as an adjective, diagram it as a participle. But if no such form exists as a verb, diagram it as a common adjective.

The *unforgiving* servant hardened his heart against his *pleading* fellow servant.

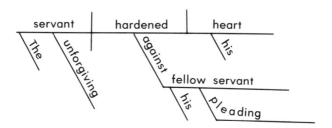

### (7) *Appositives and Omitted Words*

Both *appositives* and *omitted words* are placed within parentheses on diagrams. Following are several examples.

Appositives to the subject:

My brother *James* will be coming today.

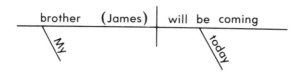

This assignment, *writing a story,* will take some effort.

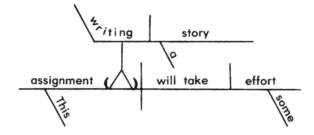

Appositive to a modifier:

This is my cousin *William's* car.

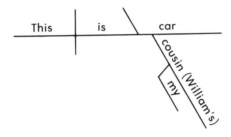

A.59b.

Compound appositives:

Two disciples, *Peter and John,* ran to the tomb.

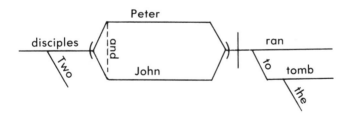

Omitted subject in an imperative sentence:

Close the door.

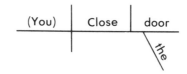

Omitted words in an elliptical clause:

Goliath was much stronger than David.

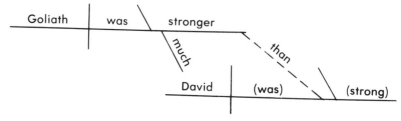

Conjunction omitted: When conjunctions are omitted in compound sentences, they need not be supplied in parentheses. However, most complex sentences need a conjunction, especially those of the type illustrated here.

The longer he waited the harder it seemed.

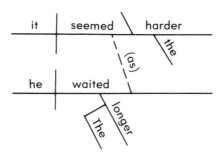

(8) *Unusual Constructions*

(a) Split or inverted order: A sentence in split or inverted order is diagramed in natural order.

How beautiful those flowers are! (split)

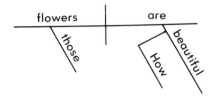

Where were you? (inverted)

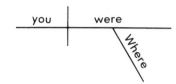

(b) Compound imperative sentence: A compound imperative sentence may be diagramed in either of two ways.

Go downstairs and get a jar of peaches.

A.59b.

FIRST:

SECOND:

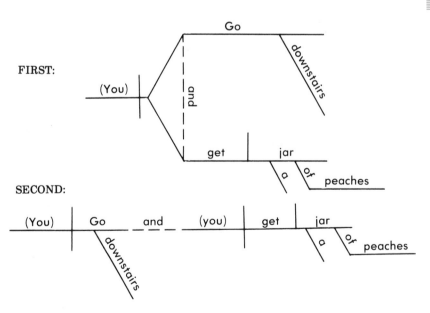

(c) Pronoun used intensively: A compound personal pronoun used intensively is diagramed as an appositive.

You *yourself* have made that statement.

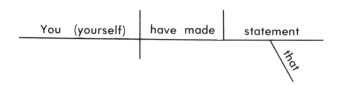

(d) Negative joined to verb: When *not* is joined to the verb, as in *cannot, doesn't,* or *won't,* the words are separated on the diagram.

I *cannot* bear my burdens alone.

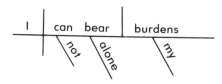

**A.59b.**    He *won't* be coming along.

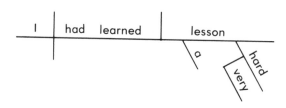

(e) Modifiers of adjectives, adverbs, prepositional phrases, or clauses: These are placed on slanted lines beneath the words they modify.

I had learned a *very* hard lesson.

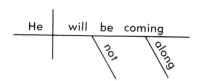

The things pleasant *to the eyes* are not always good for us.

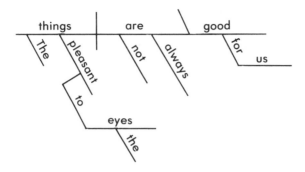

Miners often work *deep* under the ground.

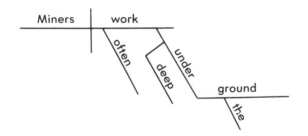

They had left *just* before we arrived.

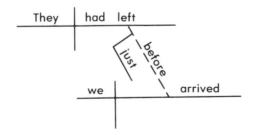

(f) Phrasal preposition or conjunction: These are diagramed in the usual position of a single-word preposition or conjunction.

We built the bird feeder *according to* the plan.

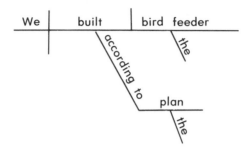

The poor boy looked *as if* he were frightened.

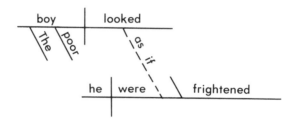

# 60.

## Variety for Emphasis

When all sentences follow the same pattern, writing becomes dull and expressionless. A variety of sentence patterns not only prevents monotony but also lends emphasis to the main point.

### 60a.

*Arrangement of Sentences:* To emphasize a point, the sentence can be arranged in split or inverted order. In the following sentences, the italicized part of the predicate is emphasized.

Jonathan loved David *very much* and asked Saul to spare him. (adverb)

The dog chased the cat around the tree. (natural)

*Friday*, observing the weather, we cut wood for the fireplace. (split)

Observing the weather, we cut wood for the fireplace on Friday. (natural)

*The plan of salvation* God gave to man because of His great love. (split)

*Because of His great love,* God gave the plan of salvation to man. (split)

*Dearer all the time become* the Psalms. (inverted)

### 60b.
*Variety of Modifiers*

Jonathan loved David *very much* and asked Saul to spare him. (adverb)

Jonathan loved David *with great love* and asked Saul to spare him. (prepositional phrase)

*Loving David,* Jonathan asked Saul to spare him. (participial phrase)

Jonathan, *who loved David very much,* asked Saul to spare him. (clause)

### 60c.
*Sentence Length:* When only short sentences are used, they can become very monotonous. When all the sentences are long, the reader can become confused. To have a pleasing effect, the sentence length should be varied.

A.60b.

### 60d.
*Variety of Classes:* A narrative can be much more interesting with a variety of sentences—simple, compound, and complex. Especially does writing require variety. In speaking, we make things interesting by tones as well as by sentence structure.

(1) *Simple Sentence*

The Psalms are meditations in poetic form.

(2) *Compound Sentence*

Most of the Psalms were written by David, but the Proverbs were written by Solomon.

(3) *Complex Sentence*

The Psalms are meditations written in such a way that they become dearer the more we read them.

(4) *Compound-Complex Sentence*

Most of the Psalms were written by David, who loved to meditate, and the Proverbs were written by Solomon, who possessed great wisdom but later turned from God.

Consider the following group of simple sentences in contrast to the former examples.

The Psalms are meditations in poetic form.
The Proverbs are wise sayings.
Most of the Psalms were written by David.
The Proverbs were written by Solomon.
The Psalms become dearer all the time.
We read them more and more.
The Proverbs show Solomon's wisdom.
He turned his heart from God.
The Proverbs cause us to think.

*60e.*

**Figures of speech:** Points can be emphasized by figures of speech. Writers can always add freshness to their writing by using unique expressions.

A.60e.

SIMILE: "Joys are flowing *like a river.*"
METAPHOR: "Jesus, *Rose of Sharon, bloom* within my heart."
PERSONIFICATION: "Let all the isles *rejoice; /* Let seas *take up the strain.*"
HYPERBOLE: "Had I a *thousand* hearts to give, Lord, they should all be thine."

*60f.*

**Conciseness:** Sometimes short sentences can be combined or long sentences can be shortened, to make them more forceful. It is well to remember, though, that readers will shy away from long, unclear sentences.

The *Martyrs Mirror* provides good reading. It was published in 1660.

The *Martyrs Mirror,* published in 1660, provides good reading.

It is my goal to finish my sewing before April.

To finish my sewing before April is my goal. (eliminates expletive)

*60g.*

*Passive voice:* Sometimes when the actor is not known it is best to write a sentence in the passive voice. Sometimes there are other reasons for not mentioning the actor.

Somebody built this house in 1885.
BETTER: This house was built in 1885. (actor unknown)

Our neighbor shot our dog because he barked excessively.
BETTER: Our dog was shot because he barked excessively.
(It is more courteous not to mention names.)

We donated ten blankets for the institution.
BETTER: Ten blankets were donated for the institution. (The receiver of the action should receive emphasis.)

*60h.*

*Order of climax:* Arrange a series of words in order of importance to gain emphasis.

The doctor kindly explained the cost, the pain, and the risk of life which would accompany the surgery.

# 61.

## Avoiding Faulty Sentences

Sometimes sentences are not clear in meaning and the sentence parts are not arranged correctly. Not only is a weak sentence "bad grammar," but it does not convey thoughts as easily. This section gives points on sentence construction.

A modifier should be placed near the word it modifies.

Covered with snow, we carried the picnic table into the garage. (What is covered with snow?)

We carried the picnic table into the garage which was covered with snow. (still not clear)

We carried *the picnic table,* **which was covered with snow,** into the garage.

A pronoun should refer clearly to its antecedent.

Lisa told Shirley she could take her letter to the post office. (personal pronoun not clear)

REVISED: Lisa said, "Shirley, I can take your letter to the post office."

I have the old chair in my living room that I bought at the public sale. (The clause introduced by the relative pronoun seems to refer to living room.)

REVISED: I have in my living room the old chair that I bought at the public sale.

Laryngitis hindered my singing, which was hard for me to accept.

REVISED: The fact that laryngitis hindered my singing was hard for me to accept.

They predict rain for tomorrow. (*They* has no antecedent to make it clear.)

REVISED: Weather reporters predict rain for tomorrow.

Bring only related thoughts together in a sentence. Use two or more sentences for different thought content.

It snowed all day yesterday, and Mary broke the eggs when she fell on the snowy steps.

REVISED: It snowed all day yesterday. Mary broke the eggs when she fell on the snowy steps.

**A.61.**  Sometimes an additional clause can unify two thoughts.

REVISED: After it snowed all day yesterday, the steps were so slippery that Mary fell and broke the eggs.

Verbals should be alike in the same sentence.

Mother taught us to cook before sewing.
REVISED: Mother taught us cooking before sewing.

To beg is better than stealing.
REVISED: To beg is better than to steal.

Eliminate excessive detail.

When David was in his tender years, healthy and strong, tending his father's sheep, he experienced God's protection from wild animals.

REVISED: When young David tended his father's sheep, he experienced God's protection from wild animals.

In writing a definition, tell *what* a thing is, not when or where.

A drought is when there is a lack of rainfall.
REVISED: A drought is a lack of rainfall.

Recognizing sentence parts means developing a sense of good sentence structure. Constructing good sentences is the key to good writing. A good sentence is grammatically correct and also says exactly what the writer wants to say.

A.61.

# B. SENTENCE MECHANICS

## 62.

### Capitalization

Most capitalized words can be put in three categories: beginning words, words in titles, and proper nouns.

*62a.*
*Beginning Words*

(1) Every sentence should begin with a capital letter.

*Hard* work should give you a satisfied feeling.

(2) A direct quotation within a sentence should begin with a capital letter.

Father said, "*We* do not do everything just for fun."

(3) Capitalize the first word of a resolution or formal statement.

Resolved: *To* provide a sound orientation program for teachers.

(4) Direct questions within a sentence should begin with a capital letter except after a colon, when either form is correct.

We wondered, *Can* such a small boy be responsible for the job?
The question to be discussed is: *Should* (or *should*) handicapped children be included in the general school?

(5) Every line of poetry should begin with a capital letter.

Remember, Lord, our mortal state,
How frail our life, how short the date!
Where is the man that draws his breath,
Safe from disease, secure from death?

*62b.*
*Words in Titles*

(1) In titles of books, magazines, articles, or stories, capitalize the first and last words and all other words except conjunctions and prepositions of less than four letters and the articles *a, an,* and *the.*

*The Christian Pathway*
"Are the Children In?"

"Developing Goals in Handwriting"
*Exploring With God*

(2) Some titles contain unusual key words. Capitalize the first word of a hyphenated compound. As a rule, capitalize the word after the hyphen if it is a noun, a proper adjective, or a word of parallel importance.

Nineteenth-Century Immigration (noun)
German-English Dictionary (proper adjective)
Hit-and-Run Driver Arraignment (parallel words)

*Note:* Capitalization of words following prefixes such as *ex-*, *pro-*, *anti-*, and *self-* in titles is of varied opinion.

Anti-Icing Device
Self-Improvement
Pro-Communist Ideals

*62c.*
*Proper Nouns*
(1) Capitalize all proper nouns.

PERSONS: John Martin
PLACES: Jerusalem
THINGS: the Capitol
ORGANIZATIONS: Michigan Conference
INSTITUTIONS: Messiah Bible School
HISTORICAL PERIODS: the Dark Ages, Civil War
MEMBERS OF POLITICAL, NATIONAL, RACIAL, RELIGIOUS, OR
  SOCIAL GROUPS: Republican, American, Jew, Anabaptist,
  Welcome Wagon
CALENDAR DESIGNATIONS: January, Monday, Thanksgiving

*Note:* Proper nouns following prefixes such as *pro-*, *anti-*, or *ex-* are still capitalized.

ex-Catholic, anti-American

(2) The names of the seasons are not ordinarily capitalized. *Book*, when it refers to a book of the Bible, is not capitalized unless the name of the book is also given.

Do we thank the Creator for snow in the *spring*?
The minister read from the *Book* of Luke.

B.62c.

(3) Directions are not usually capitalized unless they specify a particular section of the country.

> Iva turned to the *east* only to find she was on the wrong road. (a direction)
> You can tell that Grant is from the *South* by his accent. (a particular section)

(4) School subjects are not capitalized (except languages), unless they are followed by numbers.

> mathematics, geography, reading
> English, German, Latin
> Biology II, Literature I

(5) Abbreviations of capitalized words are usually capitalized.

> Mr., FBI, A.D., C.O.D.

*Note:* No. and *no.* are both correct according to their use.

(6) Nouns and personal pronouns referring to Deity should be capitalized.

> We claim *Him* as *Lord* of our lives.
> Stephen was full of the *Holy Ghost.*

*Note:* Some grammarians say that capitalization of these personal pronouns is optional except for clarification. But God is all-important in the life of a Christian; therefore, we capitalize *all* such personal pronouns.

> Jesus and *His* disciples went into a ship. (could be optional, but we always capitalize)
> God blesses man according to *His* will. (not clear without capital)

*Note:* Only personal (not relative) pronouns referring to God are capitalized. *Someone* (or a similar word) should also be capitalized when it refers to God and has no antecedent.

> We know *Someone who* can help you.
> But: God is *someone* who can help you.

(7) Major Biblical events and terms are capitalized.

> the Creation, the Fall of man, Second Coming of Christ

(8) The words *I* and *O* are always capitalized. Since *oh* almost always comes at the beginning of a sentence, it is usually capitalized also. But in a sentence like this it is not.

> He had seen such a knife only once before, and oh, how he wanted this one now!

(9) Capitalize titles that precede proper names, but not those that follow.

> King George; Elizabeth, the queen
> Mayor John Wright; John Wright, the mayor of Kent

(10) Capitalize *father, mother, sister, uncle,* and so forth, when they refer to a particular person and when they are not accompanied by a pronoun.

> I will help with the job, *Father.*
> English grammar has always been easy for *Cousin* Mary. (but: *my cousin* Mary)
> The man we call *Uncle* Matthew is not really *my uncle.*

(11) Names of plants, animals, inventions, and processes are capitalized only when they are derived from proper names. Even then some are written in lower case when they become common enough. Check an up-to-date dictionary to be sure.

B.62c.

> Canada thistle
> black-eyed Susan
> morocco leather (from Morocco, Africa)
> Pullman car (from George Pullman)
> leghorn chicken (from Leghorn, Italy)
> Holstein cow (from Holstein, Friesland)
> pasteurization (from Louis Pasteur)
> Red Haven peach

*Note:* Names of things are not capitalized when they follow brand names.

> Sunbeam toaster, Chevrolet station wagon

Capitalization can be overdone. Check a good dictionary when you are in doubt. A word which is regularly capitalized will be entered with a capital letter. There are also manuals of style for the avid writer.

## 63.

## Punctuation

*63a.*
*Period*

(1) A period should be used after declarative sentences, mildly imperative sentences, and indirect questions.

"Except a man be born of water and of the Spirit, he cannot enter into the kingdom of God." (declarative)

"Marvel not that I said unto thee, Ye must be born again." (imperative)

Nicodemus wondered how someone could be born when he was old. (indirect question)

(2) A period should be used after most abbreviations and initials.

Mr., Mrs., Dr., Jr., etc., no., A.M., B.C.

But: FBI, NATO, and other national organizations rarely have periods.

**B.63.**

(a) Do not use a period after these shortened forms or after contractions.

2nd, 3rd, can't, won't

(b) A sentence needs only one period at the end, even if it ends with an abbreviation.

The train leaves at 4:00 A.M.

(3) Use a period after numbers or letters used to enumerate items in a vertical list.

1. 45 lb.          a. definition
2. 50 lb.          b. classification
3. 52 lb.          c. structure

(4) Periods should be placed within quotation marks whether single or double quotation marks are used.

Ellis remarked, "There is no time to lose when the harvest is ripe."

Lucille's favorite song is, "I Am Thine, O Lord."

Aunt Clara told four-year-old Rodney's mother, "He said, 'I'm almost grown up.' "

(5) When a whole sentence is enclosed in parentheses, the period should be placed inside. If the enclosed part is included within a sentence, the period should be placed outside.

Mrs. Doane instructed us all on how to use the electric knife. (I had seen the demonstration before.)

If we watch demonstrations, we save wear and tear on appliances (by learning their proper use).

(6) Three periods spaced evenly (ellipsis points) indicate an omission. When a complete sentence comes before the omission, place a period before the ellipsis points. Do not use ellipsis points after a quoted sentence, except for an unfinished statement made in conversation. And be careful *never* to change the meaning of a quotation by omitting part of it.

"Blessed is the man that walketh not in the counsel of the ungodly. . . . But his delight is in the law of the Lord" (Psalm 1:1, 2).

We are glad that our journey is nearly  . . . (no period, because sentence is unfinished)

**B.63b.**

*63b.*

*Question Mark*

(1) The question mark is used after a direct question. Any interrogative sentence (including an elliptical question) ends with a question mark.

Why do people trust in riches?

Are you skilled in handling your responsibilities? In handling yourself properly? (elliptical)

(2) A double direct question or an indirect question within a direct question requires only one question mark.

DOUBLE DIRECT QUESTION: Did you hear me ask, "Where are you?"

INDIRECT QUESTION WITHIN A DIRECT QUESTION: Did Jesus ask who touched Him?

INDIRECT QUESTION: Jesus asked who touched Him.

(3) Quoted direct questions require a question mark, although the entire sentence is declarative.

> "Who touched Me?" Jesus asked.
> Jesus asked, "Who touched Me?"

(4) A question mark within parentheses is sometimes used when a writer is uncertain about given information.

> Menno Simons, born in 1496(?), wrote extensively during his lifetime.

*Note 1:* Do not use a question mark to toy with sentences, thinking it adds wit.

*Note 2:* Courtesy questions such as found in business letters do not require a question mark.

> Will you send the bill with the parcel.

### 63c.

*Exclamation mark:* An exclamation mark indicates the end of any exclamatory word, phrase, or sentence.

> INTERJECTION: Oh! Alas!
> EXCLAMATORY SENTENCE: How good God is!
> A PHRASE SHOWING EMOTION: To think of it! Not a thing saved!

Exclamation marks should be used sparingly. Excessive use weakens writing.

### 63d.

*Comma:* A comma indicates a mild separation and a place for a slight pause in reading to make the meaning of the sentence clear. The sound of a sentence is a partial guide to using commas, but sound is not always dependable.

The comma has four basic uses: (a) to divide compound sentences; (b) to set off nonrestrictive and parenthetical elements; (c) to denote certain introductory material; and (d) to separate coordinate items in a series.

(1) Dividing main clauses in a compound sentence.

> Unsaved people may enjoy life for a short time, but saved people will enjoy life eternally.

*Exception 1:* If both clauses are very short, the comma may be omitted.

Stay clear of evil desires and be content in your place.

*Exception 2:* If the clauses contain commas, it is often better to use a semicolon before the conjunction.

Before winter came on, the Jewish Feast of the Tabernacles was kept; but Jesus did not go until after this weeklong celebration was in progress.

(2) Setting off nonrestrictive and parenthetical elements.

Moses, the meekest man who ever lived, was used by God to deliver the children of Israel out of Egypt. (appositive)

God used him, with the help of Aaron, to speak to Pharaoh. (nonrestrictive phrase)

Yes, we are studying the life of Moses this quarter, John. (words in direct address)

A Sunday school meeting was held Saturday, March 5, 1960, near Staunton, Virginia. (parenthetical elements)

We planned to go; however, the trip was canceled because of snow. (after a conjunctive adverb or transitional phrase between main clauses)

*Note:* Restrictive clauses are not set off by commas because they **B.63d.** are essential to the entire meaning.

Only those *who study the Bible* will grow spiritually.

(3) Denoting introductory material.

When God corrects us, we know that He loves us. (introductory adverb clause)

After the plagues, Pharaoh promised to release the Israelites. (introductory phrase)

Seeing Pharaoh's hosts nearing the Red Sea, God's children became alarmed. (introductory gerund phrase)

God said to Moses, "Stretch out your hand toward the sea." (introducing a direct quotation)

*Note:* Ordinarily direct quotations should be set off from other sentence parts by commas.

(4) Items in a series, including words, phrases, and clauses.

Red, brown, and gold leaves fluttered to the ground. (words)

An unkindness, a lie, or a suspicion can spoil a friendship. (words)
Paul was patient in affliction, in necessities, and in distresses. (phrases)
"I have fought a good fight, I have finished my course, [and] I have kept the faith." (clauses)

(5) When the adjective next to the noun seems to be a part of the noun, no comma is needed before it.

Maude looked again at the child's beautiful golden hair. (*Golden hair* is a closely tied phrase.)

(6) Do not ordinarily use a comma before a title in quotation marks.

The local staff revised "The Church Walking With the World."

*63e.*
*Colon*
(1) A colon is used to introduce a list, statement, question, theory, or formal quotation.

One word describes disobedience to parents: vile.
The dates are as follows: January 30, February 16, and March 9.
Susannah Wesley, mother of John and Charles Wesley, once used this statement: "Whatever weakens your reason, impairs the tenderness of your conscience, obscures your sense of God, or removes your relish of spiritual things—that is sin to you."

(2) Use a colon after the salutation in a business letter.

Dear Sir:
We received your check today.

(3) Use a colon to separate numbers or references.

Genesis 3:15
4:30 A.M.
Thieleman J. van Braght: Martyrs Mirror

*63f.*
*Semicolon:* The semicolon divides the parts of a sentence more clearly—especially when there are numerous commas also.

(1) Use a semicolon between main clauses where there is no coordinating conjunction.

Martha prepared the meal; Mary listened to Jesus.

(2) Use a semicolon between clauses with connectives such as *therefore, hence, however, thus, nevertheless, likewise, consequently,* and other conjunctive adverbs.

> Satan sends out his fiery darts; therefore, we need to put on the armor of God.

(3) Use a semicolon to divide items in a series if they contain commas within themselves.

> The Millers will bring along three children: Mary, nine years old; Sara, seven years old; and Nancy, three years old.

(4) Use a semicolon to separate clauses which contain commas within themselves.

> Many people today live for things that are free, and they enjoy times when they are unoccupied; but the Christian strives instead to be helpful to others.

(5) Use a semicolon to separate phrases not joined by a conjunction.

> Christians shall serve God with fear and trembling; with diligence and carefulness.

**B.63g.**

*63g.*

*Quotation marks:* are used to enclose direct quotations, actual thoughts, certain titles, and words used in a special sense.

(1) Enclose a direct quotation with double marks.

> Paul answered Agrippa, "I would that you were altogether persuaded."

(2) A quotation within a quotation should be enclosed with single marks.

> "We need courage," the minister said, "to say, 'How . . . can I . . . sin against God?' as Joseph did."

(3) If a question mark, a dash, or an exclamation mark is part of the quoted material, place it inside the quotation mark; if it punctuates the whole sentence, place it on the outside. If it applies to both, place it on the inside.

> Cain asked, "Am I my brother's keeper?"
> When did Peter say, "I know not the man"?

Why did Isaac ask, "Where is the offering?"
He actually said, "You're having a little trouble"!

(4) Colons and semicolons should always be outside quotation marks.

Jesus said, "Whither I go, ye cannot come"; however, the Jews could not understand what He meant.
These four things are small, but "exceeding wise": the ant, the cony, the locust, and the spider.

(5) Each quotation in a conversation, no matter how short, should be enclosed in quotation marks.

"Where is my pen?" Dan asked.
"I put it back beside your desk after I used it," answered Joe.
"Now where can I look?" returned Dan.

(6) Quoted paragraphs (including Bible verses) should be enclosed in quotation marks. References to verses are enclosed in parentheses, following this pattern:

"Rejoice evermore" (1 Thessalonians 5:16).

*Note:* Sometimes in print, long sections of quoted material are set in smaller type, making quotation marks unnecessary.

(7) Titles of minor works such as short stories, essays, short poems, songs, articles from periodicals, and subdivisions of books are set off by quotation marks when used in a sentence.

After you say this week's "Memory Selection," you may read "What Made Joseph Great?" in the June 27, 1969, *Christian Example.*
Dr. Amstutz's article on "The Health Food Fad" is sensible.

(8) Words, phrases, or clauses which suggest quotation from another source may be set off by quotation marks.

The word "home" sounded good to us.
We cannot "do business" with God until we are free from Satan's entanglements.
"Hot rodding" does not fit with "being an example of the believers."

(9) Quotation marks may enclose a term which the writer does not wish to make his own. They give the idea of "so-called." But if the

term *so-called* is actually written, omit the quotation marks.

> The "unsinkable" ship lay at the bottom of the ocean.
> The so-called invincible army had been badly beaten.

Quotation marks can be overused. Do not enclose the title of your own writing. Do not enclose nicknames, technical terms, or well-known phrases. Instead of using quotation marks to denote slang, use a better term. Use good sentence structure, not quotation marks, for emphasis.

*63h.*

*Apostrophe:* The apostrophe is used to indicate the possessive case, to mark omissions in contractions, and to show occasional plurals.

(1) Add an apostrophe and *s* to form the possessive of singular nouns.

> *Mary's* concern was to learn from Jesus.

(2) The apostrophe and *s* is also used to form the possessive of plural nouns that do not end in *s*.

> The message of salvation touches *people's* lives throughout the ages.

(3) Use only an apostrophe when the plural noun ends in *s*.

> The *disciples'* amazement grew as Jesus performed miracles.

B.63h.

(4) When singular nouns ending with an *s* or *z* sound have only one syllable or have the accent on the last syllable, add *'s*. But if the last syllable is unaccented, add only an apostrophe. This rule prevents awkwardness in pronunciation.

| | |
|---|---|
| spouse's rights | James's letter |
| Moses' brother | Lazarus' death |
| Bernice's room | Lopez' presidency |

(5) An apostrophe and *s* can be used to show the plural of letters, numbers, and abbreviations.

> His *a*'s look like *o*'s.
> The 1's and 2's are scheduled to trim the church lawn this week.
> The 1970's were years of fast living.
> Ph.D's, though they are hard-earned degrees, do not take men to heaven.

(6) Personal pronouns do not require an apostrophe to show the possessive form. Several other kinds do.

his, her, its, their, somebody's, whoever's

(7) Use an apostrophe to show a contracted or shortened form. Place it at the point of omission.

is not—isn't
will not—won't
they are—they're
stir and bake—stir 'n' bake
Flood of 1969—Flood of '69

*63i.*

*Dash:* The dash is used to show a sudden break in thought, to set off parenthetical matter that is very abrupt, or to indicate interrupted speech. On the typewriter, a dash is indicated by two hyphens without a space before, between, or after. In handwriting, the dash should be indicated by a line two or three times longer than a hyphen.

(1) Sudden break in thought.

Mary hurried into the kitchen and asked Mother, "May I go— on second thought, I don't want to."

**B.63i.**

(2) Abrupt parenthetical matter.

You should remember—we all should remember—that we need to study the Bible to live according to God's approval.

(3) Interrupted speech.

"Now we'd better be careful," warned David, "or—what was that?" (no period after dash)

*Note:* Both the dash and ellipsis points may indicate unfinished speech. Use the dash to show abruptness, and ellipsis points to show hesitancy or uncertainty.

(4) Separate a series from the main part of the sentence that explains the series.

Our teacher pointed out three constellations—the Big Dipper, Orion, and Cassiopea—on a star map.

*63j.*

*Parentheses:* Parentheses are used to enclose parenthetical, supplementary, or illustrative matter and to set off numbers or letters when used for enumeration in a sentence.

(1) Parenthetical.

Jesus looked up into the tree (already knowing about Zacchaeus) and told him to come down.

(2) Supplementary or illustrative.

"Remember them that are in bonds, as bound with them"(Hebrews 13:3). This teaches us not only to remember "them that are in bonds" (are distressed), but also to sympathize (as bound with them).

(3) Enumerative.

The minister emphasized that we should allow Christ to (1) renew our thinking, (2) control our intentions, and (3) keep us at peace with our fellow men if we want peace of mind.

*Note 1:* Punctuation, when needed, should be placed outside the second parenthesis, unless the enclosed matter is an entire sentence.

*Note 2:* Commas, dashes, and parentheses can all set off parenthetical matter. The writer's intention is often the guide as to which should be used. Note the following differences.

*Commas* are used as mild separators and make the added material a part of the sentence.

Lucifer, also called Satan, wants us to share his doom.

*Dashes* are used for emphasis of the abruptness of the parenthetical part.

Lucifer—also called Satan—wants us to share his doom.

*Parentheses* are used to include outside thoughts in an obscure manner.

Lucifer (also called Satan) wants us to share his doom.

*63k.*

**Brackets** are used in quoted matter or in the writing of another to set off an explanation, correction, comment, or question. In rare cases brackets act as parentheses within another set of parentheses.

> "Be careful for nothing [Do not be overly anxious about anything]" (Philippians 4:6).
>
> "Though he [Christ] were a Son, yet learned he obedience by the things which he suffered" (Hebrews 5:8).
>
> The term for *charity* (Greek *agapē* [pronounced ag-ah′pay]) is rarely found in literature other than Christian writings.

*63l.*

**Hyphen:** The hyphen is used for joining words, for dividing words at the end of a line, and to avoid confusion between a compound word and another word. Consult your dictionary when in doubt.

**(1) Joining words**

(a) Use hyphens to join compound numbers from twenty-one to ninety-nine. This applies to both cardinal and ordinal numbers.

> twenty-five
> sixty-seventh

(b) Some compounds are separated by hyphens to avoid tripling consonants.

> cross-stitch
> shell-like

(c) When two or more words, figures and words, or letters and words are used together as an adjective to modify a noun, they should be joined by a hyphen, especially if one element is a present or past participle.

> well-to-do family
> high-priced car

(d) When a series of two or more unit modifiers has a common basic word and this word is used only in the last term, retain all the hyphens. Always leave a space after the hyphen when the basic word is omitted, unless it is followed by a comma or other punctuation.

two- and three-column pages
eight-, sixteen-, and thirty-two-page sections
8-, 10-, and 12-foot boards

(2) When dividing a word at the end of a line, be sure to place the hyphen between syllables.

"At that time there was a great persecu-
tion against the church which was at Jerusalem."

(3) To avoid confusion between a compound word and another word.

un-ionized
re-markable

## 64.

## Abbreviations

It is best to write out words and numbers in books and articles, although abbreviations are properly used in addresses, recipes, calendars, charts, tables, footnotes, bibliographies, and the following situations.

Some abbreviations are standard with proper names.

*Mr.* Graham, *Dr.* Brown, *St.* Louis

*But not: Bro.* for brother, *Sis.* for sister, *Bish.* for bishop, *Min.* for minister, *Dea.* for deacon

Abbreviated titles of offices are acceptable with full names but not with last names only.

Gov. James Rhodes
Governor Rhodes (not Gov. Rhodes)
Capt. John Smith
Captain Smith (not Capt. Smith)

Titles and degrees may be abbreviated after proper names.

Jr., Sr., M.D., D.D., Ph.D., C.P.A.
H. D. Johnson, M.D.

Words with dates or figures are normally abbreviated.

B.C., A.D., A.M. or a.m., no. or No., $

Certain organizations and agencies are named by their initial.

UN, FBI, YMCA

Chemical formulas are known by their letters.

$H_2O$, NaCl

For most purposes, write out the word, name, or measurement.

STATES: His birthplace was Hagerstown, *Maryland*.
TIMES: The family is scheduled to leave the airport *Monday*, *April* 11. (See also Numbers, section 66.)
MEASURES AND NUMBERS: Maude purchased *six yards* of fabric to make the dresses alike.

Write out *and* unless its sign is part of an official name.

Johnson & Johnson

The following are standard abbreviations for states, territories, and Canadian provinces. The two-letter capital abbreviations are the official postal abbreviations to be used with ZIP codes on addresses.

**B.64.**

| STATE | | STATE | |
|---|---|---|---|
| Alabama (Ala.) | AL | Michigan (Mich.) | MI |
| Alaska | AK | Minnesota (Minn.) | MN |
| Arizona (Ariz.) | AZ | Mississippi (Miss.) | MS |
| Arkansas (Ark.) | AR | Missouri (Mo.) | MO |
| California (Calif.) | CA | Montana (Mont.) | MT |
| Colorado (Colo.) | CO | Nebraska (Nebr.) | NB |
| Connecticut (Conn.) | CT | Nevada (Nev.) | NV |
| Delaware (Del.) | DE | New Hampshire (N.H.) | NH |
| Florida (Fla.) | FL | New Jersey (N.J.) | NJ |
| Georgia (Ga.) | GA | New Mexico (N. Mex.) | NM |
| Hawaii | HI | New York (N.Y.) | NY |
| Idaho | ID | North Carolina (N.C.) | NC |
| Illinois (Ill.) | IL | North Dakota (N. Dak.) | ND |
| Indiana (Ind.) | IN | Ohio | OH |
| Iowa | IA | Oklahoma (Okla.) | OK |
| Kansas (Kans.) | KS | Oregon (Ore.) | OR |
| Kentucky (Ky.) | KY | Pennsylvania (Pa.) | PA |
| Louisiana (La.) | LA | Rhode Island (R.I.) | RI |
| Maine | ME | South Carolina (S.C.) | SC |
| Maryland (Md.) | MD | South Dakota (S.D.) | SD |
| Massachusetts (Mass.) | MA | Tennessee (Tenn.) | TN |

| STATE | | CANADIAN PROVINCE | |
|---|---|---|---|
| Texas (Tex.) | TX | Alberta (Alta.) | AB |
| Utah | UT | British Columbia (B.C.) | BC |
| Vermont (Vt.) | VT | Manitoba (Man.) | MB |
| Virginia (Va.) | VA | New Brunswick (N.B.) | NB |
| Washington (Wash.) | WA | Newfoundland (Nfld.) | NF |
| West Virginia (W. Va.) | WV | Nova Scotia (N.S.) | NS |
| Wisconsin (Wis.) | WI | Ontario (Ont.) | ON |
| Wyoming (Wyo.) | WY | Prince Edward Island (P.E.I.) | PE |
| | | Quebec (Que.) | QC (or PQ) |
| U.S. TERRITORY | | Saskatchewan (Sask.) | SK |
| Canal Zone | CZ | | |
| District of Columbia | DC | TERRITORY | |
| Guam | GU | Northwest Territories | NT |
| Puerto Rico | PR | Yukon Territory | YT |
| Virgin Islands | VI | | |

B.64.

| MONTH OF THE YEAR | ABBREVIATION | MONTH OF THE YEAR | ABBREVIATION |
|---|---|---|---|
| January | Jan. | July | |
| February | Feb. | August | Aug. |
| March | Mar. | September | Sept. |
| April | Apr. | October | Oct. |
| May | | November | Nov. |
| June | | December | Dec. |

| DAY OF THE WEEK | | DAY OF THE WEEK | |
|---|---|---|---|
| Sunday | Sun. | Thursday | Thurs. |
| Monday | Mon. | Friday | Fri. |
| Tuesday | Tues. | Saturday | Sat. |
| Wednesday | Wed. | | |

MISCELLANEOUS ABBREVIATIONS AND THEIR MEANINGS

| | |
|---|---|
| A.D. (anno Domini) | in the year of our Lord |
| a.m., A.M. (ante meridiem) | before noon |
| Ave. | Avenue |
| B.C. | Before Christ |
| Blvd. | Boulevard |
| C | Celsius; centigrade |

| ABBREVIATION | MEANING |
| --- | --- |
| c., C. | copyright |
| c/o, c.o. | in care of |
| c.o.d., C.O.D. | cash on delivery |
| comm., Com. | committee |
| conj. | conjunction |
| c.s.t., CST, C.S.T. | Central Standard Time |
| cwt. | hundredweight |
| d. | day(s) |
| dept. | department |
| doz. | dozen |
| Dr. | Doctor; Drive (street) |
| d.s.t., DST, D.S.T. | Daylight-saving time |
| e., E, E. | east |
| ea. | each |
| e.g. | for example |
| e.s.t., EST, E.S.T. | Eastern Standard Time |
| F, Fahr. | Fahrenheit |
| FBI | Federal Bureau of Investigation |
| FDA | Food and Drug Administration |
| ft. | feet; foot |
| gal. | gallon(s) |
| Gov. | Governor |
| Govt. | Government |
| hr. | hour |
| Hon. | Honorable |
| hp, h.p., HP, H.P. | horsepower |
| hwy. | highway |
| in. | inch(es) |
| inc. | incorporated |
| Is. | island(s) |
| Jr. | Junior |
| lb. | pound(s) |
| Ltd. | Limited |
| ma'am | madam |
| M.D. | Doctor of Medicine |
| mdse. | merchandise |
| memo. | memorandum |
| mfg. | manufacturing |
| mi. | mile(s) |
| min. | minute(s) |
| misc. | miscellaneous |
| mo. | month(s) |

B.64.

| | |
|---|---|
| mph, m.p.h. | miles per hour |
| Mr. | Mister |
| Mrs. | Mistress |
| mss, mss. | manuscripts |
| m.s.t., MST, M.S.T. | Mountain Standard Time |
| mt., Mt. | mountain |
| N, N., Nor. | north |
| ne, n.e., NE, N.E. | northeast |
| no., No. | number |
| NT, N.T. | New Testament |
| nw, n.w., NW, N.W. | northwest |
| obs. | obsolete |
| OT, O.T. | Old Testament |
| oz. | ounce(s) |
| p. | page |
| payt. | payment |
| pcs. | pieces |
| pd. | paid |
| pkg. | package(s) |
| pkt. | packet |
| pl. | place; plural |
| p.m., P.M. | afternoon (post meridiem) |
| p.o., P.O. | postal order; post office |
| pp. | pages |
| ppd. | postpaid; prepaid |
| pr. | pair(s) |
| prep. | preposition |
| pr., pron. | pronoun |
| p.s.t., PST, P.S.T. | Pacific Standard Time |
| pt. | pint(s) |
| PTA | Parent-Teacher Association |
| qt. | quart(s) |
| rd. | road |
| recd. | received |
| RFD, R.F.D. | Rural Free Delivery |
| R.N. | registered nurse |
| rpm, r.p.m. | revolutions per minute |
| rte. | route |
| s., S, S. | south |
| SA, S.A. | South America |
| se, s.e., SE, S.E. | southeast |
| sec. | secretary; second(s) |
| sing. | singular |

| ABBREVIATION | MEANING |
|---|---|
| sq. rd. | square rod(s) |
| Sr. | Senior |
| S.S. | Sunday School |
| St. | Saint |
| st., St. | street |
| sta., Sta. | station |
| sw, s.w., SW, S.W. | southwest |
| syn. | synonym(s) |
| t., tsp. | teaspoon(s) |
| T., tbsp. | tablespoon(s) |
| treas. | treasurer |
| UPS | United Parcel Service |
| USA, U.S.A. | United States of America |
| v. | verse |
| vs. | versus |
| vv. | verses |
| w., W, W. | west |
| wk. | week |
| wt. | weight |
| yd. | yard(s) |
| yr. | year |

**B.65.** 65.

## Italics

Italics (indicated by underlining in writing) are used in printing to set apart or to emphasize certain material. It is good to remember that using italics too freely tends to take away emphasis.

Titles of books, periodicals, newspapers, pamphlets, and long poems are italicized. Titles of shorter works such as articles, short stories, songs, and chapters from books are usually enclosed in quotation marks. *The* before a title is not italicized unless it is part of the title.

> BOOK: Daniel Kauffman's *Doctrines of the Bible* is quite useful for Bible study.
>
> NEWSPAPER: He reads the *Daily Star* as faithfully as he eats breakfast.
>
> LONG POEM: Can you imagine memorizing all the verses of *Snowbound*?
>
> SONG: "Jesus Loves Even Me" is our family's favorite.

Names of ships, aircraft, and satellites are italicized.

The USS *Enterprise* was the first nuclear-powered carrier.

Words used as words (not considering their actual meaning), letters used as letters, and numbers used as numbers are italicized. When a definition is given, either italics or quotation marks are correct.

*Pneumonia* is a tricky word to spell.
*Reveal* (or "Reveal") means "to show" (or *to show*).
His letter *u* looks like an *n*.
Be sure to draw your *9*'s properly.

Points that need special emphasis may be italicized.

Pronouns are used *to replace nouns and to avoid repetition.*

The Bible and its parts, as well as well-known legal documents, need no italics for emphasis or clarity.

Jesus began His ministry with the Sermon on the Mount.
The Declaration of Independence changed life for America's settlers.

## 66.

B.66.

### Numbers

When cardinal numbers can be expressed in fewer than three words, they should be spelled out. Longer numbers should be written as figures. Numbers at the beginning of a sentence should be spelled out regardless of their length; but if possible, rearrange the sentence and place the number in figures within the sentence.

He needs *five dollars.*
I have only *$2.25.*

Detroit is over *one thousand* miles away.
We registered *2,450* miles on the odometer.

*Four hundred fifty* people attended the meeting. (correct)
Attending the meeting were *450* people. (better)

In scientific, mathematical, technical, or statistical text, physical quantities such as time, volumes, distances, areas, and pressures are expressed in figures.

| | |
|---|---|
| 6 days | 30 miles |
| 140 acres | 12 cubic feet |

Write the following kinds of numbers with figures.

DATES: October 18, 1980 (or "the eighteenth of October")
STREET NUMBERS: 225 Grant St.
PAGES: Turn to page 200. (not "two hundred")
DECIMALS AND PERCENTAGES: He gets 90 percent of his wages. (Use the percent sign [%] only in mathematical or statistical context.)
TIME OF DAY: The train arrived at 6:30 P.M.
SERIES OF NUMBERS: Our snow last week measured 15 inches on Monday, 2 inches on Wednesday, and 10 inches on Thursday. (Be consistent. Do not write words for some numbers and figures for others within a category.)
SCRIPTURE REFERENCES: John 16:3; John 16, verses 3 and 21

**B.67.**

Write out ordinal numbers, except those used for street names.

## 67.

## Spelling and Syllabication

Spelling has changed through the years. The silent *e* has been dropped from many words, so that now it often determines the sound of the vowel, such as *man* and *mane*. The beautiful language of the Bible has Old English phrases and spellings. We readily accept words like *honour* and *shew* in Scripture, but in our own manuscripts they are hardly acceptable. We must use words and spellings acceptable to our day and age without adopting cheap terminology.

Good spelling is a mark of careful and courteous people. Our goal should be to present a manuscript or letter without spelling mistakes. Take time to consult a good dictionary when you are not sure about the spelling of a word.

There are pointers to consider if you want to improve your spelling.
1. How does the word sound? (girl or gril)
2. Does the prefix or suffix affect the spelling? (*hoping* or *hopping*)
3. Have you used the correct homonym? (*weigh* or *way*)

These spelling rules should be helpful.

1. Drop a silent *e* when adding a suffix beginning with a vowel.

    like—likable        grieve—grievance        come—coming

    *Exceptions:* dyeing (to distinguish from *dying*), noticeable (See rule 2.)

2. Keep the silent *e* when adding a suffix beginning with a consonant, or if it is needed to keep a soft sound for *c* or *g*.

    likely              peaceable               courageous

    *Exceptions:* truly, judgment (*Judgement* is uncommon.)

3. When adding a suffix beginning with a vowel to a word ending with a single consonant, double the final consonant if all three of these are true: (a) the consonant is preceded by a single vowel, (b) the single vowel has a short sound, and (c) the last syllable of the word is accented.

    rub—rubbing         stop—stopped
    rebel—rebellion     propel—propeller

    If the last syllable of such words is unaccented, they may often be spelled either way.

    worship, worshipper or worshiper (preferred)
    marvel, marvelled or marveled (preferred)

    B.67.

4. "Use *i* before *e*, except after *c*,
    Or when it's like *a*, as in *reindeer* or *sleigh*."

    This common rule refers to *ie* sounding as a single unit. When the *i* and *e* have separate sounds (as in *experience, sufficient*), let the order indicated by pronunciation be your guide.

    chief, friend, niece, believe

    *Exceptions:* either, neither, seize (but *siege*), leisure, weird

5. For words ending with *y* preceded by a consonant, change *y* to *i* when a suffix beginning with a vowel is added, unless the suffix begins with *i*.

    fly—flies           deny—denial
    reply—replying      sly—slyly
    dry—drier           comply—compliance

6. There are only three words with /sēd/ spelled *ceed: exceed, proceed, succeed.* Only one is spelled *sede: supersede.* All other related words are spelled *cede:* secede, concede, precede, and so forth.

Following is a partial list of commonly misspelled words with the troublesome parts in italics.

| | | |
|---|---|---|
| acknowled*g*ment | fas*c*ination | o*c*cur |
| anal*y*sis | for*ei*gn | o*cc*ur*r*ed |
| an*gel* | fri*e*nd | o*pp*osition |
| app*ear*ance | gover*n*ment | prefe*rr*ed |
| benefi*t*ed | g*ua*rantee | principa*l* |
| breth*r*en | guid*a*nce | princip*le* |
| capit*al* | heigh*t* | *receive* |
| capit*ol* | independ*e*nt | s*ei*ze |
| conc*ei*ve | ju*dg*ment | signifi*c*ance |
| conscien*tious* | jus*t*ice | tremendo*us* |
| de*s*cription | maintenance | un*usua*l |
| domin*a*nt | mech*a*nics | w*ei*rd |
| e*x*aggerate | n*ie*ce | worshi*p*ing |
| e*x*ception | nineteen | wri*t*ing |
| expe*r*iment | ni*n*ety | *y*ield |

**B.67.**

Dividing words to keep the right margin straight requires an ability to spell correctly. Following are a few general rules for separating syllables at the end of a line of writing.

1. Place the hyphen at the end of the line and never at the beginning of the next line.
2. Do not divide one-syllable words. (draught)
3. Do not divide a word in a way that leaves a one-letter syllable standing alone. (a-bound, man-y)
4. Be sure to divide words between syllables. (not wi-ser but wis-er)
5. When dividing a compound word, divide it between the two words and not some other syllable. (great-grandfather)
6. Do not divide words at the end of two consecutive lines. (This is frequently done.)
7. Do not divide proper names, abbreviations, initials of names, or groups of figures. Do not divide a title of honor from a proper name.

   WRONG:

   ..................................................................................John-

son,...................................................................................................Con-
fed.,..................................................................................................J.C.
Penny,.......................................................................................... 100,-
000,...................................................................................................Mr.
Smith

8. Words with double consonants (not when they form consonant blends or digraphs) are divided between the consonants (bas-ket, din-ner), except when the word has a suffix, and the root word contains the double consonant. (fill-ing, *not* fil-ling)

# 68.

## Penmanship

"The pen is a tongue of the mind" (Cervantes). Think then what value is in penmanship when the writer has the mind of Christ! It has eternal value. Learn habits that aid good handwriting; learn to analyze the strokes that make and join letters; and learn to evaluate and improve your writing.

### 68a.

**B.68.**

*Habits for Good Handwriting*

(1) *Position and posture:* With light coming over your left shoulder (right shoulder for left-handers) and with about three-fourths of the length of both forearms on your desk, sit upright, facing the desk squarely.

(2) *Position of writing paper:* Place the writing paper directly in front of you, tilting it to the left (right for left-handers), so that the forearm forms a right angle with the lines on the paper.

(3) *Position of hand and pen:* Rest the hand on the third and fourth fingers, with the palm down. Grasp the pen or pencil with the thumb and forefinger, which should be lower than the thumb. Do not cramp them around the pencil, but hold the pencil loosely with fingers slightly curved. Keep the hand completely relaxed.

(4) *Movement in writing:* Move both the arm and fingers when you write, using the arm for forward strokes and the fingers for the delicate parts. Seek to develop a rhythm suitable for each letter.

*68b.*

*Model Letters*—capital and small:

*A B C D E F G H I J*

*K L M N O P Q R S T*

*U V W X Y Z*

*a b c d e f g h i j k*

*l m n o p q r s t*

*u v w x y z*

B.68b.

# C. SENTENCE EFFECTIVENESS

An effective sentence expresses clearly and directly what the writer wishes to say. Nine methods for writing effective sentences are explained here.

## 69.

### Completeness

To be complete, a sentence must have all the parts of one of the six basic sentence patterns. These patterns begin with the simplest arrangements and proceed to the more complex. All of them may be expanded indefinitely with modifying elements.

Pattern I is simply a noun and a verb. If the verb shows action, it is Pattern I-A. If it shows being, it is Pattern I-B.

I-A: The *children sang* happily.

I-B: The *children were* in school.

Pattern II has a noun, a linking verb, and a predicate adjective. If the verb is one like *seems, appears,* or *sounds,* it is Pattern II-A. If it is a verb of being, it is Pattern II-B.

II-A: The *clouds grew* very *dark.*

II-B: *Lazarus was sick.*

Pattern III has a noun, a linking verb, and a predicate nominative. Again, if the linking verb is one like *seems* or *appears,* it is Pattern III-A; if it is a verb of being, it is Pattern III-B.

III-A: The *children* of Israel often *became* idol *worshipers.*

III-B: *Samuel was* a *judge* of Israel.

Pattern IV has a noun, an action verb, and a direct object.

IV: The *boys did* the *chores.*

Pattern V has a noun, an action verb, an indirect object, and a direct object.

V: *Carol gave* the *teacher* an *apple.*

Pattern VI has a noun, an action verb, a direct object, and an objective complement. The objective complement may be a noun or an adjective.

             N.        A.V.     D.O.     O.C.
VI: The *captain appointed me outfielder.*
            N.         A.V.           D.O.    O.C.
VI: The *Israelites thought* Solomon's *yoke heavy.*

### 69a.

*Grammatically complete sentence:* A sentence is a group of words that expresses a complete thought. **A grammatically complete sentence contains every part necessary (for example, subject, predicate, direct object) to make the sentence complete according to the rules of sentence grammar. This is, every part is expressed; no part is "understood." These sentences are grammatically complete.**

Jesus taught the multitudes.
Many people were healed.

### 69b.

*Elliptical sentence:* An elliptical sentence omits some sentence parts. Yet it is complete because the meaning is still clear, often from preceding sentences. These sentences are elliptical.

Stop! (*You* stop!—subject understood.)
Why? (Why *shall I stop?*—skeleton understood from previous sentence.)
Because that is forbidden territory. (*You stop* because that is forbidden territory—main clause understood.)

### 69c.

*Incomplete sentence:* An incomplete sentence omits parts necessary to understand its meaning. It does not make sense by itself or in its context. **The sentence *Stop!* illustrated above is always complete because the subject *you* is always understood easily. But the two sentences following it would be labeled incomplete if they were found by themselves. Only in the proper context can they be called elliptical sentences. Be sure you understand this distinction between incomplete and elliptical sentences.**

# 70.

## Unity

A sentence with unity expresses only one connected thought in a clear, logical way. If a sentence lacks unity, it has one of two faults. Either it links together unrelated ideas or it divides into several parts a thought that should be expressed in only one sentence. Sentence unity is concerned with the ideas sentences express rather than with their basic structure and arrangement.

*70a.*

*Unrelated ideas:* If two thoughts are too unrelated to leave in one sentence, divide the sentence. But sometimes a mere change from coordination to subordination will be satisfactory.

> UNRELATED: We were quietly studying our lessons, and suddenly the fire alarm rang.
>
> CORRECTED BY DIVIDING: We were quietly studying our lessons. Suddenly the fire alarm rang.
>
> CORRECTED BY SUBORDINATION: We were quietly studying our lessons when suddenly the fire alarm rang.

If you find two closely related thoughts in separate sentences, join them into one sentence.

C.70.

> DIVIDED: Delilah had told Samson's riddle. Samson was angry about it.
>
> CORRECTED BY COORDINATION: Delilah had told Samson's riddle, and Samson was angry about it.
>
> CORRECTED BY SUBORDINATION: Because Delilah had told Samson's riddle, Samson was angry.

*70b.*

*Comma fault:* A comma fault is the mistake of joining two complete sentences with only a comma. It can be corrected by adding a conjunction or a semicolon (if the thoughts are closely related) or by dividing the sentence (if the thoughts are rather unrelated).

> COMMA FAULT: The Saracens advanced rapidly toward Europe, Charles Martel defeated them at Tours.
>
> CORRECTED BY COORDINATION: The Saracens advanced rapidly toward Europe, but Charles Martel defeated them at Tours. (The thoughts are closely related.)

> COMMA FAULT: On the one hand he hated to miss the wedding, on the other hand he was concerned about his sick daughter.
>
> CORRECTED BY DIVISION: On the one hand he hated to miss the wedding. But on the other hand he was concerned about his sick daughter. (The thoughts are somewhat unrelated.)

*70c.*

*Run-on sentence:* A run-on sentence is just one step worse than a comma fault. Two sentences are run together without even a comma to divide them. This error is also called a *fused sentence,* and its remedy is the same as that of the comma fault.

> RUN-ON SENTENCE: The Jews hated Jesus He had healed on the Sabbath.
>
> CORRECTED BY SUBORDINATION: The Jews hated Jesus because He had healed on the Sabbath.

*70d.*

*Period fault:* A period fault occurs when a writer mistakenly places a period and uses a capital letter when the sentence should all be one. This produces a *sentence fragment*; it is also called a *divided sentence.*

> PERIOD FAULT: Mary Magdalene asked Jesus where the body was. Thinking He was the gardener.
>
> CORRECTED BY JOINING: Mary Magdalene asked Jesus where the body was, thinking He was the gardener.

C.70c.

# 71.

## Coherence

A sentence should be worded in such a way that the relationships among its parts are easily understood. Such a sentence has coherence. Coherence deals more with the arrangement of sentence parts than with sentence thoughts. Thus, a sentence may have unity (only one connected thought), yet lack in coherence.

*71a.*

*Ambiguous pronouns:* A pronoun should not be ambiguous (have a double meaning). If it could be understood to refer to either of two antecedents, rewrite the sentence more clearly. Unclear pronoun reference destroys sentence coherence.

AMBIGUOUS: Joseph interpreted for Pharaoh the things which *he* had seen in *his* dream.

COHERENT: Joseph interpreted the things which Pharaoh had seen in his dream.

AMBIGUOUS: Robert told his friend that *he* had a flat tire.

COHERENT: Robert told his friend, "I have a flat tire."

COHERENT: Robert told his friend, "You have a flat tire."

### 71b.

*Unclear antecedents:* Unclear pronoun reference also occurs when there is no clear antecedent for the pronoun. *It* may be used without an antecedent in an impersonal sense: *It* is raining. But in all other uses, *it* and *they* should have specific nouns expressed as their antecedents.

UNCLEAR: Two hundred years ago *they* bled people who had a fever.

COHERENT: Two hundred years ago *doctors* bled people who had a fever.

UNCLEAR: In our science book *it* says that sponges are animals, not plants.

COHERENT: Our science book says that sponges are animals, not plants.

UNCLEAR: I was eager to go to the singing classes because I enjoy *it*.

COHERENT: I was eager to go to the singing classes because I enjoy *singing*.

### 71c.

*Misplaced modifiers:* A sentence lacks coherence when the modifiers do not clearly and logically modify the right word. Re-position modifiers in such sentences so that the meaning is clear.

Be careful with words like *almost, even, nearly,* and *only.* The meaning of the whole sentence often depends on their position.

MISPLACED: I thought you were almost my uncle.

COHERENT: I almost thought you were my uncle.

MISPLACED: Even Jesus was not free from temptation.

COHERENT: Not even Jesus was free from temptation.

*71d.*

*Misplaced or dangling phrases and clauses:* Modifying phrases and clauses must also be positioned with care. Be careful not to have dangling verbal phrases (see "Verbals," section 22), and be particularly sure that adjective phrases and clauses are placed clearly.

> DANGLING: Being late, the teacher questioned me.
> COHERENT: Being late, I was questioned by the teacher.
> COHERENT: Because I was late, the teacher questioned me.

> DANGLING: To get to heaven, Christ must be our Saviour.
> COHERENT: To get to heaven, we must have Christ as our Saviour.

> MISPLACED: Henry got the boy dry clothes that had fallen into the creek.
> COHERENT: Henry got dry clothes for the boy that had fallen into the creek.

*Note:* The nominative absolute and certain other introductory phrases are standard usage and are not to be confused with dangling verbal phrases.

**C.71d.**

> CORRECT: The bed being too soft for him, the visitor slept on the floor.
> CORRECT: Considering the advantages, he made a wise choice.

*71e.*

*Elliptical adverb clauses* can destroy sentence coherence. You can avoid errors of this kind by always including the omitted words when they are needed for clear meaning.

> UNCLEAR: While reading the part about the robbers, a noise was heard.
> COHERENT: While reading the part about the robbers, I heard a noise.

> UNCLEAR: I like peas better than Alvin.
> COHERENT: I like peas better than Alvin does.
> COHERENT: I like peas better than beans.

*71f.*

*Careless separating of closely related parts:* Coherence will suffer if closely related sentence parts are carelessly separated by modifiers or parenthetical elements. Infinitives, sentence skeletons, and verb phrases should not be divided without a good reason.

> SPLIT INFINITIVE: He wants to only make one trip.
> COHERENT: He wants to make only one trip.

> DIVIDED SKELETON: He, thinking it over, decided to wait.
> COHERENT: Thinking it over, he decided to wait.

> SPLIT VERB PHRASE: Peter had, before he realized it, denied his Lord.
> COHERENT: Before he realized it, Peter had denied his Lord.

*Note:* Occasionally you will need to split infinitives and verb phrases to avoid awkwardness. But experiment with other arrangements first, and divide related parts only if necessary for the best clarity and smoothness. (See also "Verbals," section 22, for further usage.)

## 72.

## Parallelism

Parallelism has several advantages. It helps make the meaning clear, it makes the reading smooth, and it gives the reader a sense of stability. The opposite of a parallel construction is a shifted construction. Notice how the shifted constructions illustrated in this section throw you "off balance" as you read them. Notice also how much more stable the parallel constructions seem to be.

*72a.*
*Shifted Constructions*
(1) *Words*
> SHIFTED: Haman was filled with pride, selfishness, and was cruel.
> PARALLEL: Haman was filled with pride, selfishness, and cruelty.
> PARALLEL: Haman was filled with pride and selfishness, and he was cruel.

(2) *Phrases*
> SHIFTED: The car careened wildly across the bridge, over the field, and hit the corncrib.
> PARALLEL: The car careened wildly across the bridge, over the field, and into the corncrib.

(3) *Clauses*

SHIFTED: My father is a farmer, but the teacher is Brother Alvin.

PARALLEL: My father is a farmer, but Brother Alvin is a teacher.

(4) *Parallel Sentences*

"Blessed are the meek: for they shall inherit the earth."

"Blessed are the merciful: for they shall obtain mercy."

Do not make unnecessary shifts in tense, mood, voice, subject, person, or number. Study these examples.

(5) *Tense*

SHIFTED: As he came out the door, he suddenly sees the stranger.

PARALLEL: As he came out the door, he suddenly saw the stranger.

(6) *Mood*

SHIFTED: Kneel for prayer and you should close your eyes. (shifted from imperative to indicative mood)

PARALLEL: Kneel for prayer and close your eyes.

C.72a.

(7) *Voice*

SHIFTED: Mary sewed the dresses, but the shirts were sewed by Susan.

PARALLEL: Mary sewed the dresses, but Susan sewed the shirts.

(8) *Subject*

SHIFTED: As he rounded the bend, the house came into view.

PARALLEL: As he rounded the bend, he saw the house.

(9) *Person*

SHIFTED: When one looks from the top of Loft Mountain, you see mountains and valleys for miles around.

PARALLEL: When you look from the top of Loft Mountain, you see mountains and valleys for miles around.

(10) *Number*

SHIFTED: When a person goes west, they see a different kind of country.

PARALLEL: When a person goes west, he sees a different kind of country.

Avoid needless shifts in quotations, style, and perspective, in sentences as well as in paragraphs and compositions. Consistency creates parallelism.

(11) *Quotation*

SHIFTED: The Jews asked John who he was and what do you say for yourself.

PARALLEL: The Jews asked John, "Who are you? What do you say of yourself?"

PARALLEL: The Jews asked John who he was and what he said of himself.

(12) *Style*

SHIFTED: He who refuses to comply with this law shall be kicked out, and his property shall be confiscated.

PARALLEL: He who refuses to comply with this law shall be exiled, and his property shall be confiscated.

(13) *Perspective*

SHIFTED: From the distant field Susan gazed longingly toward the house where Mother was reading the little ones a story about David.

PARALLEL: From the distant field Susan gazed longingly toward the house where she could well imagine Mother reading a Bible story to the little ones.

*72b.*

*Other Unparallel Constructions*

(1) When a compound sentence part is considered a single unit, you need not repeat the article, preposition, or sign of the infinitive (to) before the second member. But when the parts are to be understood as two (or more) separate items, be sure to repeat those introductory words to show the meaning clearly. Study these examples.

I met the owner and the manager of the shop. (two people)
I met the owner and manager of the shop. (one person)

The teacher talked to Jerry and to me. (two conversations)
The teacher talked to Jerry and me. (one conversation)

We go to church to sing and to pray. (two activites)
We go to church to sing and pray. (one worship experience)

(2)  Be consistent in the use of articles before words in a series. Study these examples.

> UNPARALLEL: We watched the bears, giraffes, and the monkeys at the zoo.
>
> PARALLEL: We watched the bears, giraffes, and monkeys at the zoo. (The first *the* is understood to refer to all the words in the series.)
>
> PARALLEL: We watched the bears, the giraffes, and the monkeys at the zoo.

(3)  Repeat introductory words before long phrases or clauses in series. If these "signal words" (such as *that* or *to*) are omitted, especially in complicated sentences, parallelism will be lost along the way.

> UNPARALLEL: Jesus told the seven churches that He knew their works, He is returning quickly, and overcomers would inherit all things.
>
> PARALLEL: Jesus told the seven churches that He knew their works, that He is returning soon, and that overcomers would inherit all things.

C.72b.

(4)  If a word in one compound part is different from that in the other compound part, it is best to include the correct words in both parts. Study these examples.

> UNPARALLEL: God has never and will never fail His children.
> PARALLEL: God had never failed and will never fail His children.
>
> UNPARALLEL: He is a carpenter, and I a farmer.
> PARALLEL: He is a carpenter, and I am a farmer.
> PARALLEL: He went to the hardware story, and I to the grocery store.
>
> UNPARALLEL: Did you bring a peach or apple along?
> PARALLEL: Did you bring a peach or an apple along?
> PARALLEL: Did you bring a peach or pear along?

(5)  Do not omit the conjunction *that* after the word *so*. Do not omit phrases or clauses after such words as *so, such,* and *too.*

> UNPARALLEL: He was so astonished.
> UNPARALLEL: He was so astonished he could not speak.
> PARALLEL: He was so astonished that he could not speak.

UNPARALLEL: The thunder was too loud.

PARALLEL: The thunder was too loud for him to sleep.

UNPARALLEL: We had such an enjoyable day.

PARALLEL: We had such an enjoyable day that we wished we could stay longer.

*Note:* The above sentences could also be changed to *He was very astonished, The thunder was extremely loud,* and so forth. Just remember to "finish" a construction if you "start" it with *so, such,* or *too.*

(6) When you define a word, use another word of the same part of speech. Define a noun with a noun, an adjective with an adjective, and so on. Use the infinitive form to define a verb.

UNPARALLEL: *Homesickness* is "when someone desires strongly to be at home."

PARALLEL: *Homesickness* is "a strong desire to be at home."

UNPARALLEL: To *strut* is "walking in a proud manner."

PARALLEL: To *strut* is "to walk in a proud manner."

(7) Correlative conjunctions (both . . . and, either . . . or, neither . . . nor, not only . . . but also, whether . . . or) should be followed by structures parallel in form. Unparallel structures caused by correlative problems can often be solved simply by repositioning one of the conjunctions.

C.72b.

UNPARALLEL: She both was an excellent cook and a good seamstress.

PARALLEL: She was *both* an excellent cook *and* a good seamstress.

UNPARALLEL: The disciples neither understood Jesus' true mission nor what His kingdom was like.

PARALLEL: The disciples understood *neither* Jesus' true mission nor His kingdom.

(8) Be sure to use a *who* (or *which)* clause before an *and who* (or *and which)* clause.

UNPARALLEL: God is the only perfect person and who knows everything.

PARALLEL: God is the only person *who* is perfect *and who* knows everything.

## 73.

## Emphasis

To present your ideas forcefully, you must know how to construct emphatic sentences. Without a knowledge of sentence emphasis, you may find your less important points being emphasized unduly and your more important points being emphasized only moderately. But with a good knowledge of sentence emphasis, you can make your main ideas shine through clearly and effectively.

### 73a.
### Sentence Style

The *loose* sentence is the simple, natural, easy-to-read kind of sentence that gives the main idea first and details later. You can understand the basic thought without reading to the very last word in the sentence. Use the loose sentence for the less important details of your topic. (The first sentence in this paragraph is loose. It could be stopped at *kind of sentence, first,* or *later.*)

C.73.

But for showing a strong contrast, for emphasizing some important point, or for summarizing a main idea, use the *periodic* sentence. This kind of sentence does not give you the main idea until you have read to the period—to the end of the sentence. But periodic sentences must not be used too frequently because too many of them make reading tiresome. (The first sentence of this paragraph is periodic.)

The *balanced* sentence uses parallel structure to give emphasis. This kind of sentence usually shows a strong comparison or contrast between two ideas. It is often a brief, summarizing statement at the end of a paragraph. Notice how the balanced sentence at the end of the following paragraph gives strong emphasis.

A man was asked, "What would you do if you had a million dollars?" He replied quickly, "I'd start on my next million." This example shows very distinctly the danger of riches. The more you get, the more you want.

The last sentence in the preceding paragraph is much more emphatic than *As you get more, you want more.*

Here are two more examples of balanced sentences.

The children were restless and eager, but the parents remained calm and composed.

The longer he delayed, the worse he felt.

*73b.*

*Sentence Length and Word Order*

(1) You may give emphasis by abruptly changing the length of the sentence you wish to emphasize. This is especially effective if you use a short sentence at the end of a paragraph of long sentences.

> Lewis and Clark had made the toilsome, winding journey over the steep Rocky Mountains and had found a river that flowed westward. Now they built boats for what they hoped was the last leg of their journey. On November 17, 1805, they arrived at a huge body of water stretching before them as far as eye could see. It was the Pacific Ocean.

(2) The way sentence parts are arranged gives emphasis to certain words. The beginning and the end of a sentence are the key positions— especially the end. Therefore, if you put unimportant or parenthetical words at the end of a sentence, emphasis will suffer. Words in series should be arranged in order of climax, with the most important word last.

> UNEMPHATIC: Such a stand would endanger his life, Daniel knew.
> EMPHATIC: Such a stand, Daniel knew, would endanger his life.
>
> UNEMPHATIC: Job lost his children, his servants, and his animals.
> EMPHATIC: Job lost his animals, his servants, and his children.
>
> UNEMPHATIC: He would never forget such an experience.
> EMPHATIC: Such an experience he would never forget.

C.73b.

(3) Use unusual word order as illustrated in the last sentence above only occasionally. Too frequent use of unusual word order—or of any method of emphasis—will make your writing sound artificial.

*73c.*

*Voice*

(1) Use the vigorous active voice instead of the weak passive voice unless you have a good reason to use the passive voice.

> UNEMPHATIC: John the Baptist was thrown into prison by Herod.
> EMPHATIC: Herod threw John the Baptist into prison.

UNEMPHATIC: They raise cotton in the South. (poor because the subject is unimportant)

EMPHATIC: Cotton is raised in the South. (*Cotton* receives more emphasis.)

(2) The following pairs of sentences are all correct, depending on what is meant to be emphasized.

ACTIVE: You must resist Satan.
PASSIVE: Satan must be resisted.

ACTIVE: We cannot change the Scriptures.
PASSIVE: The Scriptures cannot be changed.

(3) The passive voice is preferable in sentences like these.

Our dog was shot because he barked too much. (Not "Our neighbor shot our dog . . .")

Ten blankets were donated to the home. (Not "We donated ten blankets . . .")

### 73d.
### *Quotations*

C.73d.    A direct quotation is much more alive and emphatic than an indirect quotation. Use direct quotations as much as possible, especially in stories.

UNEMPHATIC: Jesus told His disciples to watch and pray.
EMPHATIC: Jesus told His disciples, "Watch and pray."

### 73e.

*Repetition:* Careful use of repetition adds directness and emphasis to writing. Careless repetition is distracting and destroys emphasis.

UNEMPHATIC: We have wrong thoughts, motives, and goals because in ourselves we are all wrong.

EMPHATIC: We have wrong thoughts, wrong motives, and wrong goals because in ourselves we are all wrong.

UNEMPHATIC: Great people are merciful and patient and show much mercy and patience toward the weak.

EMPHATIC: Great people show much mercy and patience toward the weak.

UNEMPHATIC: They took a fast ride in a fast train and got there fast.

EMPHATIC: They took a ride in a swift train and got there rapidly.

You may sometimes wish to make your sentences more emphatic, especially when you express a strong point or the main idea of a paragraph. For the effect you desire, use the right style, length, and word order in your sentences. Use the active voice, direct quotations, and careful repetition.

# 74.

## Variety

The sentences you write in a paragraph should not sound as if you were giving a list of facts. They should not all sound basically the same. Rather, they should have a pleasing variety that sounds fresh and alive and that keeps reading from becoming monotonous.

### 74a.

*Length:* Provide variety in sentence length. One error is an abundance of short, choppy sentences. The opposite error is many long, rambling sentences. Both kinds of errors should be eliminated by using good coordination, subordination, apposition, and division. Some short sentences can be changed to modifiers of another sentence.

C.74

CHOPPY: The snow was thick and heavy. It fell swiftly. It covered the trees and the ground. The next day was Saturday. The sun shone brightly. The children all enjoyed sledding.

IMPROVED: The thick, heavy snow fell swiftly, covering the trees and the ground. [Two sentences have now become modifiers.] The next day, a Saturday, the children all enjoyed sledding in the bright sunshine. [One sentence is now appositive; one sentence is a modifier.]

RAMBLING: A small boy lay on the floor, and he was about my brother's age, and he was kicking and screaming, and his parents hardly seemed to notice, and it was a shame.

IMPROVED: A small boy about my brother's age lay kicking and screaming on the floor. But to their shame, his parents hardly seemed to notice. [Two clauses are now modifiers of first sentence; sentence is divided; one clause is now modifier of second sentence.]

*74b.*

*Beginning*

(1) About half of your sentences should have the normal, subject-first beginning. The other half should have varied beginnings. You may begin with an adverb word, phrase, or clause, or with a conjunction, for variation.

> SUBJECT: *Cornelius* sent men to Joppa after the angel spoke to him.
>
> ADVERB WORD: *Immediately* Peter went down to the men which were sent to him by Cornelius.
>
> ADVERB PHRASE: *On the following day,* the men went to Joppa.
>
> ADVERB CLAUSE: *After the angel spoke to him,* Cornelius sent men to Joppa.
>
> CONJUNCTION: Cornelius fell down before Peter to worship him. *But* Peter said, "Stand up; I myself also am a man."

(2) You may also begin sentences with transposed appositives (appositives that come before the nouns they refer to) or with participial phrases. Be careful, however, to avoid dangling sentence parts.

**C.74b.**

> TRANSPOSED APPOSITIVE: Always a faithful man, Abraham obeyed God immediately.
>
> PARTICIPIAL PHRASE: Breathing threats and slaughter, Saul severely persecuted the Christians.

*74c.*

*Basic Pattern*

(1) Sometimes the word order of the basic sentence pattern can be changed for variety. Here are several examples.

SUBJECT-VERB

The rain came down.
A man stood at the window.

SUBJECT-VERB-COMPLEMENT

We must have God-confidence.
Edwin was a butcherer.

VERB-SUBJECT

Down came the rain.
At the window stood a man.

COMPLEMENT-SUBJECT-VERB

God-confidence we must have.

A butcherer Edwin was.

(2) Another variation within the basic pattern is placing a word or phrase between the subject and verb. But do this with caution; it may cause awkwardness or confusion. (See also "Coherence," section 71.)

*Cornelius* gladly *received* Peter into his house.

*Peter* immediately *recognized* that the *Lord* also *wanted* Gentiles in His church.

### 74d.

*Structure:* Use simple, compound, and complex sentences in your writing. None of these structures is the "best" to use; rather, use all three for variety. Using all three kinds also helps you achieve variety in sentence length.

### 74e.

*Use:* Most of the sentences you write are declarative. But an occasional imperative, interrogative, or exclamatory sentence lends freshness and life to writing. Notice how the following declarative sentence could be written for variety.

DECLARATIVE: We will serve the Lord.

IMPERATIVE: Let us serve the Lord.

INTERROGATIVE: Who of us will not serve the Lord?

EXCLAMATORY: Serve the Lord!

C.74d.

Remember that effective writing does not consist of discovering a "best" pattern of sentence wording. Rather it means combining a pleasing variety of patterns to present your thoughts naturally, clearly, and interestingly.

## 75.

### Vocabulary (Exactness)

You do not need a huge vocabulary to be able to express yourself well. Neither should you strive to master big words so that you can impress people with your intelligence. A much better reason for expanding your vocabulary is to know enough words so that you can select exactly the one you need to express your meaning clearly.

*75a.*

*Dictionary use:* Your dictionary is a valuable tool with which to expand your vocabulary. Therefore, know it well. Besides giving definitions, dictionaries tell the level of usage of words or of certain definitions. Some common terms are listed here.

Standard
{
*Formal:* General English vocabulary (unlabeled words in dictionaries). Used mostly in writing, such as in legal papers.

*Informal:* Acceptable in conversational-style writing.
}

Non-Standard
{
*Colloquial:* More often spoken than written.

*Dialectal:* Spoken in certain localities.

*Illiterate:* Improper for good English.

*Slang:* "Street language," should be avoided.
}

*75b.*

*Denotation, connotation:* Every word has a denotation (a literal meaning) as well as a connotation (a suggestion or feeling). For example, whispering, conversing, speaking, and shouting are all methods of talking. Yet each word has a different connotation which makes it suitable only for certain situations.

C.75a.

Christian courtesy requires that we use words of acceptable connotation to avoid being offensive to others. It is improper to call an overweight person fat, a thrifty person stingy, or an uneducated person dumb.

*75c.*

*Euphemisms:* We must also avoid the opposite extreme—too many euphemisms. These are expressions that substitute unpleasant words with more pleasant ones. While this is entirely justifiable within the bounds of Christian courtesy (*passed away* instead of *died, odor* instead of *stink*), it can lead to terms that avoid realities—even spiritual realities. We may find ourselves writing *weakness* instead of *sin, rededication to Christ* instead of *repentance from sin,* or even *that other place* instead of *hell.* A proper balance is important.

*75d.*

*Synonyms:* Synonyms are words with similar meanings (no two words have *identical* meanings). A list of synonyms in a dictionary or thesaurus can, of course, help you find a more exact word than the one you think of at first. But *beware* of pulling out a word with which you are not thoroughly familiar. It may have a connotation that will mar the entire effect you are working for. For example, you may be writing about reverence in God's house, and you want a synonym for *speaking*. In a thesaurus you find *chant*, and decide to use it. But imagine how irreverent your composition will sound when you mention the minister *chanting* to the congregation. Therefore, know the word before you write it.

### 75e.

*Prefixes and suffixes:* Prefixes and suffixes are keys that unlock many word meanings. Here are some common prefixes and their meanings. Others can be found in your dictionary.

| | | |
|---|---|---|
| *non-, un-* not | *super-* above, beyond | *fore-* front |
| *dis-, in-* not | *hemi-, semi-* half | *micro-* small |
| *pre-* before | *inter-* between, among | *tele-* distant |
| *post-* after | *under-* insufficient | *trans-* across |
| *mono-, uni-* one | *re-* again, back | *peri-* around |
| *bi-* two | *anti-* against, not | *sub-* under |
| *tri-* three | *para-* beside | *ex-* out |

C.75e.

Suffixes are usually added to words to change their part of speech or to show inflections. Suffixes that form verbs are *-ize, -fy, -ate, -en, -ed, -ing.* Those that form nouns are *-ness, -ment, -(t)ion, -ence, -ance, -or, -er, -ity, -al, -ure.*

Check your dictionary before writing a prefix or suffix with a word unless you are positive about the correct one to use. You may make a wrong word. Or you may write a word with a meaning different from what you want. Notice the difference in the meanings of these sentences.

The boy was unsatisfied by his lunch. (He was still hungry.)
The boy was dissatisfied with his lunch. (He did not like it.)

### 75f.

### Exact words

Good sentence vocabulary requires that you write words that convey an exact and clear message. Notice the difference between these paragraphs.

GENERAL: I cut the opening larger so that the moth could get out. Out came the insect, looking very different from what

I had imagined.

EXACT: With the point of my scissors I snipped the confining threads to make the exit just a very little easier, and lo, immediately, and with perfect ease, out crawled my moth dragging a huge, swollen body and little, shriveled wings.

Keep out of the rut of using overworked words such as:

| | | | | | |
|---|---|---|---|---|---|
| awful | big | fine | great | little | pretty |
| bad | fast | good | happy | nice | wonderful |

The word *good*, for example, can usually be replaced by synonyms such as *beneficial, valuable,* or *serviceable.*

Avoid also the opposite extreme—using bigger or heavier words than necessary. The smaller and more familiar exact words are better. The following words, though sometimes good to use, can be replaced by the simpler words beside them.

| | | |
|---|---|---|
| manner—way | possessed—had | pronounce—say |
| informed—told | secure—get | signify—mean |

**75g.**

*Idioms:* To form an accepted English idiom, in addition to choosing exactly the right word, you must also use the right preposition. Here are several examples.

| | | |
|---|---|---|
| hope to (for) | comply with | able to |
| want to | disappointed in | more than |
| superior to | afraid of | stand for |

Consult your dictionary whenever you are in doubt. An unidiomatic expression hinders effectiveness.

**75h.**

*Similar words:* Proper spelling of similar words is essential. One wrong letter in one word can make the difference between clarity and confusion. Do you always know when to use *to, too,* and *two*? Do you know the difference between *affect* and *effect*? A standard dictionary, as well as the "Glossary of Usage," Section D, under "III-Usage" in this handbook, will help you clear up these problems.

**75i.**

*Reading:* The best way to gain and maintain a good vocabulary is to read many good books. The Bible is the best book you can read; its truth will inspire you, and its style sets an excellent pattern to follow. Other books by Christian authors will also provide you, page after page, with enriching experiences in methods of expression and development of style. Remember, you can never expect to write well unless you read extensively.

## 76.

## Conciseness (versus Wordiness)

Wordiness results when more words are written than are necessary for clear meaning. Such writing is discourteous because it forces the reader to spend more time and effort with it than necessary. He may even decide to read something more worthwhile.

*76a.*

*Deadwood:* Words that add no meaning whatever to a sentence are called deadwood. This is the simplest kind of wordiness and is remedied merely by crossing out the extra words.

The ~~warm~~ noonday sun blazed ~~fiercely~~ over the land and the people ~~living on the land~~. (*Noonday* is more exact than *warm* and implies the same thing. *Blazed* implies fierceness. And anyone knows that people live on land.)

Be especially careful to avoid the kind of deadwood that hides an important truth in a bundle of wordy details.

WORDY: While Zacchaeus, a publican and a very rich man, was seeking Jesus by running ahead of the crowd and climbing into a sycamore tree, Jesus was also seeking Zacchaeus by coming to Jericho, where he lived, and they found each other.

CONCISE: While Zacchaeus was seeking Jesus, Jesus was also seeking Zacchaeus, and they found each other.

*76b.*

*Redundancy* is a deeper kind of problem. It occurs when ideas are repeated in an illogical or disorderly way, giving the feeling of traveling in circles. Whole sentences and sometimes whole paragraphs must be reorganized to correct redundancy.

REDUNDANT: The carnal nature within us must be dealt with. It causes problems in our Christian lives and must be dealt with by a diligent, daily application of the Word of God. The carnal nature causes problems not only in personal life but also in school and church life.

REVISED: The carnal nature within us causes problems not only in our personal Christian lives but also in school and church life. It must be dealt with by a diligent, daily application of the Word of God.

The *reduction process* is a systematic method of correcting wordiness by changing sentences to clauses, clauses to phrases, and phrases to single words whenever it is practical. Here are several examples.

WORDY: The Lord plagued the children of Israel. This was their punishment because they had worshiped the golden calf.

REDUCED: The Lord plagued the children of Israel because they had worshiped the golden calf. (sentence reduced to clause)

REDUCED: The Lord plagued the children of Israel for worshiping the golden calf. (clause reduced to phrase)

REDUCED: The Lord plagued the Israelites for worshiping the golden calf. (phrase reduced to word)

**C.76c.**

These examples are only given to show the possibilities of the reduction process. They do not mean, for example, that *Israelites* is better than *children of Israel*. Overuse of this process will result in a clipped, cut-and-dried writing style. However, wordiness is usually the more common problem, and the reduction process can be a valuable help in finding the proper balance between the two extremes.

*76c.*

**Wordy expressions:** Study these wordy expressions and their revisions. Notice how concisely the same ideas can be expressed.

| WORDY | CONCISE |
| --- | --- |
| as a usual rule | as a rule; usually |
| ascend up | ascend |
| join together | join |
| large in size | large |
| circulated around | circulated |
| repeat again | repeat |
| similar to | like |

| WORDY | CONCISE |
|---|---|
| red in color | red |
| it is necessary that we | we must |
| man who is friendly | friendly man |
| be aware of the fact | know; realize |
| in the near future | soon |
| when the sun was shining | sunny |
| made-up fiction | fiction |
| appeared to be | seemed |
| meet up with | meet; encounter |
| tiny particle | particle |
| things that he could do | things to do |

## 76d.

*Pretentious writing:* This type of wordiness, also called the over-written style, results from the attempt to sound like a great writer. The author has the notion that big, flowery, unusual words are better than simple everyday words. But such writing is disgusting. Pretension is hypocrisy, and all such evils must be cleansed from our hearts before we are in any position to write. A simple, natural style is far better.

C.76d.

PRETENTIOUS: While journeying through the remote regions of that section of the country located in the direction of the setting sun, our eyes beheld with profound awe the magnificence of that abysmal rift in the crust of the earth designated the Grand Canyon.

NATURAL: On our trip through the West we marveled at the awesome sight of the Grand Canyon.

## 76e.

*Trite expressions:* Wordiness can sometimes be avoided by the use of colorful figures of speech. But when a certain figure becomes stale through overuse, it has become a trite expression. A person who uses trite expressions freely in his writing shows that he would rather use expressions he has heard someone else use than write straightforward expressions of his own. This is because trite expressions come much more naturally than original thinking does. How many of these trite expressions appear in your writing?

| hungry as a bear | high as a mountain |
|---|---|

| | |
|---|---|
| quiet as a mouse | slow as molasses |
| dead as a doornail | quick as a flash |
| old as the hills | big as an elephant |
| straight as an arrow | sharp as a tack |
| after all was said and done | make a long story short |
| needle in a haystack | practice makes perfect |
| | make a beeline |

It is probably impossible to eliminate wordy and trite expressions in your everyday spoken language, where you must constantly express yourself without much time for forethought. But in writing you have plenty of time for revision. When you find wordy or trite expressions there, rewrite them to make fresh, concise expressions of your own.

## 77.

## Figurative Language

Through the use of a figure of speech, a writer can give very briefly a clear picture of what he means. Figurative language is effective especially because it compares something unfamiliar to something familiar. For example, to help us understand Him, Jesus said, "I am the good shepherd." Then He did not need to say such things as, "I love you and care for you because you are Mine. I provide you with everything you need, and I protect you from harm." We know all these things because we know what a good shepherd does.

Learning to observe in terms of comparisons is one secret of becoming an interesting writer. What did the windstorm make you think of? Was it like a savage beast, clawing and chewing at the house? Or was it more like a powerful river current, threatening to sweep the house away? Such comparisons add life and color to your description.

### 77a.
### Kinds of Figurative Language

(1) The *metaphor* compares by saying that one thing is something else which it resembles, or that something happened that is true only in a figurative sense. The Bible has many of these.

"He washed his garments in wine."
"Thy word is a lamp unto my feet."

(2) The *simile* compares by using words such as *like* or *as*. Here are

several Bible examples.

"Is not my word like as a fire?"
"He shall be like a tree."

(3) The *metonym* compares by giving something the name of the thing it resembles. *Metonym* means "changed name."

"Go ye, and tell that fox." (Herod)
"I will lift up mine eyes unto the hills." (heaven)

(4) *Personification* has a quality or a thing speaking or acting like a person. In the Bible, personification is often used in parables or illustrations.

"Doth not wisdom cry?"
"Wisdom hath builded her house."
"The voice of thy brother's blood crieth unto me from the ground."

(5) *Hyperbole* is an exaggeration or overstatement intended to produce a result without being taken literally.

It seems as if I have been working at this for hours.
We thought they would never arrive.

*Note:* Great caution needs to be exercised in using hyperbole. Frequent use of hyperbole can lead to a habit of telling lies.

**77b.**

*Trite figures:* Be careful to avoid common, worn-out figures. If a certain figure of speech comes readily to your mind, it has probably come just as readily to the minds of many other writers. Strive for fresh figures of your own. (Review, if necessary, the list of trite expressions under "Wordiness," section 76e.)

**77c.**

*Mixed figures:* Be careful also to avoid the mixed figure, a figure that starts with one comparison and ends with another. If you find a mixed figure, either revise it to keep all the comparisons matched, or change to straightforward language.

MIXED: Pilate tried to keep a fence around the boiling mob.
REVISED: Pilate tried to keep a lid on the boiling mob.
REVISED: Pilate tried to control the raging mob.

*77d.*

*Inappropriate figures:* Inappropriate figures do not fit with the tone or style of your composition. Revise to match the rest of your article.

> INAPPROPRIATE: The glorified Jesus had feet like shiny jewelry and a voice like a roaring tempest.
>
> APPROPRIATE: The glorified Jesus had feet like fine brass and a voice like many waters.

C.77d.

# V. The Paragraph

## A. INTRODUCTION

## B. PARAGRAPH REQUIREMENTS
78. Form
79. Unity and Coherence

## C. PARAGRAPH SENSE

## D. PARAGRAPH DEVELOPMENT
80. Adding Details
81. Adding Facts
82. Adding Descriptions
83. Adding Definitions
84. Adding Examples
85. Relating an Incident
86. Developing by Comparisons, Contrasts, or Arguments

## E. PARAGRAPH UNITY

## F. COHERENCE IN A PARAGRAPH
87. Chronological Order
88. Spatial Order
89. Order of Importance
90. Use of Linking Expressions

## G. EMPHASIS IN A PARAGRAPH

## H. KINDS OF PARAGRAPHS
91. Expository
92. Argumentative
93. Narrative
94. Descriptive

## I. TRANSITION BETWEEN PARAGRAPHS
95. Using Connective Words
96. Repeating a Key Idea

# V. The Paragraph

## A. INTRODUCTION

The Christian writer has a message to present to readers. His aim is to make the message appealing and forceful. God may lay many thoughts upon a writer's mind, but if they are presented to the reader in a rambling way, they will not be effective. Only when they are organized into good paragraphs will they appeal to the reader and be forceful in conveying the intended message.

## B. PARAGRAPH REQUIREMENTS

78.

### Form

Almost anyone who can read could pick out a paragraph from a page of writing. Rules for form say that the first line of a paragraph must be indented and that the margins must be kept as straight as possible. Thus we recognize a paragraph as a section of writing from one indentation to the next.

79.

### Unity and Coherence

To be a true paragraph, a group of sentences must comprise a *unit of thought*. Sometimes (especially in stories) only one sentence makes a paragraph because the next sentence begins on another aspect of the composition. But whether long or short, all paragraphs are units of thought.

A conventional paragraph has an *introduction*, some manner of *development*, and a *conclusion*. The first sentence usually states the main idea, and is then called the *topic sentence*. However, it may merely hint at the main idea, which is then expressed later in the paragraph as a regular topic sentence.

Those sentences following the introductory sentence consist of ideas that support or lead up to the main idea expressed in the topic sentence. The manner in which this is handled will have a large bearing on the success or failure of the paragraph. We can fairly easily state our main ideas as grand topic sentences; but to provide sound, logical support for them is another matter. In fact, this matter of paragraph development takes up a major portion of this section on paragraphs. It is of utmost importance to your success as a writer that you master this aspect of composition.

After you have adequately supported your main idea, you must not leave the issue hanging. Finish with a conclusion that summarizes what you have been saying; or, if your developing sentences have been leading up to your main idea, conclude with a well-written topic sentence. Be sure to bring a satisfying conclusion to what you have begun to say.

# C. PARAGRAPH SENSE

To become an effective writer, you must develop a *paragraph sense.* You must be able to sense what the main idea of a paragraph is, whether it has been developed sufficiently, and whether it has a satisfactory conclusion. If you have good paragraph sense, you can quickly tell when a sentence does not belong in a paragraph. You can also tell which sentence is the topic sentence or which paragraphs are so closely knit that they need no topic sentence. And the best way to gain this paragraph sense is to read widely those materials which older Christians have approved as being sound and well written.

One good way to cultivate your paragraph sense is to practice spotting topic sentences. The following paragraph has a topic sentence at the beginning.

*"There are more works of darkness around us than ever before.* Though men claim to be enlightened, they write books and articles on works of darkness such as witchcraft, fortunetelling, astrology, and spiritism. Most bookstores have such dangerous books for sale; and some popular magazines carry articles that arouse interest without pointing out the evil. These books are so dangerous that we are 'playing with fire' to even allow our curiosity or interest to be aroused. The death penalty is pronounced upon people who have anything to do with the works of darkness."

This paragraph illustrates a topic sentence at the end.

"Most of you know what a keystone is. It is that wedge-shaped stone that is put in the top center of the arch and thus gives strength and solidarity to the whole structure. The practice we are about to examine has about it something that makes it the keystone in the whole structure of Christian nonconformity. A study of the history of church groups would reflect the fact that when this practice falls by the way, it is only a matter of time until every other mark of Christian nonconformity becomes extinct. *Let us therefore never become apologetic about teaching and practicing the Christian Woman's Head Covering.*"

In analyzing the paragraph, we conclude that the topic is not "keystone" but, instead, an important Christian doctrine.

# D. PARAGRAPH DEVELOPMENT

The importance of adequate paragraph development has already been emphasized. In this section you will find various methods of development explained and illustrated. Study them well.

## 80.

### Adding Details

D.80.

Letters often provide examples of topic sentences without sufficient material to develop them. Details help explain information. Study this excerpt from a letter.

"We are all well now that the little ones have recuperated from flu.

"The weather is so nice after five gloomy, rainy days.

"Rebecca hit a wet spot on the pavement yesterday and the car landed in the ditch. She's a bit shaken up, but not hurt.

"We're planning to see Uncle Johns when they travel through Indiana on their way to Oregon."

There might be much more to say about each topic. The first paragraph could be:

We are all well now that the little ones have recuperated from flu. Ronald was sick first. Then Father contracted the germs. I myself began to feel ill from getting up so often at night. Finally the twins were affected. It was a real blessing, however, that the family remained cheerful through the experience.

The third paragraph is greatly in need of details.

While driving toward home yesterday, Rebecca hit a wet spot on the pavement and lost control of the car. The back end swung completely around and the car skidded into the ditch. The mishap occured just a mile from home, so we took the tractor and pulled the car out of the ditch. The car has a few small dents. Rebecca is all right except for being "shaken up."

## 81.

## Adding Facts

Adding facts to the topic sentence is an effective way to develop a paragraph. Textbooks often use this method.

"*One outstanding characteristic of many plants is that they contain cells having chlorophyll.* Chlorophyll is a complex, green chemical. This chemical allows plants to make food from water and carbon dioxide with the aid of sunlight. This process, called photosynthesis, provides the food for all living things. Either directly or indirectly, all living things depend on the plant's ability to make food. This is according to God's plan for His world. 'He causeth the grass to grow for the cattle, and herb for the service of man: that he may bring forth food out of the earth' (Psalm 104:14)."

D.81.

## 82.

## Adding Descriptions

Adding descriptions is another means of developing the topic sentence. Nature stories can readily use descriptions as shown by the following paragraph about a thunderstorm.

"*In the afternoon clouds began to gather in the west, over the mountains.* Billows of white at first, touched with gold at the edges. Then ominous gray and black ones moving in, moving in, to engulf the white. Soon great tumbling cloud masses were pushing up the sky toward the sun which still glistened like a golden ball on blue satin. Snowy peaks were cut off by the heavy line of gray. Flash! Crash! Clouds seemed to roll together, head on, and the noise echoed from height to height in a tremendous roar. A cold wind began to blow."

—Aileen Fisher, *All on a Mountain Day*

## 83.

### Adding Definitions

Definitions can make up the paragraph. Notice how the topic sentence is developed in this definition.

*A promise is simply an agreement to do or not to do something.* It includes at least two parties and is recognized on the basis that one is able to perform and the other to receive that which is promised. This produces expectation and devotion on the part of those who look forward to its fulfillment. By man to God or by man to man, promises ought to be significations of the divine will of God. The promise is the binding element of all vows, pledges, contracts, affirmations, bargains, stipulations, and so forth.

## 84.

### Adding Examples

The following paragraph is developed by several examples, each one referring to the opening sentence.

*"Do we not make a mistake in supposing that some people have a 'gift' of prayer?* A brilliant Cambridge undergraduate asked me if the life of prayer was not a gift, and one which very few possessed? He suggested that, just as not everyone was musical, so not everyone is expected to be prayerful! George Müller was exceptional not because he had a gift of prayer, but because he prayed. Those who cannot 'speak well,' as God declared Aaron could, may labor in secret by intercession with those that speak the Word. We must have great faith if we are to have great power with God in prayer, although God is very gracious, and oftentimes goes beyond our faith."

—Taken from *The Kneeling Christian* (Zondervan).

## 85.

### Relating an Incident

Enlarging the topic sentence by relating an incident is an interesting method of bringing out a point.

*"Insincerity is revealed by one's attitude toward the stewardship*

*of example.* During the course of his travels, Charles Haddon Spurgeon had occasion to visit many lands. The story is told of his frequently having an occasion to pass through the principality of Monaco. In his spare time he enjoyed loitering on the grounds of the Casino of Monte Carlo. The gardens were lavishly landscaped and Spurgeon considered them among the most beautiful in the world. In conversation with a friend, Spurgeon resolved that he would never visit the gardens again." (Virginia Ely, *Devotion* [Revell, 1960], p. 78. The story goes on to say that many entered the Casino to gamble because they followed good folks into the garden; thus this incident makes a pointed lesson.)

## 86.

### Developing by Comparisons, Contrasts, or Arguments

The topic sentence can be developed by means of comparisons, contrasts, or arguments. Comparisons and contrasts should be based on facts, whereas arguments are actually a point of view either in favor of or in opposition to certain reasoning. Many editorials and articles need this type of writing when the reasoning is based on the Word of God. When the thinking has a sound foundation, the writing can be considered authoritative.

Here is an example of a comparison used to develop the paragraph.

> *The underlying philosophies of the Bible-centered and the Bible-integrated textbooks are totally different.* The Bible-integrated approach is to take the world's textbooks and put a Bible slant on them by adding Bible verses while keeping the original structure of the content. The Bible-centered approach, on the other hand, has a content structure that is grounded in the absolutes of Scripture and is carried all the way through on Scriptural principles.

D.86.

## E.  PARAGRAPH UNITY

In developing the thought of a paragraph, *every sentence must relate to the topic sentence.* For this to be possible, the writer must first have clear and unified thinking about the main idea of his paragraph. To revise a paragraph that is weak in unity, sometimes a writer can simply eliminate a single sentence. However, the paragraph must often be rewritten.

Young people can learn many things from older people if they will take the time to chat with them. My uncle had been a missionary to Israel years ago, and he has a wealth of knowledge about foreign peoples and customs. Although I have never been abroad, I have seen many things through his eyes. *Sometimes he gets off his subject to bring out a point.* He has stories to tell from living among the natives that one would hardly learn from a two-week tour. (The italicized sentence is not entirely unrelated to the topic, yet it does detract from the unity of thought.)

Saturday the whole family was working diligently to prepare for weekend guests. The Biblical principle of hospitality was lived up to by providing accommodations acceptable to those who stopped to visit. Joan baked a cake, Joyce dusted the furniture, and I swept the walks. Father brought in some wood for the fireplace in case of cool weather. We are not always sure about October weather. By noon we were satisfied that our guests would be comfortable at our house. (This paragraph needs more unified expression, and the easiest way to achieve it is to rewrite the paragraph.)

Saturday the whole family worked diligently to prepare for weekend guests. Father firmly believes that preparation is a part of the Biblical principle of hospitality, and so he set us to work. Mother, as usual, was the general overseer. Joan baked a cake, Joyce dusted the furniture, and I swept the walks. Father brought in wood for the fireplace in case of cool October weather. By noon we were satisfied that the needs of our guests could be taken care of while they stayed with us.

# F. COHERENCE IN A PARAGRAPH

## 87.

### Chronological Order

"Brother Wesley leaned back in his swivel chair and ran his hand through his fast-graying hair. His mind ran back over the nine years that they as a family had been laboring for the Lord in this area. With his growing family of five, they had moved into the more hilly section of the state to begin mission work. They enjoyed the more easy-going way of life; in fact, they preferred it to the busy schedules of many churches. They loved the people and, in return, felt the love of their neighbors."

This idea—one thing following another—can be an example to help us understand *coherence in paragraphs*. *Coherence* is "sticking together" or presenting thoughts in logical order so that they fit together. The thoughts should flow along smoothly from beginning to end. Every sentence must relate to the same topic, and also follow in logical sequence to produce coherence.

Yesterday morning I got up late. I did not have time to finish my mathematics assignment. There were chores to be done. English class is fourth period. I hurried through a chapter in the Bible. I discovered my shirt was wrinkled. There must be a better way than this.

In rewriting this paragraph, we might arrange everything in order and add transitional material to give continuity to the thoughts, rather than having everything happen at once.

Yesterday morning I got up late. I hurried through a chapter in the Bible with little satisfaction. The chores had to be done, so I eliminated my math assignment. Since English class is fourth period, I decided I could forget that for a while. After all my hurrying to get ready in time, I discovered I did not have a fresh shirt to wear. Going out the door, I resolved that there must be a better way than this to start the day.

Another type of paragraph that uses chronological order is a paragraph which explains a process. Recipes or instructions for putting something together are common examples of this type of paragraph. The instructions are given in the order they are to be carried out.

To make a bright chalk drawing, follow these directions. First, spread newspapers on your working space. Next, wet your paper. Let the extra water drip off your paper. Then lay it on the newspapers. Draw on the wet paper with colored chalk. If you want to preserve the picture, spray it with "fixative," available at a craft shop.

## 88.

## Spatial Order

Spatial order (order of space) is an excellent way of achieving coherence in descriptive paragraphs. The scene is described from left to right, from near to far, from details of minor importance to those of major importance, or in the reverse of any of these. This paragraph illustrates spatial order.

"Some of the doorways had heavy curtains hanging over them, and one into which they peered, since the door was wide open, showed the great banqueting hall, with tapestries on the walls, casques and bucklers, antlers, and many other relics of the chase in the forest. Across the hall at the upper end ranged the high table at which the lord of the castle sat, and the other tables ran down by the walls, leaving the central space clear."

## 89.

## Order of Importance

Presenting thoughts in order of importance is another method of obtaining coherence.

Our mallards look attractive swimming in the creek. They also keep the creek clean and clear by catching minnows and eating moss. Most of all, they are useful because they pick up the corn which is spilled when we feed the pigs.

## 90.

## Use of Linking Expressions

Effective use of linking expressions helps in presenting thoughts coherently.

Sometimes we load our schedules too heavily to allow ourselves time for meditation and prayer. *With this in mind,* we should learn to say no to some activities. *Although* all our plans might be good, we must remember that we need time with God.

Following is a list of connectives that can be used to link ideas.

| | |
|---|---|
| again | in addition |
| also | in a like manner |

| | |
|---|---|
| furthermore | first |
| further | with this in mind |
| moreover | second |
| meanwhile | |

The concluding thought of a paragraph can be tied in by connectives such as the following.

| | |
|---|---|
| finally | consequently |
| as a result | as shown |
| therefore | as a conclusion |

# G. EMPHASIS IN A PARAGRAPH

*Emphasis* is giving the most force to the main idea. In every paragraph one thought should be outstanding and the other statements should be used to develop that main thought. The beginning or the end of the paragraph is the most emphatic position.

*The person who laughs at any sin has not dealt with sin in his own life.* The person who laughs at the drunkard is in as pitiable a condition as the drunkard himself. The person who can enjoy a lustful joke is as great a concern as the one who tells the stories. Smiling at another's spiritual fall is just as sinful as it is for the other to have fallen.

# H. KINDS OF PARAGRAPHS

Every paragraph shows one or a combination of the four kinds of writing: *expository, argumentative, narrative,* and *descriptive.*

## 91.

### Expository

Expository writing is a presentation of detailed facts, and this sometimes includes colorful and descriptive words. Vague and abstract ideas are not a part of an exposition. This type of paragraph presents a clear explanation.

In the last days of Eli, when Israel when out to battle, they sensed a need for renewal; so they took the ark of God with them to battle. The earth rang again because of their renewal effort. Older folks expected that now God would show Himself strong in their behalf as He had done aforetime. But it did not work that way. The Philistines won the battle. The renewal effort failed because sin was not repented of and put away from their midst.

## 92.

### Argumentative

An argumentative paragraph is an arrangement of facts to prove a point. Job asked, "But what doth your arguing reprove?" (Job 6:25), and usually not much is accomplished through arguing. Yet this type of paragraph is considered because it covers persuasion, a useful tool. Argumentation is the presentation of facts in a logical order to arrive at an answer; however, this will often require a number of paragraphs rather than only one.

"The Calvinists have an easy and many times arrogant type of Christian assurance. While living in open disobedience to many Scriptures, they testify of their peace and openly declare, 'The Spirit itself beareth witness with our spirit, that we are the children of God.' Never, never would they quote, 'Hereby we do know that we know him, if we keep his commandments.' "

## 93.

### Narrative

The narrative paragraph, to explain simply, is telling a story. It is the relating of incidents, whether real or imaginary. Usually, expository and descriptive writing is mixed into the narration to give it details. Narrative writing should flow smoothly from one happening to another.

"Yes, this is the place," James Mann said. Everything was familiar in a rather vague way. He had been keenly disappointed to find the home place locked up. But if there were a meeting tonight, his parents would be there. Scarcely able to control his emotions, James walked to the door. He had refrained from writing because he wanted most of all to tell them of his conversion, face to face. The trip had seemed short in his eager anticipation of reaching his beloved home—love, peace, and understanding.

94.

## Descriptive

A descriptive paragraph gives a picture in words. It is full of words which describe the topic. Many times, descriptive expression is mixed with exposition or narration to give it movement or make it meaningful. Descriptive words are italicized in the following paragraph.

"What a *beautiful, magnificent* day! The *sparkling, frost-covered* trees and bushes *glimmered* in the *early morning* sunlight. The earth seemed to be *slowly awakening* from its winter nap. *Huge mounds of snow* were still piled high, but this morning the sun was victor. It seemed to be rejoicing in its effect upon the work of the Master's creation during the past week of heavy snow."

# I. TRANSITION BETWEEN PARAGRAPHS

95.

## Using Connective Words

When the thoughts of a paragraph are well organized, it is yet another matter for thoughts to flow smoothly from one paragraph to another. Certain connective words can tie thoughts together. The topic or time may change as the writing proceeds, but there are words to refer back or forward. The possibilities include:

| likewise | after | next |
| in the meantime | since | then |

96.

## Repeating a Key Idea

Another effective link is to repeat important words or ideas in one paragraph that were mentioned in the paragraph before. This *shows* the reader the connection between the two paragraphs, rather than simply *telling* him by the use of linking words. Notice how the introductory sentence following the paragraph below repeats a key idea of the paragraph.

When one has many things, he tends to forget God. He turns his eyes from God who gave the blessings, to the blessings themselves. He has so many things, that he forgets his responsibility to thank and to obey the One who gave the blessings.

*Another tendency of those who possess many things* is to think that they got them by their own power.

Both of these methods are valuable for linking paragraphs. Use them interchangeably to provide variety in your writing.

I.96.

# VI. The Composition

## A. THE CALL TO WRITE

## B. CHOOSING A SUBJECT
97. Choose a Subject That Interests You
98. Limit the Subject

## C. GATHERING INFORMATION
99. Know Where to Find Information
100. Take Notes
101. Determine a Central Purpose

## D. ORGANIZING IDEAS

## E. DEVELOPING AN OUTLINE

## F. WRITING THE COMPOSITION
102. Develop an Effective Introduction
103. Keep the Composition Body Interesting
   a. Follow a Central Theme
   b. Be Direct—Not Vague
   c. Make Your Writing "Readable"
   d. Write Authoritatively
   e. Give Accurate Information
   f. Build Effective Paragraphs
104. Conclude Forcefully
   a. Summarize the Central Theme
   b. Repeat the Title in Some Way
   c. Make a Conclusive Statement
   d. Use an Impressive Illustration
   e. Mistakes to Avoid

## G. REVISING THE COMPOSITION
105. Check for Style
106. Check for Grammar
107. Reread Carefully
108. Recopy According to Specifications

## H. OTHER KINDS OF COMPOSITION
109. Letter Writing
   a. Friendly Letters
   b. Social Notes
   c. Business Letters

VI

110. Writing a Report
    a. Develop a Burden
    b. Acquaint Yourself With the Library and With Reference Material
    c. Take Notes, Including Biographical Data
    d. Include Footnotes and Bibliography
    e. Write in Your Own Words
111. Poetry
    a. Types of Poetry
    b. Rhythm in Poetry
    c. Writing Poetry

VI

# VI. The Composition

## A. THE CALL TO WRITE

Needs for written material for the home, the school, and the church are always current, yet how many people read without ever thinking of what was required to supply the material for their enrichment? If you ask somebody whether he has thought about writing a meditation for a periodical, he will probably answer that he is not a writer. Students shrug off a poor grade in composition, saying, "After all, that is not my gift." Who, then, shall write?

*An opportunity constitutes a call.* "As we have therefore opportunity, let us do good unto all men, especially unto them who are of the household of faith" (Galatians 6:10). There is no end to the opportunities to write, and by conveying a message, we can do good.

*What are the requirements for a writer?* The simplest answer is much dedication to the task. If there is a message to be presented, then you need a determination to make the message clear. An understanding of English grammar and composition will help you along, but perseverance is the main requirement. Therefore you need to pray earnestly that God will grant you the dedication and the time necessary to produce the composition for which He has already given the burden.

As you begin to write, as you struggle along, and as you hold up the finished paper, one question should always stand out: *What is the purpose of this piece of writing?* Any article, report, or book does have a purpose. This purpose corresponds to the four types of writing: *exposition* (informing the reader), *argument* (convincing others), *narration* (relating a story), and *description* (a sensory impression). By keeping your purpose before you, you can better accomplish what you have set out to do.

When God speaks to you with a message, it is usually best to begin immediately. Jot down any thoughts that enter your mind, because they might slip away. If you have a deadline to meet, a prompt beginning gives you more time for improving your work. Usually there is just as much time for a task at one time as at another.

On the other hand, you may have a hard time getting started. It may be that God is asking you to wait for various reasons. You must then simply depend on Him, for He is giving the message. Only when we are empty can He fill us. By feeling dependent on Him, we also gain humility. Since others can tell how we feel—even in writing— how important it is to be clothed with humility!

# B. CHOOSING A SUBJECT

Many times a writer is given an assignment and his thoughts are directed to the subject given. But what about the times *you* need to decide?

If you feel the call to write, ask the Lord to show you the next step by giving you a subject. He may open your eyes to observe something of special interest. He might touch you concerning some ordinary happening, and enable you to make it special enough to write about. Ask the Lord to keep you alert.

## 97.

### Choose a Subject That Interests You

*Being interested in your subject* is a necessity if you are to give the composition any life. You need to enjoy gathering material and thinking about your composition. Your enthusiasm must show or you will not convince your readers.

## 98.

### Limit the Subject

B.97.

A subject that is too broad will give you trouble organizing your thoughts, especially if you plan to write a short composition. *Be sure to limit your subject* so that you can handle it adequately.

Following are some examples of general and specific topics.

| BROAD SCOPE | SLIGHTLY LIMITED | LIMITED |
|---|---|---|
| Habits | Developing Habits | Using Sound Speech |
| Birds | Birds on the Farm | Our Friends, the Pigeons |
| Prophecy | Jesus in the O.T. | Isaiah and the Crucifixion |
| Church History | Martyrs | Conrad Grebel |

In the first column, the topics are so general that your writing would turn out to be long and rambling. The second column contains topics suitable to be developed into lengthy articles. By limiting the scope of your thoughts as in the third column, you can concentrate on details.

# C. GATHERING INFORMATION

How simple it would be if you could go to memory's storehouse and pick out material as you need it! True, God has given you the gift of remembrance and you can store many things in the brain. Yet, to prepare for writing or speaking, you need to go to a source of information that makes what you have to say accurate. The material you gather will determine whether you have something worthwhile to say.

## 99.

### Know Where to Find Information

*Knowing where to find information is as important as knowing facts.* The only infallible source of information is the Bible. It is accurate in every point and it can be depended upon for its finality. All information gathered must agree with the Bible. The Christian writer depends on it.

## 100.

### Take Notes

*Learning to collect ideas is a needful step for the writer or for anyone using the thinking process.* Suppose that you were scheduled to speak at the parent-teacher's meeting, or that you had been asked to teach a Sunday school class instead of writing a composition. What specific things would you want to present? You would need to draw from your own experience and hunt out books or articles on the subject. The same is true for writing a composition.

*Gathering notes* is something like preparing a meal. You raised a beef, you tended an orchard, and you planted a garden; now at mealtime you can draw from the various sources to bring out a variety of colors and tastes. All the food is eventually put on the table, a combination of good taste and nourishment in one single meal. In exactly the same way, your variety of notes blends into one composition.

*Take notes as you study.* Some writers use a stack of small (three-by-five-inch) cards and list each item separately along with its source. Other writers use larger sheets of paper and list items as they read. With either method, when you feel that you have collected a variety of material, you may be able to make a rough outline. But you will need to trim off some fat or throw out the peelings. Just as with a meal where some items only take up space or give an unpleasant taste, so some of your notes will be nonessential. (See "Reference Resources," section VIII, and "Writing a Report," section 110.)

## 101.

### Determine a Central Purpose

*Considering the purpose* of your writing will help you decide what to include. Ask the Lord to guide your thinking. The purpose of your writing and the length of your paper must be clear in your mind.

*It is wise to write the central purpose* and keep it before you. The central purpose is to your composition what a topic sentence is to a paragraph. All that you write must relate to the central theme, with subordinate ideas arranged to support the central purpose.

Suppose you make notes for the subject "Using Sound Speech." The purpose would be to inspire the reader to develop the good habit of using sound speech. Your list might look like this (no need to consider form at this point).

C.101.

> Definition of sound speech
> What is slang?
> The Bible talks about idle words.
> Swearing and cursing
> Being angry
> Names
> The destiny of liars
> Animals talking in the Bible
> Using an oath

Now examine your list and decide whether each item relates to the subject and whether it contributes to the purpose of your composition.

"Being angry," for instance, may lead you away from your subject. Although it has some relation to what you wish to say, it would be better to list "words of anger."

"Animals talking in the Bible" does not really relate to sound speech habits, so eliminate it altogether.

# D. ORGANIZING IDEAS

With only essential notes on your list, next arrange them in some definite order. Order of time, order of importance, or order of logic (with the strongest reason coming last) are elements to consider for arranging your thoughts.

# E. DEVELOPING AN OUTLINE

An *outline* is a blueprint for your composition. It should be a method of organizing your preliminary information to make a working plan for the job of writing. Outlines, just as blueprints, are not so final that they cannot be improved; however, a builder must know what materials he needs before he begins his project, and so must a writer. There must be an accumulation of data, ideas, and reasoning before anything of value can be written. When the job of writing has begun, you may need to add yet more details.

Sometimes the experienced writer outlines his material mentally, but even then he uses these guidelines to plan his composition. A certain logical arrangement will cause the thoughts to fall into their natural places.

The three most common types of outlines are the topic outline, the sentence outline, and the paragraph outline. The topic and sentence outlines follow the same pattern of numerals and letters, while the paragraph outline has no headings, but simply gives a statement for each paragraph. Each time you use an outline, follow one pattern rather than mixing the types.

**Rules for outline form.**
1. Center the title above the outline.
2. Use number and letters before each point to show main and subordinate headings. Indent each subordination as follows.

   I. This is a main point.
      A. This is a subpoint of I.
      B. This is a subpoint of I.
         1. This is a detail about B.

2. This is a detail about B.

3. This is a detail about B.
   a. This is a detail about 3.
   b. This is a detail about 3.
      (1) This is a detail about b.
      (2) This is a detail about b.
         (a) This is a detail about (2).
         (b) This is a detail about (2).

II. This is a main point.
   A. This is a subpoint of II.
   B. This is a subpoint of II.

3. Make the number or letters of the same rank follow directly in order, arranged in a column, being careful to keep each separate rank indented to the same degree vertically. See the preceding example.

4. Begin each line with a capital letter.

5. End each topic in a sentence outline with a period. (See 2 above.) But do not use periods for the topic outline. (See 8 and 9 below.)

6. There must always be two subordinate topics—nothing can be divided into fewer than two parts. If there is only one subordinate idea, make it part of the main topic.

INCORRECT

I.
   A.
      1.
   B.

CORRECT

I.
   A.
      1.
      2.
   B.
II.

7. In a topic outline, make each kind of heading of the same form. If the main topic is a noun, each main heading should be a noun. If a subtopic is a modifier, each related subtopic should be a modifier.

INCORRECT:

I. God planned for a pair of eyes
   A. For good focus
   B. To see more
   C. One for a spare
II. Movable eyes
   A. To see better
   B. Easier reading

CORRECT:

    I. A pair of eyes
       A. For good focus
       B. For greater vision
       C. For a spare
   II. Movable eyes
       A. To see better
       B. To read across a page

8. Determine which material will be main topics and which will fall into subordinate headings. Use proper numbers and letters to show coordinate topics and subordinate topics.

INCORRECT:

    I. Reasons for effective study
       A. Usefulness to God
       B. Essentials for effective study
   II. Motivation
  III. Skill
  IV. Concentration

CORRECT:

    I. Reasons for effective study
       A. God's plan for life
       B. Usefulness to God
   II. Essentials for effective study
       A. Motivation
       B. Skill
       C. Concentration

9. Be sure your outline covers the subject and central purpose indicated by the title.

POOR:

    I. Effective study
       A. How
       B. Why
   II. Essentials
       A. What kind
       B. How many

BETTER:

I. Reasons for effective study
   A. God's plan for life
   B. Usefulness to God
II. Essentials for effective study
   A. Motivation
      1. How to challenge students
      2. How to have it yourself
   B. Skill
   C. Concentration
      1. How to restrain the roving mind
      2. How to increase attention
   D. Organization
      1. How to be systematic
      2. How to review
   E. Independence

10. Arrange the outline in a logical order, and do not allow headings to overlap in thought. Consider the different kinds of order: time, place, space, importance, and so forth. By using one pattern, you can keep your outline logical.

Sometimes beginning writers resist the idea of outlining. Usually this indicates that either they have not learned to use their outline or they are not willing to think. An outline is a method of putting a composition in order by doing some preliminary thinking. Besides, any extensive writing must have an outline so that it does not lose its direction. A long work such as a book can stay in the writer's mind, even if he spends a year writing it, because he always has the outline to refer to.

An outline shows the proportion of the various topics. Too much space for one topic may take away space from another equally important topic. Checking the outline to give each item proper space will prevent spending too much time on a single thought in the composition.

A well-organized outline with sufficient coverage helps the writer to express his thoughts freely and smoothly. He is ready to go into the introduction and the actual task of writing. The outline is his tool for efficiency.

INCORRECT:

**Mennonite History**

   I. The first hundred years (time)

  II. In Germany (place)

 III. The Anabaptists (people)

Mennonites in Germany and also the Anabaptists could be included in the first hundred years; thus the subjects overlap.

CORRECT:

**Mennonite History**

   I. Period before 1600

  II. Period from 1600-1800

 III. Period since 1800

This is in logical time order from earliest to latest.

# F. WRITING THE COMPOSITION

## 102.

### Develop an Effective Introduction

*Every composition needs a good beginning.* Your reader must have necessary introductory information so that he can follow you. You will want to catch his attention and relay some of your enthusiasm so that he will desire to continue reading. Therefore, be sure that your introduction *introduces* your subject—quickly, interestingly, and clearly.

Using the title somewhere (directly or indirectly) in the first paragraph can make an effective beginning.

F.102.

#### Spiritual Stability

We know of little that is more distressing than an individual who is *spiritually unstable.* One never knows where to find him. He may be very agreeable to any proposition if it strikes him right, or he may be downright disagreeable otherwise. Such a person is hard to work with in the church. . . .

Give important information in the opening paragraph to get your composition going.

Butterflies have God-given instincts to provide for their young. They place their eggs very near to the plant where the caterpillar will feed.

Many introductions could be eliminated because they ramble and really do not say much.

It is good to spend time in meditation. Have you ever stopped to think of the marvels of metamorphosis? Surely God has created all things well.

This opening paragraph is more specific and sets the pattern for an entire theme.

The change of an ugly caterpillar to a lovely butterfly is one of the marvels of God's creation. Finding a caterpillar on a parsley stem can lead to interesting observation and inspire your thoughts.

News articles tell who, what, when, and where in the first paragraph.

Brother John Martin spoke on "How Parents Can Prepare Their Children for School" at the October parent-teacher's meeting of the Zion Christian School.

By asking who, what, when, or where of your composition throughout, you can check your writing for directness and clarity.

Relating an incident in the introduction is an effective method of arousing the reader's attention. Be sure that the incident is related to your topic. From the story, you can surely and smoothly move on to your topic.

Elizabeth Glyde had been told by her doctors that she would never be well again. With this outlook, she returned home. There she received a message from a dying youth, fourteen years old: "Tell her that when I came to the valley of the shadow of death, Jesus was there to meet me." The dying woman was greatly inspired by the words of comfort, so much so that she went on to write "Be With Me in the Valley."

Suffering and death do not really look pleasant to those who enjoy health and vitality. Even the ill who are about to "cross over" sometimes possess doubts. We can look to Jesus through these experiences and rest assured that He will meet us.

Avoid making uninteresting statements that the reader can obviously see.

*Do not say:*

This is an introduction to the subject of butterflies.

*or:*

This composition is written to prove smoking is harmful and wrong.

Avoid sounding apologetic. It makes the reader feel uncomfortable and wastes time and space that could be devoted to the topic.

I hardly feel qualified to write about ways to study a Sunday school lesson. There are many people who seem to bring better thoughts to class than I can. I trust you will bear with me as we move through this article.

By all means, avoid a long, drawn-out introduction. Using the pointers you have already learned, go directly into the main body of your paper.

## 103.

## Keep the Composition Body Interesting

From the introduction, you can go on writing the entire composition. Assuming that your outline is complete, you should follow it from one point to another. Do not be overanxious about form, but rather keep your ideas rolling. Ideas are the necessary ingredient for any kind of writing.

### 103a.

*Follow a central theme:* Always keep the purpose of your writing before you and follow a central theme from beginning to end. Unified thoughts are a necessity for clarity. You want your readers to know exactly what you are trying to say.

VAGUE: Some of the artwork appeared as though cleanliness should be taught first of all.

CLEAR: Some of the art papers had smudges from the children's dirty hands.

### 103b.

F.103.

*Be direct—not vague:* Sometimes an important message never gets to the reader or hearer because it is presented in a vague way. Learn to be direct—yet tactful.

The type of writing you engage in will set the style you adopt. A report on the monarch butterfly could be formal, stating facts. An article on the Christian's relation to the government might be formal or informal. An essay on good manners could sound conversational.

In Christian writing, the chief concern is that somebody reads and understands what you have written. You can capture your reader's attention. For some reason, people always enjoy human interest; in other words, they like to relate to what they are reading. This is the practical way to make reading beneficial.

*103c.*

*Make your writing "readable":* Using an abundance of nouns is the best method of making your writing "readable." Count the nouns in different types of writing, both in the types you enjoy and in those upon which you find it hard to concentrate. Did the number of concrete words make the difference?

Jesus gave the charge, "Feed my lambs" and "Feed my sheep." In relating spiritual truths, you can apply this to making your writing fit the people with less understanding as well as those with deep minds. The reader's time is another element that decides whether he is going to read. He does not feel his time is wasted if he knows exactly what the article says or if his interest is held from one point to another.

*103d.*

*Write authoritatively:* Be sure your composition is authoritative. What you say must agree with the information that the reader has. For example, it would be unwise to write about: how students should act at school, when the school policy does not agree with what you are saying. Outside reading will give backing to your opinions. Most important of all, give Biblical information, for it will never be out of date, nor can its authority be questioned.

*103e.*

*Give accurate information:* Doing anything less would be dishonest! Sometimes writers (and speakers) are tempted to exaggerate in order to impress their readers (or audience). If five inches of rain fell in half an hour, causing the creek to flood, tell it the way it was. If the blizzard lasted seventy-two hours, squelch the temptation to say many days—it was only three.

Use sound reasoning to back your statements. Some statements might apply to a given situation but are entirely wrong for the next. For instance: John Miller was often tempted to steal in his youth. He begged the Lord to help him, and after many trials he won a victory. Now it would be erroneous to write as though every young person had the habit of stealing. Suppose a writer, knowing that John Miller was dishonest, would say that no young person should be permitted to handle money. How unfortunate this would be since youth who would be subjected to the results of this reasoning would be greatly hindered in learning principles of Christian stewardship.

*103f.*

*Build effective paragraphs:* Keep your composition in paragraphs according to topics. In some cases you may devote a paragraph to each heading in your outline. At other times you might need two or three paragraphs to cover one idea. Develop your paragraphs according to the principles of good paragraph writing discussed in section V, "The Paragraph" (especially "Unity and Coherence," section 79).

Remember to make smooth transitions between paragraphs, using one of these methods.

(1) Repeat the idea of the former paragraph in the new paragraph.

*Example:*

Taking notes from the lesson text is commonly known as outlining. Most lesson texts are based on an outline. Some are quite obvious, while others are obscure. *It is good for a student to be able to pick out the outline* from the text, also to bring out important subpoints.

*To outline correctly,* the student should be trained . . .

(2) Use logical order.

*Example:*

Farmer Brown looked at the water standing in the fields after the downpour. "I won't be making hay for a week," he decided.

*He walked on.* "That bridge across the creek is either unsafe or washed away. I'll need to attend to that first thing."

(3) Use connective expressions.

*Example:*

Did you ever check your ability to "listen"? When you read a verse of Scripture, do you reach out eagerly to understand it and live according to it? Did you hear all the words but not really wait before the Lord for a message?

*Likewise,* can you hear others speak and never really absorb what they are saying? You might be more eager to speak than to listen.

F.103f.

# 104.

## Conclude Forcefully

The conclusion of your composition should be forceful and impressive. It should have a unifying effect on the entire composition.

Several methods of writing an effective conclusion can be used.

*104a.*

*Summarize the central theme:* Each one of us must then decide *that sound speech is important.* What we say tells what is inside us. As Peter's speech betrayed him, so also our bad expressions give us away.

*104b.*

*Repeat the Title in Some Way*

### A Lesson Learned

All the eighth graders apologized to each other with sincerity and depth that had been missing for a month. Brother Ray was satisfied that a *lesson* had been *learned.*

*104c.*

*Make a conclusive statement* from the data you have presented.

### Which Version?

The King James Version is a bulwark of protection against the subtle additions and subtractions of the modernists. . . . *So, since the Word of Truth does not change, it is well for us to stay with a version that has made us wise unto salvation and has been loved* by many generations.

*104d.*

*Use an Impressive Illustration*

A boy ran away from home and went to the city. Soon he fell into sinful ways and neglected even to write to his mother. She longed to see her boy, so she went to the city and searched for him. In vain she looked. Then one day she was run over by an automobile. They took her to a hospital where she died a few hours later. Before she died she whispered to one of the nurses, "If you see my boy, tell him that God and his mother never gave up."

—W. Hershel Ford, *Simple Sermons on Heaven, Hell, and Judgment* (Zondervan)

*104e.*

*Mistakes to avoid* in ending your composition.

(1) A weak, rambling conclusion that hardly comes to an end.
(2) New material aside from the main purpose of your paper.
(3) Apologetic statements about yourself.
(4) Simply "stopping" without a logical conclusion.

F.104a.

# G. REVISING THE COMPOSITION

A student once wrote this paraphrase on the inside cover of her composition book: "Now abide plan, write, and rewrite; and the greatest of these is rewrite." No composition is complete without this operation. Never underestimate the value of rewriting.

Your first draft should include every idea you wish to present; your second paper should present every idea in the best form. If possible, allow some time to elapse before you look critically at what you have written. Perhaps you are in a hurry to finish your composition for class, or you promised material to an editor by a certain date. But you still have no excuse to skip the revision.

Rewriting requires perseverance. It also requires considerable thought. When the cause is the Lord's, you will want to present your best workmanship. He can supply you with time. He can also supply you with a new perspective from which to view your work. A new perspective is essential for rewriting.

## 105.

### Check for Style

a. Is your title appropriate?
b. Are your ideas clear? If you were the reader, would you understand them?
c. Is the composition in logical order? Sometimes this means deviating from the outline when you see a better order.
d. Did you stick to your topic? When you look over your writing, you may decide to add or subtract a sentence, or perhaps a whole paragraph.
e. Do your introduction and your conclusion contribute to the composition?

G.105.

## 106.

### Check for Grammar

a. Have you developed paragraphs according to the principles you have learned?
b. Did you use a variety of sentence lengths and structures?
c. Is your grammar correct?

d. Did you follow the principles of capitalization and punctuation, and did you spell each word correctly?

## 107.

### Reread Carefully

When you feel that you have done your best and you call your composition finished, read over it carefully. Reading aloud is helpful. Asking a friend to analyze your paper is another method of checking.

## 108.

### Recopy According to Specifications

Assured that everything is exactly the way you want it, copy your composition carefully, typed or hand written according to specifications.

#### Brief Outline of the Steps of Composition Writing

a. *Choose the subject.* The subject should be proportioned to the number of words you are attempting to write. Know the purpose for working on this subject.

b. *Gather information.* Make a list of all information that might be included in your composition. Reading and thinking are your two main sources.

c. *Organize ideas.* List your material in logical order. Discard anything that does not relate to the subject.

d. *Make an outline.* The outline is your working plan. Include sufficient material to make your writing complete. Follow acceptable patterns of form.

e. *Write a first draft.* Following your outline, write rapidly as ideas come to your mind. Use your knowledge of grammar to arrange sentences and paragraphs.

f. *Revise.* Lay your paper away for a time and then check it in every detail.

G.107.

# H. OTHER KINDS OF COMPOSITION

## 109.

### Letter Writing

Letter writing is the most often used type of writing, and, with hardly an exception, people need to try their hand at it some time or other. In a letter, the writer "talks" to his reader. It should follow all the rules of courtesy. There are two kinds of letters—friendly and business.

*109a.*

*Friendly letters* are usually written to friends and families, although occasionally you may need to write to a stranger. They may be a friendly visit on paper, a note of thanks, an invitation, a reply to an invitation, an apology, or an expression of sympathy.

Friendly letters may be written on any type of paper the writer chooses. However, he should make it appropriate to the occasion.

Since letter writing is a means whereby God uses you to relate to others, you should be open to His leading. Many times a letter has arrived just in time to cheer a lonely or discouraged heart. You can be an instrument to do that very thing.

**Guidelines for Friendly Letters**

a. Jot down your main thoughts so that when you write, your train of thought is orderly.
b. Be natural and do not use unnecessary words. "I will close now" is obvious enough without writing it.
c. Be courteous and truthful.
d. Use correct grammar and mechanics.
e. Share things that are interesting and edifying. Reflect Christ as you write. Provide interesting details and be specific.

**H.109.**

**Form for Friendly Letters**

Heading
Address
Date

Greeting

Body

Closing
Signature

*109b.*

*Social notes:* Sometimes you have a definite reason for writing a letter such as a thank-you note, an invitation, or an apology. Do not neglect writing these types as the need arises.

**(1) Guidelines for Notes of Thanks**

(a) Promptness is especially important when you receive something by mail; a thank-you note will assure the sender that the gift arrived safely.

(b) Mention what you appreciate about the gift or favor.

(c) Express a direct "thank you."

INCORRECT: I would like to thank you for the comfortable bed and delicious breakfast you provided.

CORRECT: Thank you very much for the comfortable bed and delicious breakfast you provided.

**(2) Guidelines for Invitations**

(a) Tell what, when, and where. Be specific about times, dates, and places, to avoid misunderstandings.

(b) Make your invitation warm and friendly.

(c) If activities are planned, such as chore time or hiking, mention that suitable clothes will be needed. It is embarrassing to be unprepared.

**(3) Guidelines for a Reply to an Invitation**

(a) Answer promptly.

(b) Express appreciation for the invitation.

(c) If you accept the invitation, repeat the time, date, and place so that the hosts will know you understand correctly.

(d) If you cannot accept, express regret, and give a reason if possible.

**(4) Guidelines for Notes of Apology**

(a) Be clear about what you have to say.

(b) Express regret.

(c) Offer to make amends.

**(5) Guidelines for Notes of Sympathy**

(a) Make your note brief and full of feeling.

(b) Offer a portion of God's Word or a few lines of poetry with your words of sympathy.

**(6) Ways to Improve Your Letter Writing**

(a) Answer letters promptly, while the impressions you received are fresh in your mind.

(b) Write with your reader in mind, as if you were talking to him.

(c) Ask questions and write in a way that prompts an answer.

(d) Keep your thoughts organized to avoid a jumbled effect.

(e) "And whatsoever ye do in word or deed, do all in the name of the Lord Jesus, giving thanks to God and the Father by him" (Colossians 3:17).

See "Paragraph Development" (especially section 80, "Adding Details").

*109c.*

*Business letters:* You may write a friendly letter as the mood strikes you, and you may use anything from scrap paper to lovely stationery. Not so with a business letter. You should always use appropriate, lined or unlined white paper and always place the parts in their proper location according to accepted conventions.

The business letter is written to accomplish a transaction. Its tone may be warm and friendly, but it should always conform to standard practice. Business letters should be typewritten or neatly hand written with blue or black ink.

Become familiar with the parts of a business letter: (1) heading, (2) inside address, (3) salutation, (4) body, (5) closing, (6) signature.

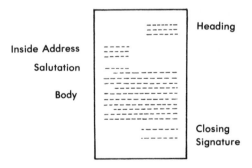

1. The *heading* includes the writer's address and the date of the letter. If letterhead is used, only the date is needed. The heading should be placed in the upper right corner.

> 2260 Kimmens Rd.
> Canton, OH 44720
> March 1, 1983

**2.** The *inside address* names the person or company to whom the letter is written and gives the address. Allow four spaces below the date, and place the inside address at the left margin. See examples below with salutations.

**3.** The *salutation* or greeting is also placed at the left margin, two spaces below the inside address. Capitalize the first word of a salutation and all the nouns in it. The form of salutation is determined by the inside address and is followed by a colon.

To a company:

Real Estate Showcase
243 E. Liberty St
Wooster, OH 44691

Gentlemen:

To an individual whose name you do not know:

Editor of *Gleanings in Bee Culture*
A. I. Root Company
Medina, OH 44256

Dear Sir:

Dietary Consultant
Walnut Hill Retirement Center
Millersburg, OH 44654

Dear Madam:

(Never write *Dear Mrs.:*
or *Dear Miss:* unless
marital status is known.)

To an individual whose name is given:

Mr. Howard Clark
Insta Sales Company
1965 Orr Street
Cleveland, OH 44106

Dear Mr. Clark:

To a government official:

The Honorable James Scott
Senate Office Building
Washington, DC 20515

Dear Senator Scott:

4. The *body* of the business letter is the message you are sending. It should begin two spaces below the salutation. (If your letter is very short, the complete letter should be centered on the page to look balanced.)

Make a business letter brief and clear. Decide what you want to say before you begin writing. Always use tact and courtesy, even if you are making a complaint. Be sure to read your letter carefully to make sure it can be understood. In fact, all the rules for writing a good composition apply especially to the business letter.

5. The *closing* should be placed two spaces below the body (unless you need to center the letter on the page), slightly to the right side of the page. Some appropriate closings are *Very truly yours, Yours truly, Sincerely yours, Cordially yours* (for an acquaintance), *Respectfully yours* (for very formal letters).

6. The *signature* should be typed (if your letter is typed) four to six spaces below the closing, with a hand-written signature just above it. Never give yourself a title unless it is to show Mrs. or Miss.

## Business Letter Forms

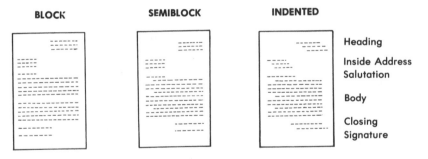

## Steps for Folding Business Letters

### *For Small Envelopes*

1. Fold from bottom with crease a little below the center of the page, leaving a small margin at top.

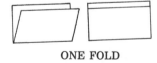

ONE FOLD

2. Fold from right side to within one-third of the space from the left. Then fold the left side over, leaving one-fourth inch along the right.

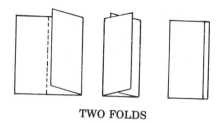

TWO FOLDS

3. Place in envelope with last fold along the bottom.

### For Large Envelopes

1. Fold in thirds by first folding bottom third up and then folding top third down, leaving a slight margin.

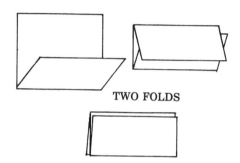

TWO FOLDS

2. Place in envelope with last fold down.

Business letters are written to transact business. An office uses letters for all kinds of business. But at home, you will need only five basic kinds of business letters.

A *letter of inquiry* is used to ask for information, help, or any kind of favor.

A *letter of information* is written to answer an inquiry.

A *letter of introduction* is written to acquaint some person or business with a new individual. It may be written by the person himself or by a former employer or teacher. It is usually used when applying for a job.

*An order* must be absolutely accurate and complete. Check your catalog numbers, quantities, and other figures to be sure you are asking for what you want. If possible, use an order blank provided by the company. If you have none, be sure to list everything an order blank would ask for.

A *letter of adjustment or complaint* is written to a company when your transaction is unsatisfactory. Tell what has happened and ask politely for an adjustment. In this age of computers, you may need to write several times before the right individual handles your letter. Remember to be courteous at all times. Not only is it Christlike to be kind, but your complaint will have more influence when you have registered it politely.

*Envelopes* for business letters should be standard business size, 3⅝ by 6½ inches or 4 by 10 inches. A business office handles many letters, and one that is not a uniform size can be a nuisance. Order and courtesy are Christian responsibilities. We need to pay attention to even the more minor details.

## 110.

## Writing a Report

A report is a formal presentation of facts. To write a report you will need to spend much time gathering information. Knowing how to find information and to assemble it in your own words is a skill that you will need all your life. *Presenting information that could be read word for word out of a book has little value.* Gathering information from an encyclopedia is good, but it is only a beginning in learning to make a report. You will need to avail yourself of other sources of information. This may require the occasional use of a library.

Research and study give you lasting knowledge as well as permanent study habits. Learning how to study on any given subject should help you learn how to study the Bible. The Bible is the richest source book available, and with good habits, your study anywhere from cover to cover will be meaningful.

*110a.*

*Develop a burden:* You must be interested in and concerned about a subject if you are going to study it extensively. Imagine spending hours on something in which you have no interest. Neither can you give your audience anything convincing if you are in such a state of mind.

*110b.*

*Acquaint yourself with the library and with reference material* before you start your report. (See "Reference Resources," section VIII.) The *card catalogue* and the *Readers' Guide to Periodical Literature* found in every library will give you clues on almost any subject.

*110c.*

*Take notes, including biographical data:* Getting down to the business of writing the report is the real work. You will need to think.

And you will need to continue reading. You may be tempted to think that reading and recording notes is a poor way to spend writing time. But think instead of the benefit you can be to your readers by the information you convey.

Find several books or periodicals that relate to the subject you are writing about. Be sure you have sufficient material to give your report a thorough coverage. Keep a note paper for every bit of information you consider valuable, or make three-by-five-inch note cards and write each idea separately. If you wish to quote, write the passage on a card. As you make notes, check that you have everything you will need for a bibliography; nobody wants to hunt for information after the paper is written.

Following are examples of notes to begin reports.

### The Conscientious Objectors and World War II

*On paper*

How the Christian feels about revenge
    Confession of Faith
    Article XIV. Defence by Force
    Dortrecht Edition 1632. Reprint 1976


"My kingdom is not of this world: if my kingdom were of this world, then would my servants fight" (John 18:36).
                      Bible


Civilian Public Service—testing times
    "Camp Life," page 85
                Nonresistance Under Test
                E. J. Swalm

How the program was operated
                Mennonite Encyclopedia

### The Monarch Butterfly

*On cards*

(each card containing one idea)

> The larva or caterpillar eats milkweed. In two or three weeks it changes into a chrysalis.
>
> Audubon Nature Encyclopedia

> Swarms of Monarch butterflies go south. About 240,000 pass through a gap in the Appalachian Mountains.
>
> Wings in the Meadow, p. 163

*110d.*

*Include footnotes and bibliography:* When you write, you will need *footnotes* at the bottom of the page and a *bibliography* at the end of your report to give credit for any information you borrowed. Along with your notes, make a bibliography which gives the author, title, publisher, and date of each book from which you obtained information.

For the preceding examples you need a bibliography something like this:

Bender, Harold S., and Smith, C. Henry, eds. *The Mennonite Encyclopedia.* Volume 1. 1955; rpt. Scottdale, Pa.: Herald Press; 1969

Coffman, S.F., ed. *Mennonite Confession of Faith.* Dortrecht edition, 1632. rpt. Bartel Printing Co., 1976.

Swalm, E.J., *Nonresistance Under Test.* Nappanee, Ind.: Indian E.V. Publishing House, 1949.

Brewer, Jo. *Wings in the Meadow.* Boston: Houghton, Mifflin Company, 1967.

National Audubon Society. *The Audubon Natural Encyclopedia.* Volume 2. 1955; rpt. Curtis Publishing Company, 1971.

Many questions arise about listings for a bibliography. Here, basically, are the facts to be included.

Name of author, or authors, editors, or organization writing the book

Title of the book

Volume number if in a series

Edition if a revision
City, publisher, and date

For a periodical give the following facts.

Name of author
Title of article
Name of magazine, date issued, page number of article

Any quoted material requires footnotes at the bottom of the page.

"The veterans had their GI Bill of Rights to back them up and promise future security, but the CPS man had no legal right to expect to return to his old job. Some, by their choice of CPS, knowingly forfeited the privilege of returning to their former jobs. This problem was a very real issue during CPS days, but the promise that God will not forsake those faithful to Him proved true in the many opportunities which opened for these men upon their return to civilian life."[2]

[2] E. J. Swalm, *Nonresistance Under Test* (Nappanee, Ind.: Indian E. V. Publishing House, 1949), p. 110.

Following are examples of footnotes for various types of listings.

*One author, one edition:*
James Gilchrist Lawson, *Deeper Experiences of Famous Christians* (Anderson, Ind.: Warner Press, 1911), p. 285.

*One author, and a revision:*
George R. Brunk, *Ready Scriptural Reasons*, rev. ed. (Scottdale, Pa.: Herald Press, 1954) p. 127.

*A book by an editor:*
John C. Wenger, ed., *The Complete Writings of Menno Simons* (Scottdale, Pa.: Herald Press, 1956), p. 228.

*Several volumes:*
National Audubon Society, *Audubon Nature Encyclopedia* (Philadelphia—New York: Houghton Mifflin Co., 1971), 2:336.

*Encyclopedia articles:*
"Nutrition," *World Book*, 1971.

*Article from a publication, magazine, and suchlike:*
Paul M. Landis, "Discouragement," *The Christian Contender*, August 1977 pp. 8-12.

Using another writer's words without giving him recognition is *plagiarism.* Even when an article is written in your own words but the ideas are mainly borrowed ones, some recognition should be given.

The Christian writer, whose desire is to be honest, will try to avoid this type of literary theft.

Be sure that you copy quoted material accurately and that you do not change its tone. This is just another way of being courteous to others.

When footnotes require much of a page, it is best to put them at the end of the writing. Some writing depends almost entirely upon borrowed material. An article of history using old news clippings, interviews, and old books is an example of this.

*110e.*

*Write in your own words:* Always write your report in your own words, adopting your own style, and use direct quotes as needed to make the report authoritative. Follow the procedure given in "Writing the Composition," (section VI, F.) to make your report well organized. Keep your reader in mind as you write.

# 111.

## Poetry

Poetry is a form of writing in verse which produces emotional response. It requires correct grammar and even rhythm. It must be constructed so that its message is profound and its thought pattern clear.

*Verse* is a line of rhythmic composition.

A *stanza* is a group of lines following a pattern of rhythm.

H.110e.

*111a.*

*Types of Poetry*

(1) *Descriptive* poetry describes something.

### The Love of God
Like a cradle, rocking, rocking,
  Silent, peaceful, to and fro—
Like a mother's sweet looks dropping
  On the little face below—
Hangs the green earth, swinging, turning,
  Jarless, noiseless, safe and slow,
Falls the light of God's face, bending
  Down and watching us below.

—Helen Hunt Jackson

(2) *Lyric* poetry expresses desires and is good to set to music.

> O Master, let me walk with Thee
> In lowly paths of service free.
>
> —Washington Gladden

(3) *Narrative* poetry tells a story and can be lengthy; sometimes entire books have been written in verse.

> 'Twas battered and scarred, and the auctioneer
> Thought it scarcely worth his while
> To waste much time on the old violin,
> But held it up with a smile.
>
> —Myra Brooks Welch

(4) *Didactic* poetry teaches a lesson and can include the previously named types.

> Over and over again,
> No matter which way I turn
> I always find in the Book of Life
> Some lesson I must learn.
>
> —Unknown

(5) Other types are *dramatic* poetry and *light* or *humorous* verse, but they are not commonly suitable for Christian writing.

(6) *Occasional* verse is the name given to the lines on a greeting card or to poetry commemorating a special occasion.

*111b.*

**Rhythm in poetry:** Poetry is known by its *rhythm*—its pattern of accented and unaccented syllables arranged in lines. A line of poetry is measured by feet. A *foot* is one accented syllable and one or more unaccented syllables. The five most common feet are *iamb* ( ˘ ´ , eṅduṙe); *trochee* ( ´ ˘ , fádĕd); *anapest* ( ˘ ˘ ´ , dĭscoṅteṅt); *amphibrach* ( ˘ ´ ˘ , ădmíriṅg); and *dactyl* ( ´ ˘ ˘ , fiṙmămĕnt).

A line is defined by naming the foot by its number and type. Number: one foot—*monometer;* two feet—*dimeter;* three feet—*trimeter;* four feet—*tetrameter;* five feet—*pentameter;* six feet—*hexameter;* seven feet—*heptameter;* eight feet—*octameter.* Thus a line with four iambic feet is called an *iambic tetrameter.*

> Hŏw swéet / the chaṙm / of coúr/t̃e śy    (*iambic tetrameter*)
> Aṅd gra/ciŏus woṙds, / hŏw swéet!    (*iambic trimeter*)
>
> —From *Politeness*

> ╯ = accented syllable
> ∪ = unaccented syllable

Téll me / nót, iň / moúrn fŭl / núm beřs.    (*trochaic tetrameter*)
—"The Psalm of Life"

Variations are permissible in writing verse; feet may be interchanged, and unaccented syllables may be added if the thought and word demands them. Although you may use a variety of feet, keep the same pattern in every stanza. Read your lines aloud to be sure that the rhythm is smooth and natural.

Poetry is most easily identified by *rhyme*, the repetition of a corresponding accented vowel sound. Because good rhyming is definitely a matter of sound, the rhyming words must have a pleasant effect. The rhyming words may be placed in consecutive lines or alternating lines.

|  |  |
|---|---|
| Alternating lines rhyme | No! Rest is not quitting<br>   The busy career;<br>Rest is the fitting<br>   Of self to one's sphere.<br>      —Goethe |
| Consecutive lines rhyme | I shot an arrow into the air,<br>It fell to earth, I knew not where;<br>For, so swiftly it flew, the sight<br>Could not follow it in its flight.<br>      —Longfellow |

### 111c.

*Writing poetry:* Since poetry is the expression of the writer's desires or inner meditations, you must draw from the storehouse of thoughts. You need to add to your thoughts constantly if you want to use them. Let a poem flow unhindered as it comes to your mind. Sometimes only a line or two may form; and again, you may have an entire stanza. Write it as it comes; grasp every part, so that you do not lose your inspiration. Rewrite your poem later to adjust it to the rules of rhyme and rhythm.

Poetry should follow the rules of correct grammar. For good thought, the words must come in their natural order. The rules for punctuation are the same for poetry as for prose.

AWKWARD:

In deep humility I bowed
And asked the Lord to take
My worry and presuming,
*Which things worse do make.*

*The first line of poetry and lines rhyming with it are never indented.*
Here are varying patterns of indentation.

| | |
|---|---|
| All lines rhyming and no indentation | Come, let us reason now and *see* <br> This little Baby—who is *He?* <br> Our Saviour, Master, Lord, if *we* <br> Give up ourselves and bow the *knee.* |
| Second and fourth lines rhyming and indented | Do not look for wrong and evil— <br> You will find them if you *do;* <br> As you measure for your neighbor <br> He will measure back to *you.* |
| First and third lines rhyming as well as second and fourth; alternating lines indented. | Life is real! Life is *earnest!* <br> And the grave is not its *goal;* <br> Dust thou art, to dust *returnest,* <br> Was not spoken of the *soul.* <br> —Longfellow |
| Varying patterns of rhyme; thus, indentation of varying lines | If ever I see <br> On bush or tree, <br> Young birds in a pretty *nest* <br> I must not, in play, <br> Steal the young birds away <br> To grieve their mother's *breast.* |
| First three lines rhyming and only the last line indented | Just as I am, without one plea, <br> But that Thy blood was shed for me, <br> And that Thou bidd'st me come to Thee, <br> O Lamb of God, I come! <br> —Charlotte Elliott |

The writer of poetry should be inspired so that those who read the thoughts in verse receive inspiration also. Along with rhythm and rhyme, the poem should contain meaningful thoughts. Just as the writer of a composition needs to know what he is trying to say, so does a poet. Add thought upon thought, going from one concept to another in an orderly manner just as you would in prose.

Although not all people write poetry, everyone should have some degree of *poetry appreciation.* Reading well-written poetry is the first essential. Filling needs of the inner life with poetry is another beginning element in enjoying poetry. You might start with *hymns about heaven,* and dwell on those pleasant prospects for a blessing. The *Book of Psalms* is a form of poetry that has been very inspiring to many. Although the Psalms do not rhyme, they do follow orderly patterns of thought.

*Parallelism* is the name given to the thought patterns you find in the Psalms.

*Synonymous parallelism* is a pattern of similar thoughts used together to build a verse or verses.

> I will sing of the mercies of the Lord for ever: with my mouth will I make known thy faithfulness to all generations.
>
> —Psalm 89:1

*Antithetic parallelism* is a pattern of opposite thoughts used together.

> The face of the Lord is against them that do evil, to cut off the remembrance of them from the earth.
> The righteous cry, and the Lord heareth, and delivereth them out of all their troubles.
>
> —Psalm 34:16, 17

> Every wise woman buildeth her house: but the foolish plucketh it down with her hands.
>
> —Proverbs 14:1

*Synthetic parallelism* is a pattern of adding thought upon thought.

> Lord, thou hast been our dwelling place in all generations. Before the mountains were brought forth, or ever thou hadst formed the earth and the world, even from everlasting to everlasting, thou art God.
>
> —Psalm 90:1, 2

Poetry (as well as prose) can be made more descriptive by using *figures of speech*. The Scriptures are rich with these. The four most often used figures of speech are simile, metaphor, personification, and hyperbole.

**H.IIIc.**

SIMILE: A comparison made using *like* or *as*.

> He shall be like a tree planted by the rivers of water, that bringeth forth his fruit in his season.
>
> —Psalm 1:3

METAPHOR: A comparison made without using the word *like*, but rather using one of the forms of the verb *to be*.

> The Lord is my rock, and my fortress.
>
> —Psalm 18:2

PERSONIFICATION: Giving to a thing some human qualities.

> How amiable are thy tabernacles, O Lord of hosts!
>
> —Psalm 84:1

HYPERBOLE: An exaggeration used for emphasis (not a deceiving statement).

*From a hymn:*

Had I a *thousand* hearts to give,
Lord, they should all be thine.

—Samuel Stennett

H.111c.

# VII. The Short Story

**A. INTRODUCTION**

**B. GATHERING IDEAS**
112. Use Familiar Material
113. Keep a Notebook or Journal
114. Decide on a Character
115. Keep the Story Realistic

**C. PLANNING THE STORY**
116. Decide Your Ending First
117. Introduce Main Character Near the Beginning
118. Eliminate Unnecessary Details and Descriptions
119. Decide How to Tell the Story

**D. WRITING THE STORY**
120. Use Conversation
121. Show Action
122. Build Sympathy for the Right
123. Keep the Story Natural
124. Show Correct Spiritual Values
125. Let the Story Bring Out the Lesson

**E. DEVELOPING THE PLOT**

**F. ENDING THE STORY**

**G. CHOOSING A TITLE**

**H. REWRITING THE STORY**
126. Lay the Manuscript Aside for a While
127. Read Manuscript Again Critically and Revise

**I. BENEFITING FROM EDITOR'S CRITICISM**

**J. PREPARING THE MANUSCRIPT**
128. Specifications for the Manuscript
   a. General Appearance
   b. Paper
   c. Reference Copy
   d. Margins
   e. Spacing
129. Manuscript Changes
130. Mailing the Manuscript

# VII. The Short Story

## A. INTRODUCTION

If you would take a poll of reader's opinions, you would probably find that the *short story* is the most widely read type of writing. *Narrative* writing catches attention and therefore is a means of conveying a message to many people. In stories, readers find situations they can relate to. Through stories you can move people to love, disdain, sympathize, work, campaign, and more.

The Christian writer should endeavor to be more than a mere entertainer. The story should lend information, build character, or teach a spiritual truth, as well as captivate the interest of the reader. The story should reveal the working of God in human lives.

You will find story writing an enjoyable experience because you are relating to things close at hand. Story writers are not always exceptional people with noteworthy experiences. More than finding exciting and unusual incidents, the story writer learns to make the most of ordinary happenings. Common day-to-day events are the basis for most of life's lessons.

The Christian is concerned with writing that is either true or true to life. Good writing is the product of *much observation.* Details are made authentic by using the right words to portray actions, sounds, appearances, or thoughts.

## B. GATHERING IDEAS

Narrative writing is similar to composition writing in that you *must have something to write about.*

### 112.

#### Use Familiar Material

Be a careful observer and you will find many ideas for stories. Experience rather than research is the source from which to draw material for a story. Take a close look at the things people do and say. Think about the trials and triumphs of ordinary people—your friends, your classmates, or the people you work beside. Notice your surroundings—shapes, sounds, and movements in familiar places.

## 113.

### Keep a Notebook or Journal

If you jot down happenings, the ideas will not slip away so easily. You will also be more alert if you make a habit of recording your observations.

## 114.

### Decide on a Character

Decide on a character or specific incident for the story. Build your story around one central idea. As you learned in composition writing, refrain from trying to cover a wide range of material.

## 115.

### Keep the Story Realistic

Make your story natural by choosing words carefully. Think of words that will portray the people and the setting accurately. If you need help in choosing words, try using a thesaurus to broaden your vocabulary.

# C. PLANNING THE STORY

## 116.

### Decide Your Ending First

The first thing you must have in mind is *the end of your story.* By thinking of the outcome, you can decide the conflicts and solutions that are involved. All the various incidents you relate must follow each other smoothly to bring you to the end. You can introduce happenings as you go, to hold the interest of the reader, knowing that they all lead to the end. Knowing where you will end your story also helps bring out the purpose of writing.

B.113.

## 117.

### Introduce Main Character Near Beginning

Introduce your *main characters near the beginning.* The reader should be able to decide who, what, when, and where before going very far into the story. At the same time, arouse the curiosity of the reader enough that he will want to continue reading.

## 118.

### Eliminate Unnecessary Details and Descriptions

*Start right off with your story.* Short stories are often used in periodicals where there is limited space; therefore, begin immediately to tell the story. Eliminate elaborate description or lengthy characterizations, yet work in details that answer the above questions and help the reader to see and feel the setting.

## 119.

### Decide How to Tell the Story

*Narration* is the telling of a story. You will need to decide the method of narration you want to use. First-hand accounts may be told in the first person. The third person is most often used—and rightly so—to tell about others' experiences.

# D. WRITING THE STORY

Writing the story requires skill; and, for the most part, skills are developed by practice. Readers subconsciously eye the page. They find an abundance of quotations and short paragraphs much more inviting to read than long, solid paragraphs. A buildup in the plot to bring your story to a climax also makes the story more interesting.

C.118.

## 120.

### Use Conversation

Let conversation "tell the story."

By all appearances, somebody had cheated, because the test papers had the same error. The teacher quizzed the three eighth graders and then gave admonition about being honest. Then one of the three girls explained that they had studied together and that she had given the others the wrong method.

Brother Kurtz stood in front of the class, holding the test papers. "Three papers have the same wrong answers," he said sadly. "It appears as though one looked over another's shoulder."

All the eighth graders looked up questioningly to hear what he would say next.

"You will never learn to think for yourself by wrongly depending on others." Brother Kurtz went on, "Remember, too, that God's eye is on us continuously. He sees each sparrow that falls and He knows the intents of our hearts.

Rosa raised her hand.

"Yes, Rosa."

"Brother Kurtz, this morning at recess, Mary, Janet, and I studied mathematics together. I explained percentages wrong, and now all three of us working these problems have made the same mistakes." She hesitated, then added simply, "I'm sorry I explained it wrong."

The teacher breathed a sigh of relief. "How nice it is to know that nobody was cheating," he said.

## 121.

## Show Action

Show action instead of telling it. You may need three times as many words, but the account is more interesting.

John and Mary had a rough ride to town in the old truck.

Mary scratched her leg on the rusty door as she pulled herself into the dilapidated truck.

"I hope this truck gets us to town and back with the medicine for the cow," John mused aloud.

The truck lurched forward as John steered onto the road. Mary grasped the dash as they straddled a hole in their path.

## 122.

## Build Sympathy for the Right

D.121.

Cause your readers to make wise choices as they go along, by building a sympathetic feeling for the right.

"I know Mother looks tired," thought Sue, "but I'm going to get this birthday letter off to Cousin Leanna anyway."

Outside Beth was singing as she hung up the clothes. "The sunshine is so brightening, it makes me feel more speedy," she mused. "Maybe I can help Sue with the dishes yet, then we can both write a letter."

**123.**

## Keep the Story Natural

Make your story sound natural. You need command of an adequate vocabulary, yet you must choose words that the reader understands. Do not attempt to copy another's style, but write in your own words. For a test, read your story aloud to check if it sounds like you!

**124.**

## Show Correct Spiritual Values

Be sure to show correct spiritual values. For instance, show real penitence as the characters see themselves in the light of God's Word, rather than showing them refraining from wrongdoing because they are bound to be caught. For another example, compromise is fine when two neighbors share a piece of farm machinery, but compromise is wrong when two young men decide between spending Saturday evening washing the car at the filling station or going to church.

**125.**

## Let the Story Bring Out the Lesson

Refrain from adding your personal explanations; let the story bring out the lessons. This is especially tempting at the end of a story.

> Robert and David stumbled into the basement, dripping wet. "Why didn't we believe Father when he said the ice was getting thin?" murmured Robert.
> *So you see that parents usually know what is best and it pays to heed their advice.*

D.123.

The same is true of action.

> Bozo looked through the gate and yipped loudly. Then he stopped the noise and began to dig underneath the gate. The chickens on the other side continued to cackle. *By now you can guess that the dog delighted in chasing the chickens.*

# E. DEVELOPING THE PLOT

There are many ways to tell a story, but not all the methods will hold the interest of the reader. A child might tell about "A Week at My Uncle's House," giving a day-to-day account. But experienced writers will build a *plot* with sufficient conflict to make a story interesting, rather than merely relate happenings from one time to another as children do. *The plot must be developed around the purpose of the story.* Holding your readers in suspense without a lesson or inspiration is, in essence, wasting time.

The plot can be illustrated on a graph.

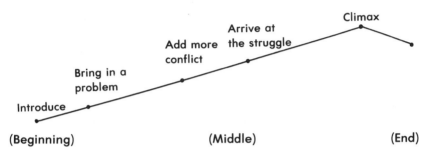

Every story should have enough conflict to make the reader wonder how the story will turn out. Even though the problem is only a small one, most of us want to know "what happened." If you write a story about the time you got your finger in the meat grinder, first of all decide the purpose for telling it. You could plan to show how God marvelously designed the human body to heal itself. Therefore, the conflict will be whether or not the mangled finger can be saved.

Or consider the evening Mother sent little George to throw the scraps over the fence, and he came back reporting that he saw "lights moving" back there. Did he imagine something in the dark? Think of the lesson you want to weave into the story.

## F. ENDING THE STORY

*The end of the story should satisfy the reader. Find a good stopping place shortly after the climax.* The inexperienced writer might show various weaknesses in his story endings.

1. Do not cut off your story too abruptly. Be sure that the reader's curiosity is satisfied and he need not wonder, "What then?"

> UNFINISHED: The opossum was still trying to get into the chicken house when Philip came with his gun.

2. Avoid tacking admonition to the end. The lesson should be so well woven into the story that the reader knows what is to be learned.

> POOR: Harold found that the habit of faultfinding had rooted deeply. You, too, will find that there is no one who thinks exactly as you do; so concentrate on the good characteristics of your fellow church members.

3. Do not give the impression that the story is endless.

> "John," said Dawn seriously, "I feel that I must cease to keep company with you. Unless you stop seeing your rowdy friends, I do not feel that we will grow spiritually."
> John's face turned red. "If that's the way you feel . . ." He stalked out the door into the early evening.
> Then Dawn decided to get a job at a home for retarded children. She gave herself willingly and spent long hours in behalf of the needy ones. Seeing the gradual development of the various children gave her new satisfaction. Daily she prayed to be in God's will. [And so on.]

# G. CHOOSING A TITLE

Giving your story a title is an important job. You will need to consider the theme of your story and make the title relate to it. At the same time, you should not reveal the outcome of your story in the title. "It Pays to Share" leaves little doubt about the ending. "The Twins See a Bear" steals the climax from the story. "The Twins' Surprise" will do more to arouse interest. The title should also speak to the age of the readers. The already-mentioned titles give a hint of stories for children. For mature readers, try, "Great Things He Has Promised" or "When the Clock Stopped Too Soon."

**G.**

# H. REWRITING THE STORY

## 126.

### Lay the Manuscript Aside for a While

If any kind of writing ever needs a "second thought," the narrative does. In telling a story, you need to be concerned about how it sounds. Lay your manuscript aside for at least a day, and then read it over carefully.

## 127.

## Read Manuscript Again Critically and Revise

Following is a list of things you will want to consider as you reread your manuscript.

1. *Are your details general or concrete?* You might describe scenery, flowers, fabric, or personalities as *beautiful* when you could say the *picturesque* hillside, the *gay* pansies, *becoming* clothes, or a *gentle* manner.

> GENERAL: Spring brings us warm days and new sounds. We think of God as the giver of life as the birds make their nests and as grass and leaves appear again.

> CONCRETE DETAILS: The *awakening of spring* brings new *reminders* that "while the earth remaineth, seedtime and harvest . . . shall not cease." The *cheerful robin* builds her nest in the *apple tree where the first buds unfold* when the sun sends its warm rays. The *sparrows twitter gaily* as they pull at the *new blades of grass* while searching for early insects.

To give colorful details, avoid using old, worn-out adjectives. Without thinking, you might call puppies cute. Now take some time to describe them with more concrete words. (For practice, try describing common articles with a fresh choice of adjectives. Look around you—describe a head of lettuce, or the road that goes past your house.) Now look over your story and decide whether you have given concrete, fresh details.

2. *Have you been repetitious?* The story will sound wrong if the same word appears too often in a paragraph. A selection of synonyms at your command might help in making the sentences follow each other in a more satisfactory way.

H.127.

> Mary Miller is *ambitious*—anyone would agree. She seems to enjoy having several projects in progress at the same time. In the basement you find her loom and boxes of rug rags. In the living room stands a quilt where she "rests" when *ambition* wanes. Her greatest *ambition* is memorizing Bible verses which she has posted near her various crafts. Truly, at the age of seventy, she is *ambitious.*

> Mary Miller is ambitious—anyone would agree. She seems to enjoy having several projects in progress at the same time. In the basement you find her loom and boxes of rug rags. In the living room a quilt is waiting for her to spend some time in quiet stitching. Along with all this

work, she memorizes Bible verses which she has posted near her various crafts. Truly, at the age of seventy, she is far from idle.

3. *Are your paragraphs varied in length?* Readers automatically label a page containing only long paragraphs as hard to read. On the other hand, a steady pattern of short paragraphs gives the impression that the writer lacks ability.

4. *Does the conversation sound natural?* Weaving conversation into a story requires thought and time. *Said* is an overworked word which in many cases can be substituted with *called, grumbled, demanded,* and so on. However, dialogue often needs no "John said," or "Mary asked," where the paragraphs show the change from one to the other. A sentence or two of action mixed with the conversation subtly identifies the speaker. And then after you have tried all these devices for conversation, at times either *said* or *asked* will still be most appropriate to use!

POOR:

John asked, "Where were you, Tim, when I was ready to bring the cows home?"

Tim said, "I was at the back of the barn, fixing the broken window."

John said, "Well, I managed, but your help would have made the job easier."

BETTER:

John panted as Tim appeared at the open gate. "Where were you when I was ready to bring the cows home?"

"At the back of the barn, fixing the broken window," Tim replied. "Did you need me?"

John shrugged. "Well, I managed, but your help would have made the job easier."

UNNATURAL:

"Will you study with me for the math exam?" Mary *requested.*

"Certainly," *stated* Jane. "I have gone over all the pages in this section once. Twice should give me an *A* in the test."

BETTER:

"Will you study with me for the math exam?" Mary asked.

"Certainly," Jane answered with a smile. "I have gone over all the pages in this section once. Twice should give me an *A* in the test."

*Note:* Be sure the words you use denote speech, not action.

WRONG: "It's over in that cupboard," pointed Mother.
RIGHT: Mother pointed. "It's over in that cupboard."

# I. BENEFITING FROM EDITOR'S CRITICISM

When you are satisfied that your story is written to the best of your ability, send it to an editor. Do not be discouraged if it is returned to you with notations. You may be tempted to think that you had asked the Lord for guidance and had not received it. But a returned manuscript may be an answer to your prayer for assistance in learning to write effectively. When an editor takes time to make comments on your writing, count it as an opportunity to learn from an experienced person. Thank the Lord for this blessing.

If you feel prompted by the Holy Spirit to relay a message through this rejected story, make improvements and try again. Some experienced authors have been known to try a dozen times before their manuscripts were accepted. If you keep in touch with God, you should not have repeated rejections, as a rule, because He is leading you. Whether your manuscripts are accepted or rejected, strive to follow on as the Lord is bidding you.

### Steps for Short Story Writing Briefly Stated

1. Be conscious of story ideas all around you.
2. Plan the story with the ending in mind, so that you know how to lay out the plot.
3. Write freely as the incidents come to your mind. To make your story interesting, keep in mind the pointers you have learned.
4. Give your story an appropriate title.
5. Lay the manuscript aside for a short time; then give it new consideration. Revise it to make it sound natural.

# J. PREPARING THE MANUSCRIPT

## 128.

### Specifications for the Manuscript

If you are a student preparing a manuscript for your teacher, you have been given certain specifications to follow. If you are stepping out to present your manuscript to a publisher, you will also need an acceptable standard. Your work should look as neat and proper as possible. An instructor will tell you what he expects; a publisher does not usually see your work until it is completed.

*128a.*

*General appearance:* The appearance of a manuscript depends on the tools you use, as well as on your workmanship. *Make sure your typewriter is clean and the ribbon is in good condition.* The print on your manuscript should have clear letters with good ink.

*128b.*

*Paper* for the manuscript should be uniform and white. The standard is typewriter paper—8½ inches by 11 inches. The weight of the paper should not be too light.

*128c.*

*Reference copy:* It is important that you make a carbon copy for your own reference. If an editor would wish to consult you, the duplicate would be a necessity. At times when papers are lost, the carbon copy is quite valuable.

*128d.*

*Margins* should be uniform throughout the manuscript. The page should look well balanced, and there should be space to allow for editorial notations. One- to 1½-inch margins at the sides are commonly acceptable. The top and bottom margins should be at least an inch. If notations are to be at the bottom, leave sufficient space for them. (A pencil mark one inch from the bottom will help you to know when you are near the end of the page.)

The first page should contain the author's name and address and a notation of the size of the manuscript. Following is an illustration of a suggested heading.

J.128a.

```
Mary Martin                          About 500 words
547 Blake Road
Lancaster, PA 17602




              Blessings in Disguise
                 By Mary Martin
```

128e.

Spacing: *The manuscript should be double spaced, using only one side of the paper.* Typing is standard, but if you have not acquired this skill, neat penmanship with black ink may be substituted. Black ink can be photocopied the most satisfactorily if the publisher needs to do so.

Pages should be numbered at the top, either in the center or at the right. To save trouble, every page should contain your name, the title of your work, and a page number such as the following.

| Mary Martin | Blessings in Disguise |
|---|---|
| -2- | |

# 129.

## Manuscript Changes

If you have completed your manuscript and, at the last minute, decide to change a part of it, be sure that your changes are clear to the editor. Rare are the writers who do not think of changes upon making a final reading. Notations can be made directly above the line to be changed, and inserts are often added in the margin or on a separate sheet. Material to be deleted should be marked so that there is no question.

> When we prayed that the Lord would increase our love, He sent Muriel into our home. She appeared thin and uncoordinated at the first glance. In the first hour, she had begun a quarrel with each of her foster sisters. We soon understood why the caseworker said he was desperate for a home in which to place her.
>
> When Muriel brought the bread knife down on the table, putting nicks in the varnish, we were horrified. When she bit Cousin Jean, we were at the end of ourselves.
>
> In the solitude of the orchard, we knelt and asked God to help us love the unlovely. Only His perfect love to us could help us to love this seeming "least of these." Like Jacob, we stayed until we had received a blessing— the blessing of more love for Muriel. That new sense of feeling brought new determination to set her feet in the straight paths.

J.128e.

# 130.

## Mailing the Manuscript

When sending a manuscript of several pages, it is wise to label the last page "the end." With the pages numbered and the ending marked, no editor or typist need question whether any part of the manuscript is lost.

# VIII. Reference Resources

**A. GOD'S INFALLIBLE WORD**

**B. BIBLE STUDY AIDS**
131. Concordance
132. Bible Dictionary
133. Bible Atlas
134. Bible Encyclopedia
135. Commentaries
136. Topical Bibles
137. *Doctrines of the Bible*

**C. USING THE LIBRARY**
138. Dewey Decimal System
139. Card Catalogue
140. Parts of a Book
141. Visual and Auditory Aids, Periodicals, and Government Documents
142. *Readers' Guide*
143. Reference Volumes

**D. DICTIONARIES AND THEIR FEATURES**
144. Spelling
145. Syllabication and Pronunciation
146. Capitalization
147. Definition of a Word
148. Parts of Speech and Inflections
149. Word Origin
150. Word Usage
151. Synonyms and Antonyms
152. Diacritical Marks

VIII

# VIII. Reference Resources

## A. GOD'S INFALLIBLE WORD

God is sovereign ruler of the universe. His Word is Law, and all that we believe or say or write must agree with divine law. At the end of time, God's Word will judge every man (John 12:48). How important it is that we make this Law our foremost source of knowledge!

We need the Scriptures to reveal God's will for us. The Word of God should be so much a part of our lives that we can detect anything that is not in harmony with it. Remember, Satan is ever trying to get us to believe the untruth.

A variety of helpful material is available to aid the serious Bible student. Bibles often include abbreviated helps in the back for handy reference. There are also unabridged volumes for intensive study.

## B. BIBLE STUDY AIDS

131.

### Concordance

A concordance is an alphabetical list of words and the passages in which they are found. It is an easy means to gather passages on a given Bible term.

a. *Cruden's Unabridged Concordance* lists every word in the Bible and the text in which the word is used. The table of contents gives other features about the book.

b. *Young's Analytical Concordance* is a more complete concordance in which the Greek and Hebrew words are given along with the text. A lexicon is given in the back to further explain the original meaning.

c. *Strong's Exhaustive Concordance of the Bible* is a complete concordance of every word in the Bible. It also features a "Hebrew and Chaldee Dictionary" of the Old Testament and a "Greek Dictionary of the New Testament" to explain the original meaning of important words.

d. The *Greek-English Concordance of the New Testament* is a work that compares the English text with the original language. Exact understandings are made possible by explanations of the use of the words in the original Greek.

## 132.

## Bible Dictionary

A Bible dictionary gives descriptive material and information about outstanding words in the Bible. Some Bibles include a combination dictionary and concordance in the back.

a. *The Westminster Dictionary of the Bible* by Davis is a conservative, scholarly work. It gives descriptions of places as well as explanations of words.

b. *Unger's Bible Dictionary* is a more complete work. It gives details of many people and places.

## 133.

## Bible Atlas

A Bible atlas is a book of maps showing countries, cities, lands, and waters of Bible times. Many Bibles have a limited atlas at the back, but a separate atlas has a more comprehensive selection of maps. Studying maps gives one knowledge of the location where many Bible stories took place.

## 134.

## Bible Encyclopedia

A Bible encyclopedia gives supplementary information to Bible terms. It is, in a sense, a detailed Bible dictionary in that it explains Bible passages.

B,132,

## 135.

## Commentaries

Commentaries are books resulting from scholars of the Bible compiling their information. They are arranged in the same order as the books of the Bible. Among their features is that of linking related passages from various parts of the Scripture. They explain ancient customs as well, giving a better understanding of Bible terms. But commentaries are also sources of varying opinions of Bible scholars.

They do lend much information, but they also expose man's opinions—either those of the editor or of the scholars he quotes. Not all Bible scholars are "rightly dividing the word of truth"; we must be careful, therefore, to accept interpretations only if God's Word as a whole supports them.

## 136.

### Topical Bibles

Topical Bibles have a system for studying the Scriptures by topics. *Anger, blessings, fellowship,* and *envy* are examples of words that might be used. For instance, you may choose the word *honesty*, and a topical Bible will have various references listed on that subject. Each topical Bible will give an explanation for its use.

## 137.

*Doctrines of the Bible,* by Daniel Kauffman, is a study of the teachings of the Scriptures. The various doctrines are arranged in sections and thoroughly investigated. This book is a means of studying the Bible in topics and understanding God's Word as rules to live by.

All these books, designed to aid in study of the Bible, contain introductions or recommendations for their use. Take time to study the explanations. You can receive the most help from these Bible-study aids by following their suggestions.

# C. USING THE LIBRARY

The world has countless stores of books—in fact, there is no end to the making of books (Ecclesiastes 12:12). Primarily, the Christian finds knowledge and wisdom by studying the Scriptures. His first concern is to know the will of God. Is there then a place for other reading in the Christian's life, or shall all other sources of information be ignored? There certainly is a place for it; one individual's research can benefit other people as their study is harmonized with the Bible. This involves having books censored before we read them, and reading only those that are not dangerous.

The *library* is a source of information you may need to use to make a report. There you can borrow books for use and save yourself the expense of buying volumes you may seldom use.

B.136.

## 138.

## Dewey Decimal System

To find the books you need, you must first understand how libraries are arranged. Libraries use a classification system to arrange the books according to subject matter. The *Dewey decimal system* is most commonly used by school and public libraries. This system consists of numbers and decimals (000 to 999). Some very large libraries use the Library of Congress system, which consists of the alphabet and numbers. The number given to a book is its *call number*.

The numbers for classifying books by the Dewey decimal system are:

| | |
|---|---|
| 000–099 | General reference works |
| 100–199 | Philosophy |
| 200–299 | Religion |
| 300–399 | Social Sciences |
| 400–499 | Philology or Language |
| 500–599 | Pure Sciences |
| 600–699 | Useful Arts (Engineering, Agriculture) |
| 700–799 | Fine Arts (Landscaping, Architecture, Music, Painting) |
| 800–899 | Literature |
| 900–999 | History, Geography |

Each class can be divided into finer parts such as:

| | | | |
|---|---|---|---|
| 500 | Science | 530 | Physics |
| 510 | Math | 540 | Chemistry |
| 520 | Astronomy | 550 | Earth Science |

Even finer subdivisions can be made by using smaller numbers and decimals.

| | |
|---|---|
| 630 | Gardening |
| 631 | Organic |
| 634 | Fruit Growing |
| 635.7 | Herbs |
| 635.9 | Shrubbery |
| 635.933 | Roses |
| 635.977 | Evergreens |

The Library of Congress divisions are:

A    General works
B    Philosophy—Religion
C    History—Auxiliary Sciences
D    Foreign History
E-F  American History
G    Geography—Anthropology
H    Social Sciences
J    Political Science
K    Law
L    Education
M    Music
N    Fine Arts
P    Language and Literature
Q    Science
R    Medicine
S    Agriculture
T    Technology
U    Military Science
V    Naval Science
Z    Bibliography—Library Science

For more-narrow classifications, books are further divided by combinations of numbers and letters. A history of the English language would begin with PD.

## 139.

## Card Catalogue

You will not need to memorize all these numbers; the library has a *card catalogue* to help you find the material you need. The card catalogue looks like a cabinet with many, many small drawers. It is placed in the heart of the library, conspicuous enough for any newcomer to find it. The drawers, filled with three-by-five-inch cards, are arranged in alphabetical order. Every book placed in the library is listed three ways in the card catalogue: by a *title* card, an *author* card, and at least one *subject* card.

TITLE CARD

---

Amateur Beekeeping

638.1   Sechrist, Edward Lloyd,   1873-1953
S

*Amateur Beekeeping;* with illus. by Frank Norris Todd.
Devin-Adair, 1955
148 p. illus.

Written for the ordinary backyard beginner. This book offers
step-by-step plans for starting out in bee culture. It gives systematic
direction for year round management of bees, correct equipment,
and how to use it.

1 Bees
1 Title
3-9-56                     ◯

---

AUTHOR CARD

---

638.1   **Sechrist, Edward Lloyd,**   1873-1953
S

Amateur Beekeeping
*Amateur Beekeeping;* with illus. by Frank Norris Todd.
Devin-Adair, 1955
148 p. illus.

Written for the ordinary backyard beginner. This book
offers . . .

1 Bees
1 Title
3-9-56                     ◯

---

SUBJECT CARD

> **Bees**
>
> 638.1    Sechrist, Edward Lloyd,    1873-1953
>   S
>
>     *Amateur Beekeeping;* with illus. by Frank Norris Todd.
>     Devin-Adair, 1955
>     148 p. illus.
>
>     Written for the ordinary backyard beginner . . .
>
> 1 Bees
> 1 Title
> 3-9-56                          O

By looking at the subject cards, you may find other books about the same thing. The card catalogue gives a complete listing of all books kept in the library on the same subject.

Libraries differ in contents of the cards. You might find the size of the book given in centimeters, as well as the Library of Congress card number and call number given at the bottom.

## 140.

## Parts of a Book

Become familiar with the various parts of a book. You can analyze a book by checking the preliminary information given. Not all books have every part in the following list.

> *Frontispiece:* A full-page illustration at the front of the book.
>
> *Title page:* Gives the complete title of the book; names of authors or editors; name and address of publisher.
>
> *Copyright page:* Shows information concerning the copyright. Tells the year of copyright and by whom (either by the publisher or the author himself).
>
> *Dedication page;* Recognition to some outstanding individual in the author's relationship.
>
> *Introduction, Preface, or Forward:* Preliminary material to introduce the book. May be written by the author or by someone also interested in the work. The purpose of the book, directions for using it, and acknowledgments for outside help may be entered here.

C.140.

*Table of contents:* Listing of chapters and the pages where they begin, placed in the front of the book. Some books also give a list of illustrations, maps, or other information in the front.

*Index:* More detailed than the table of contents and found in the back. Alphabetically arranged for quickly finding topics discussed in the book.

*Additional material:* Called the appendix, glossary, or bibliography, according to its contents.

*End sheets:* The inside of the front and back covers. May contain illustrations or maps useful for understanding the book.

## 141.

## Visual and Auditory Aids, Periodicals, and Government Documents

The library contains other features besides its rows and rows of books. Many libraries lend records and Braille volumes for the blind. An information center will give facts to those who call in by telephone. Periodicals, pictures, and government documents are filed in the library. You should avail yourself, however, of only the things that help you to understand the work and will of God. You should shun the temptation to waste your time reading worthless material or studying subjects that call you away from serving the Lord.

## 142.

## Readers' Guide

Occasionally you might want up-to-date information from a magazine or periodical. The library contains a *Readers' Guide to Periodical Literature,* which gives a listing by author or subject (not the title of the article). But many magazines contain enticing advertisements, short stories portraying ungodliness, and news articles denying our sovereign God. You do well to remember this and to always fill your mind with knowledge that increases faith.

An entry in the *Readers' Guide* appears thus.

**Brain disorders**
What you should know about epilepsy, Parkinson's disease, multiple sclerosis, and others; Gerald Knox. Bet Homes & Gard. 52:6, 8, 114-118 Je. '74

The title of the magazine is abbreviated. The number before the colon gives the volume, and the numbers after the colon refer to the pages where the article is found. The date of the issue is abbreviated.

## 143.

### Reference Volumes

While the *Readers' Guide* is the most familiar, libraries may offer certain specialized guides.

The library also holds many reference volumes called general works. These vary from place to place. General works are numbered from 0-99. Here is a short list, but the possibilities are innumerable.

> Indexes to government documents and periodicals
> Library guides
> Catalogs of books in print
> Biographical dictionaries
> Encyclopedias
> Yearbooks and Almanacs
> Atlases
> Dictionaries and Wordbooks

# D. DICTIONARIES AND THEIR FEATURES

The *dictionary* is a necessary tool for your writing. Not only can you find the meanings of words there, but you can also find homonyms, synonyms, and antonyms to increase your vocabulary. *Funk & Wagnalls Standard College Dictionary* contains many special sections of added information. Dictionaries vary in arrangement and additional information.

There are basically three sizes of dictionaries: large, unabridged volumes not easily carried along, but useful in a library; the college dictionary which students and families keep in their personal possession; and pocket dictionaries which contain fewer entries and give little information other than spelling and a brief definition.

C.143.

The latest revisions bring you up to date on acceptable language; however, some editions are governed by more permissive standards than others. The *Funk & Wagnalls Standard College Dictionary* carries a conservative approach. Look up the word *God* in several dictionaries, for an example. Some do not even carry it as a capitalized entry.

In order to use a dictionary efficiently, you must become familiar with the introductory pages. Every dictionary gives explanations for pronunciation and word study, and many give a table of symbols and abbreviations. The following entries represent the various classifications of information found in a dictionary.

## 144.

### Spelling

The dictionary can answer your questions about spelling a word. If a word has two acceptable forms, the preferred term is given first. If the spelling of the derivative of a word is a question in your mind, consult a good dictionary.

crochet—crocheted
worship—worshiped or worshipped

## 145.

### Syllabication and Pronunciation

Each entry is divided into syllables, with either a dot or a space to show the division. The accented syllable is marked by varied methods—an accent mark, italics, or bold letters. When you are not sure where to divide a word that falls at the end of a line, check the marking of syllables in the dictionary. To show the pronunciation of a word, some dictionaries use diacritical marks, and others use a combination of vowels and consonants to mark the sound.

hôr′tə•tôr′ē    *hor* tuh tor ee

A speaker should always be sure of the pronunciation of words. A dictionary used freely adds to one's vocabulary before he finds himself in front of people.

D.144.

## 146.

### Capitalization

The dictionary will show proper nouns and proper adjectives by listing them with capital letters.

Nazarene    Scotch terrier

## 147.

### Definition of a Word

Probably more people consult a dictionary for a meaning of a word than for any other reason. Never hesitate to take that extra minute to be sure of the definition of the word you are wondering about. An entry might have as many as ten definitions. Dictionaries vary in the methods of listing. In many cases, the definitions are listed according to frequency of use, with the most common meaning first. Some dictionaries enter definitions in historical order, giving the oldest meaning first. Some also give a bit of historical information so that you can make a detailed word study.

## 148.

### Parts of Speech and Inflections

The part of speech of a word is given in abbreviated form immediately after the pronunciation: (vij′ə•lənt) *adj*. If the word can be used as different parts of speech, each one is listed with an example.

Other forms of the word are entered, such as unusual plurals of nouns or irregularities of verbs. Words such as adjectives or adverbs from the same basic word are listed at the end of the entry.

| | |
|---|---|
| PLURAL OF NOUN: | **deer** *n.* (**deer** pl.) 1. A ruminant having deciduous antlers . . . |
| IRREGULAR VERB: | **go** *v.* (**went, gone, going**) 1. To move from one place to another . . . |
| OTHER FORMS FROM SAME BASIC WORD: | **in•sist** *v.i.* 1. To make an assertion or demand with emphasis. 2. (obs) To find support. **in•sis•tence, in•sis•ten•cy** *n.* |

## 149.

### Word Origin

D.147.

Most English words come from other languages. A good dictionary will show you the *derivation* of a word.

**Re•peat** . . . [<F. repeter <L. re- again + peto, seek]. (meaning that *repeat* is derived from French which was earlier derived from Latin)

## 150.

## Word Usage

A dictionary will show you whether a word is archaic, provincial, dialectal, informal, or slang. It might also show you whether a word belongs to a specific field such as medicine, agriculture, or engineering.

## 151.

## Synonyms and Antonyms

The dictionary will often supply other words of similar meaning and words of opposite meaning along with the entry. Upon reading the definition of a word, you might decide that a listed synonym is a better word to use. By thinking of opposites, you can better choose words that say exactly what you want them to say.

The dictionary may list the synonyms of *doubt* as *disbelief, distrust, hesitancy, incredulity, suspicion,* and *uncertainty.*

Antonyms of *doubt* are *assurance, belief, certainty, confidence,* and *determination.*

There are also dictionaries of synonyms and antonyms. If you want a good word finder, one to aid you in choosing right words, keep *Roget's Thesaurus* at your desk.

## 152.

## Diacritical marks

One method of showing pronunciation is the use of *diacritical marks.* Following is a list of their names and examples of their use.
a. *Macron* (mā'krən) (-); used to mark a long vowel with the sound of the vowel itself.

āte    ē'vil    fīne    ō'pen    ūse

b. *Breve* (brēv) (˘); mark for a short vowel sound.

ăs    fĕd    sĭt    blŏt    ŭp

c. *Schwa* (shwä) (ə); a weak, neutral vowel sound found in most unaccented syllables, such as the o in *equator* (i•kwā'tər).
d. *Dieresis* (dī•er'ə•sis) (¨); marks a broad *a* such as *cär.*
e. *Tilde* (til'də) (˜); marks an *e* in unaccented *er* sounds such as un'dẽr and o'vẽr.

f. *Circumflex* (sûr′kəm•fleks) (ˆ); marks other vowel combinations with *r*.

glôry    tûrn    câre

Dictionaries vary on markings. Be sure to study the key to the dictionary you are using.

# IX. Oral Communication

**A. INTRODUCTION**

**B. VISITATION**

**C. USE OF THE TELEPHONE**
153. Placing a Call
154. Receiving a Call

**D. INTERVIEWS**
155. Interviewing Another Person
156. Being Interviewed

**E. INTRODUCTIONS**

**F. PARLIAMENTARY PROCEDURE**
157. Duties of Officers
158. Agenda of a Business Meeting
159. Motions
160. Rules of Order

**G. SPEAKING TO AN AUDIENCE**
161. Gathering Information
162. Organizing Your Thoughts
163. Presenting the Topic
164. Brief Summary of Public Speaking

IX

# IX. Oral Communication

## A. INTRODUCTION

People use language every day in speaking to one another and give little thought to correct grammar. Rightly so. Correcting each other as a conversation moves along would be a very uncomfortable way to exchange information.

Good habits should be planted as soon as a child learns to speak. "Baby talk" is a useless dialect that should not be imitated by those who talk to the beginner. Give the right names to objects and use correct verbs to express motion.

As English students, use correct grammar in your everyday conversation. Learning to use *don't* and *doesn't* in English class is wasted effort if John still informs Father, "The calf don't drink the milk." Poor usage is partly a bad habit. You must use correct forms if they are to become a permanent part of your vocabulary.

You use conversation to convey information, to pass the time, and to encourage one another as you travel through life. Right words in conversation cheer the downhearted and strengthen the weak. "How forcible are right words!" (Job 6:25).

## B. VISITATION

Visitation is a form of Christian service in which everyone at some time becomes involved. This kind gesture of communication should be spontaneous action and not just the fulfillment of duty. Right and wrong practices should be kept in mind when visiting. Your presence and conversation should strengthen the other person's faith in the Lord. Therefore, speak things that edify and encourage. Never stay long when you are visiting a sick person. Keep commotion to a minimun—which means your voice should be soft yet clear. Young people should make a practice of sitting calmly, and small children should remain outside when a patient is very sick and weak. Do not engage in a discussion of the illnesses or misfortunes of other people which would lead to the discouragement of the one you are visiting.

# C. USE OF THE TELEPHONE

Nearly everyone has used the telephone as a convenient means of communication. You may have answered it for your mother before you were old enough to go to school, and may feel you have had much practice already. Even so, it is good to review proper procedures for making or receiving a call. Keep in mind that the other person does not see any facial expressions or gestures of your hands, and can depend only on what you are saying. Use a natural tone of voice and choose words that make your explanation clear.

## 153.

### Placing a Call

In placing a call, certain points should be observed.

a. Be sure of your number.

b. Let the telephone ring a sufficient number of times to let the one you are calling reach the telephone.

c. Say who you are and give your purpose for calling.

> EXAMPLE: "This is Twila Martin calling. I am looking for helpers to serve dinner at the barn raising on Friday."

d. If you must ask for the person you wish to speak to, do so politely.

> EXAMPLE: "This is Carl Nickles. May I speak to your father, please?"

> DO NOT SAY: "What is your father doing? Call him to the phone."

e. If you are not sure of the party you have reached, ask politely.

> EXAMPLE: "Is this Stoners?" or "Is this 263-3993?"

> DO *NOT* SAY: "Who is this?" (Sometimes widows and other women living alone have been harassed by calls and do not find it wise to say who they are. It is better for *you* to give away the name you are calling.)

C.153.

f. Do not make your telephone call lengthy and inconvenient. If the matter requires ten or fifteen minutes, ask whether it is convenient and whether a party line is to be considered.

## 154.

### Receiving a Call

Here are points to keep in mind when receiving a call.

a. In answering, say "hello" and give your name.
b. Let the caller give his message.
c. If the caller asks for someone who is not at home, ask politely for information.

>    EXAMPLE: "May I ask who is calling?" or "May I take a message for Tom?"

d. Do not give undue information if the call is not for you.
e. If you take a message be sure that it is accurate. Write it down.

Making a call on a party line is not the best means of clearing a misunderstanding or conveying personal information. But neither should you listen in when someone else is conversing on a party line. Always follow Christlike procedures when using a telephone.

# D. INTERVIEWS

An interview is a businesslike conversation conducted for the purpose of gathering information. Since the interview is intended for a definite purpose, it consists of questions and answers that bring the desired results. Interviews are used by employers wishing to find qualified help, by writers gathering information for articles, and by reporters seeking information about an event that has occurred.

## 155.

### Interviewing Another Person

If you have need to interview someone, apply Christian courtesy. Form a pattern in your mind to get the most benefit from the time spent.

a. Make arrangements beforehand. State the purpose and set a time, perhaps suggesting several times and letting the other person choose.
b. Have a list of questions on hand that need to be answered. Ask questions that invite conversation instead of a simple yes or no. If you are working on a story, get enough facts to make it complete. If you are hiring help, ask questions that expose the character of the

C.154.

one being interviewed.

c. Be punctual. Allow extra minutes for delays so that you can keep your appointment. Most latecomers and forgetters simply do not allow enough last-minute time for little irregularities.

d. Get down to business and avoid irrelevant topics so that you do not take extra time. If the discussion should lead to disagreements, be sure to come to an understanding.

e. If you are gathering information for publication, ask permission to take notes or to quote the one you are interviewing. If you are writing a story about him, you will need his approval because readers will probably identify him.

## 156.

### Being Interviewed

If you apply for a job, you will likely be called for an interview. The employer will wish to know something about your character and abilities. Follow certain pointers for your interview.

a. Make sure of the time and place.

b. Be pleasant and well groomed.

c. Answer questions with good English, not with lazy slurs (*workin'* instead of *working,* or suchlike). Give honest answers. If you have had no experience at a job, say so, but also give related experience if it is of any benefit.

> EXAMPLE: "I have never worked for a mason, but I did help my father lay a block wall around the barnyard. I am willing to mix mud."

d. Give some personal information that might help the employer understand you.

> EXAMPLE: "I have always enjoyed showing my brother and sister how to make things such as mottoes and baskets. On the other hand, I have had to think long hours to do a math assignment. I feel that I can depend on God's grace added to my interests, to give me the wisdom I need to teach crafts."

D.156.

# E. INTRODUCTIONS

As you travel from place to place, you will need to make *introductions* at times. Knowing how to make introductions helps you to be considerate and informative as you learn to know people.

When you bring one or more young people into the presence of an older person with whom they are not acquainted, always be considerate by making introductions.

YOU MIGHT SAY:

"Aunt Mary, I'd like you to meet my friends from Wisconsin. This is Wanda Martin, and this is her cousin, Rachel Witmer."

TO YOUR FRIENDS

"Aunt Mary lives with our family when she's not busy taking care of sick folks."

As a matter of politeness, always inform the older person first. If all are about the same age, make introductions from one to the other without hesitation about who should be first.

Introducing yourself is necessary sometimes when you visit a new place or if you befriend a visitor when you are at home. Make an attempt to open a friendly conversation along with learning to know each other's name.

"Might you be Glen Martin's brother? I am Abe Shrock. My family lives just across the road from the Martins."

The familiar old introduction "Miller is my name" might be polite enough, but it does little for getting a conversation started. Making an acquaintance should help you to know that person better and will help to provide richer fellowship.

# F. PARLIAMENTARY PROCEDURE

You will likely become involved in business meetings at various times in your life. Choosing classmates to produce the school paper is one example of working together in a meeting. Carrying on some of the concerns of the congregation in an annual meeting is another example of business procedure.

To begin organization of a group, interested individuals draw up a *constitution* or statement of bylaws. This constitution states the name, purpose, and standards of the organization. It also provides for election of officers and means of carrying on business.

A method of carrying on the business in a meeting is necessary. *Parliamentary procedure* is the most common method for conducting a meeting to carry out the business. It is so named because this method with all its details is used by the British Parliament. The methods of order may vary from simple rules for small organizations to complex, detailed rules for large groups. All members—not only the chairman—should be familiar with the rules of order for conducting a meeting.

## 157.

## Duties of Officers

a. *Chairman (or President)*
  • To be in his place before the opening time of the meeting
  • To preside over the meeting (call for reading of the minutes; introduce business; rise to give the floor to a speaker, and be seated during discussion)
  • To appoint committees
  • To carry out the bylaws

b. *Vice-Chairman (or Vice-President)*
  • To preside in the absence of the president
  • To assume duties according to the constitution

c. *Secretary*
  • To keep minutes of the meetings and read minutes of the previous meetings
  • To be in charge of correspondence

d. *Treasurer*
  • To be responsible for monetary matters of the organization (keeping the record of income and expenses, giving a financial report, and yielding to an audit)

**F.157.** ## 158.

## Agenda of a Business Meeting

The agenda of a business meeting should come in order as follows.
  • Call to order
  • Roll call (if needed)

- Reading of the minutes
- Treasurer's report
- Committee reports
- Unfinished business
- New business
- Adjournment

a. *Call to order:* The call to order is a statement by the chairman, or president.

> CHAIRMAN: The meeting will come to order. Brother Dan Miller will bring a meditation and lead in prayer.

b. *Roll call;* The roll call, when needed, is recorded by the secretary. When voting is done by a board of directors, it is especially necessary to have a quorum (a sufficient number to make a balanced decision) in attendance.

c. *Reading of the minutes* is carried out as follows:

> CHAIRMAN: The secretary will read the minutes of the last meeting.
>
> (The secretary reads.)
>
> CHAIRMAN: Are there any additions or corrections?
>
> (Changes are made.)
>
> CHAIRMAN: If there are no other changes, the minutes stand approved as corrected. (or "as read" if there were no changes)

d. *Treasurer's report:* This report is given when called upon.

> CHAIRMAN: Brother Allen will give the financial statement. (cash on hand, receipts, expenditures, and so forth.)

e. *Committee reports:* Not all organizations need committees, but if certain members are assigned to study into a matter, they will be called upon to present information at a meeting.

f. *Unfinished business* refers to business that was tabled (or postponed at the last meeting or was assigned to a committee and is now ready to be presented at this meeting.

g. *New business* may be introduced by the chairman or by the members.

> CHAIRMAN: Are there any new matters to be presented?
>
> BROTHER M.: I move we resurface the school drive to eliminate the mud holes.

ANOTHER MEMBER: I second it.

CHAIRMAN: It has been moved and seconded to resurface the school drive. Is there any discussion?

Discussion follows. Anyone who wishes to voice his opinion must first receive the floor and then present his view. A vote may or may not be taken. The matter may be tabled for extra consideration.

*Nomination and election of officers* is new business that is a serious function of the organization. Provisions should be made in the bylaws to carry out election of officers, and all members should understand them.

Nominations might proceed in this manner:

CHAIRMAN: Nominations are open for assistant secretary.

BROTHER G.: I nominate Dean Martin.

(The nomination is recorded.)

BROTHER H.: I nominate Dallas Good.

(The nomination is recorded.)

BROTHER J.: I move nominations cease.

BROTHER K.: I second the motion.

Voting takes place. Elections should always use the secret ballot or raised hands with closed eyes in honor of feelings. Lesser matters can be done by show of hands. The chairman casts a vote if it is necessary to break a tie.

h. *Adjournment:* The chairman controls the meeting. If there is a speaker, the business should be brief so that he is allowed enough time to give what he has. When the speaker is seated, the chairman should *adjourn* the meeting with brief closing remarks. It is not necessary to repeat the words of the speaker.

## 159.

## Motions

Motions in a meeting need a second but not always a discussion. a. *Procedural motions* concern the procedure of the meeting and are not discussed. The chairman simply restates them (after they are seconded) and asks for a vocal vote. Such motions might be:

"I move this motion be tabled until the next meeting."

"I move we close discussion and take a vote."

"I move we adjourn."

The chairman then says, "All in favor say 'aye' [pronounced like eye]. . . . Those opposed say 'no.' " Only if the vocal vote is close does he ask for a show of hands on procedural motions.

b. *Main motions* are the heart of parliamentary procedure. Any new business to be carried out should be put in the form of a motion. Another member seconds the motion, and the chairman asks for discussion. Each member may give his opinion when the chairman gives him the floor. The chairman should restate the motion before he asks for a vote. But before a motion is passed, another member may suggest an amendment, which must then be voted on. If the amendment is passed, the chairman reads the entire motion with its amendments, and a final vote is taken.

> BROTHER H.: I move that the mothers bring hot soup to school during the winter.
>
> BROTHER K.: I second the motion.
>
> CHAIRMAN: It has been moved and seconded that the mothers bring hot soup to school during the winter. Is there any discussion?
>
> (Discussion follows.)
>
> BROTHER A.: I move that the motion be amended to say that two sisters shall be responsible to have the mothers bring hot soup to school.
>
> BROTHER H.: I second the motion to amend.

After discussion, the chairman takes a vote on the amendment. Then he calls for a vote on the motion itself.

c. *Point of order* is the term used to restore a meeting to proper order. There is no need to vote on such a motion. Typical incidents might be a motion which violates bylaws, difficulty in hearing the speaker, or lack of a quorum. Anyone in the meeting may call for order.

> BROTHER G.: I rise to a point of order.
>
> CHAIRMAN: You may state your point.
>
> BROTHER G.: I understand the bylaws to assign to the secretary the work which Brother H. has moved to assign to the vice-president.

F.159.

## 160.

### Rules of Order

Don'ts in following rules of order.

a. *Chairman*
  - Don't start a meeting late.
  - Don't try to sway opinions in discussion, unless you ask the vice-president to preside.
  - Don't give numbers of votes in elections—expose only the name of the leading candidate.

b. *Members*
  - Don't be late.
  - Don't delay giving a second to a motion.
  - Don't refuse to give your opinion at a meeting, and then criticize later.
  - Don't be critical of members who have little knowledge of parliamentary procedure, but try to do your best in keeping a meeting in order, "in honour preferring one another" (Romans 12:10).

# G. SPEAKING TO AN AUDIENCE

At first you might think that you are primarily involved in private conversations, which have been covered in these last sections. But you might be surprised if you think of the many times someone stands before a group. Every Lord's Day you depend on Sunday school teachers and on ministers. Teachers in Christian schools, brethren in charge of devotions at cottage meetings or prayer meetings, and speakers at parent-teacher meetings are all examples of speakers before audiences. This section will give you points for doing your best when you receive a speaking assignment.

The teacher never knows which of his pupils will, in the future, need a knowledge of speaking, but it is likely that every Christian who makes himself available for the Lord's work will have some public speaking to do. Giving oral reports and answering essay questions orally provide good practice in thinking while you are among people, and are a necessary part of study in school.

# 161.

## Gathering Information

When you receive a request to speak, your first question will be, "What shall I say?" Even if you think of a topic (or if a topic is assigned), you must have "supporting ideas" or "plenty to say." Studying the sections entitled "The Composition" (VI) and "Reference Resources" (VIII) will help you in learning to gather material and in thinking logically.

*Make a note* of anything you might use for your topic. A speaker should have more ideas than he will use so that he will not appear to have exhausted the subject. The Bible is the principal source of study for many assignments; effective methods of studying it are therefore a must. Studying each word in a verse and finding other references for that word is one method. Finding a number of verses on a topic is another.

All your notes are useless, however, if your study fails to inspire you personally. Let yourself be used of the Lord to hear His message, and then you will have the enthusiasm you need to relay it to others.

*Listening* is an important prerequisite for speaking. Many of your ideas will come from other speakers who have inspired you. The problem with many people is that they *hear* but do not discipline themselves to grasp the message. Careless listening habits hide as a snare, snatching away your benefits of listening to a sermon or any other inspirational message. Think of how discourteous it would be to turn on a tape recorder while conversing with a friend. But if you find yourself in a worship service reminding yourself of the things you must tell someone afterward, you are just as discourteous. And you are only hearing, not listening.

You may blame a minister for being a poor speaker, but much of his presentation depends upon the listeners. If he must expend all his energy to command attention, he will have a hard time letting his thoughts flow freely. Poor listeners can increase their ability to grasp and retain a message by spending time in prayer before the meeting in behalf of the speaker. When you have prayed beforehand, the Lord will give added grace, and you will be better prepared to concentrate on the message.

G.161.

## 162.

## Organizing Your Thoughts

*Preparing for your speaking assignment* is the next step. You must arrange all the material you have gathered into a logical order. See "Developing an Outline" (section VI, E.). Decide whether every point has enough supporting material to make it clear. Use facts, illustrations, and reasoning to strengthen each main point.

In organizing your material, use only a few main points. People in an audience, unlike readers, must rely on memory or note-taking because they cannot page back. "A Dozen Rules for Christian Courtesy" might sound good, but twelve points are hard to remember. Three to five points are more of an ideal for speaking. It is better to organize and enlarge on a few points than to touch lightly on many.

Every speaker has his method of making notes as he prepares to speak. When proper preparations are made, Christian speakers are promised help to the memory through the Holy Spirit (John 14:26). Writing out thoughts while you are alone establishes your vocabulary for public use and plants phrases in your mind, even if you choose to discard the notes later. Study in the fear of the Lord; make notes as the Holy Spirit directs; and present to your listeners those things revealed to you.

Many incidents could be related where people were deprived of a blessing because they had difficulty following the speaker's rambling thoughts. Before you speak, be diligent in organizing your thoughts so that they fit together logically and can thus be followed easily by your listeners.

Outlines show your thinking.

| CENTRAL THEME: | **The Love of God** | |
|---|---|---|
| TWO MAIN IDEAS: | Is great enough for all people | Saves and keeps from sin |
| SUPPORTING MATERIAL: | 1. Greater than tongue or pen can tell (song) | 1. Plan of salvation (Rom. 5:8) |
| | 2. For the world (John 3:16) | 2. Will of God (Matt. 7:21-23) |
| | 3. Blessing to His children (Matt. 7:7-11) | 3. No clearance for the guilty (Ex. 34:6, 7) |

G.162.

A sentence outline helps you think in complete thoughts.

### The Importance of Learning Music

I. Music needs a prominent place in our lives.
  A. Singing is to be a part of our worship service.
    1. Ephesians 5:19 speaks of hymns and melodies.
    2. Colossians 3:16 mentions admonishing one another in hymns.
  B. Singing should be a part of us.
    1. We should sing often at home and in a worship service.
    2. We can cheer others by singing.
      a. Singing lightens burdens as we sing when we work.
      b. Singing for the sick and aged brings cheer and inspiration.
II. The study of music is necessary.
  A. Singing "by ear" is not always accurate.
  B. Blending of voices aids the message.
  C. Characters in music are as important as punctuation is to reading.
  D. You can learn more songs by reading music.

You can glance at a *word outline* more quickly than at a *sentence outline* when you are in front of an audience. If you are very familiar with all your points, a glance will keep your talk moving. You could arrange your thoughts in a sentence outline to begin, and then make a brief word outline for use when you are speaking.

### Learning Music

I. Its prominence
  A. Worship
    1. Eph. 5:19
    2. Col. 3:16
  B. A part of us
    1. Sing often
    2. Cheer others
II. Study of music a necessity
  A. For accuracy
  B. For blending
  C. Importance of characters
  D. New songs

G.162.

## 163.

## Presenting the Topic

After planning your talk and preparing to give it, you face the most important part of oral communication—*the presentation.* You will want to concentrate on passing your knowledge to the listeners. You have studied your topic, acquired information for yourself, and are eager to pass it on. Now "do it with thy might."

Giving a report in the classroom may differ from teaching the class or speaking at a parent-teacher meeting; but no matter who you are, you will benefit by knowing how to appear in public. *Your first appearance* could well be the index listeners use to catch your thoughts. How you look is the quality people notice first; how you act is the trait people notice longest. Do your best in both. Be sure that your clothes are clean and neat (no food spills, no collars turned up) and that your shoes are polished. Equally important to neatness is your conduct before your turn arrives. Sit naturally—neither slumped nor so stiff that you look uncomfortable. Enter every part of the meeting; listen to every speaker; do not be engrossed in your own notes; and remember that the entire class or meeting has something to benefit you also. The spirit of the meeting will be an aid to you as you speak.

A nervous feeling when you rise to your feet is a good sign. It shows that you are serious about the assignment and about conveying your thoughts to the audience. God can work best through the humble spirit. He can give you words when you depend on Him. However, do not be overcome by self-consciousness; it makes the listeners uncomfortable. "For God hath not given us the spirit of fear; but of power, and of love, and of a sound mind" (2 Timothy 1:7).

When you rise to speak, take your time. Give your audience a few seconds to get their eyes adjusted your way. Give yourself time to position any notes and get your mind "rolling." By starting slowly you can remain more calm and think more clearly. You will also find it easier to say things as you mean them without getting your words mixed up.

Speaking, teaching, or preaching is not an exhibition of skill, but an opportunity to convey ideas, information, and exhortations. If your manner detracts from your subject matter, you would do better to remain seated. One older minister who had preached many valuable sermons was once asked to speak before a group composed of many non-Christians. He tried so hard to be proper that he failed to present a convincing message from the Word of God.

In every way avoid drawing attention to yourself, either by too little or too much assertion. A mock humility is as wrong as putting on airs. Do not look at the floor, the walls, or the ceiling, but at the people to whom you are speaking. Avoid using a chanting or monotonous voice; talk in a clear, natural tone.

Use correct English. Try to avoid colloquial terms, yet be careful not to speak "over the heads" or your audience.

| POOR: | | BETTER: |
|---|---|---|
| lopsided | — | unbalanced |
| mess | — | predicament |
| peck of trouble | — | problems |

Avoid clearing your throat habitually or adopting other undesirable mannerisms. Adjusting your clothes, brushing back your hair, and fumbling with a pencil are poor habits. Using pet phrases such as "We believe," "You already know," "It tells us here," or a simple yes between sentences becomes a habit. Some speakers are marked for undesirable habits; do not be one of them.

Do not make references to yourself unless they contribute to your topic. "I do not feel qualified to speak on this subject" is a very unnecessary comment. "I studied late last night until I had this topic mastered" offers no inspiration. Do not play on the feelings of your audience to bring glory to yourself. Rather, endeavor to glorify God.

Do not read a passage more than once, but rather present what you have to say. A Sunday school teacher once read the lesson text, then read it verse by verse with comments, and later read it to clinch his closing. Remember that your listeners could have stayed at home and read the lesson three times. Give yourself to study and deep meditation so that you have thoughts to share.

What you say should relate to your listeners. Use directness in your manner of presentation. Too many speakers fail to get a point across to their audience because what they say is too vague. Compare the following paragraphs.

G.163.

The Lord uses people to spread His Word. Individuals can tell others of His great love and of His justice. There are opportunities everywhere. The Bible has answers for those who are confronted with trouble and sorrow. Every soul could benefit from the message of salvation.

The Lord uses people to spread His Word. You can tell your neighbor about His great love and His justice. You can find the sick, the sad, and the sinful souls wherever you look. The Bible has a message of comfort for those who are troubled, and admonition for those who are tempted. Look about you. Bring the great message to those in need.

Talking comes with exhaling. Learn to breathe deeply to give your body a better supply of oxygen, and then exhaling lasts for a longer period of time. By having sufficient breath, a speaker can produce better tone. Excessive voice and breathing tensions cause hoarseness. Practice breathing deeply while you are working or studying so that you attain the habit for speaking.

In closing your talk, remember that your audience cannot turn back the pages as readers can. Briefly repeating your main points will plant them more firmly in the listener's mind. Make a fitting statement to close your thoughts, and then be seated. If you see the allotted time running out, waste no words on the time; keep your words for the topic, ending it gracefully.

## 164.

## Brief Summary of Public Speaking

**a.** Seek the Lord's help in planning a topic.
**b.** Gather material.
**c.** Be filled by what you have learned.
**d.** Make an outline.
**e.** Present your topic according to what you have prepared.
**f.** Seek to have your audience concentrate on the message and forget you.
**g.** Make the closing a fitting one.

All communications, written or oral, should glorify God.

"Let the words of my mouth, and the meditation of my heart, be acceptable in thy sight, O Lord, my strength, and my redeemer."

—*Psalm 19:14*

G.164.

# Index